We Pass Knowledge to One Another

By
Scott Martin Locke

We Pass Knowledge to One Another
An Original work by Scott Martin Locke
© Copyright 2013

Published by Elemental Publishers
Raleigh, North Carolina, USA

ISBN 0-9765403-2-0
Library of Congress Control Number 20079034

Cover Artwork: Ken Morrison
Seattle, Washington
sleepingmind.com

Front Cover: Our first recollections of time and events are of family and home. Our roots, held by our perceptions at birth, mature to the final passage into heaven, rebirth, or nothing at all. We grow, as does our knowledge, from the roots of our perception and branch out into the world, heading towards the sky with anticipation while still grounded in our earthly environment. Every branch is our knowledge; the leaves are our wisdom; but before the leaves, the blooms are pure inspiration.

Back Cover: The extreme challenge we all face in life is not a choice but the event horizon of change, handed out like candy on Halloween. We eat it and survive. The hand holding on to the rope is our grasping of found knowledge, belief, and faith. At one end of the rope knowledge splinters from physical and spiritual. At the other end our human intellect grasps with all its strength and will to understand what it holds on to. We only let go when at our mortal end we find the truth of spirituality.

Contents

Foreword	vii
Author's Notes	ix
Prologue	xxi

Part One

In the Beginning: We Pass Knowledge to One Another	1
Foundations for Noumenal Reason	19
Intellectual Necessity	25
Facient Interpretation	32
Logic and Simplicity	36
Elements of Thought	40
Intelligence and Survival	45
Language and Expression of the Will	48
A Theoretical Matrix of Patterns of Thought	53
The Aesthetic Feeling of Knowledge	58
Our Intelligible Character	62
Experiencing Relationships of Knowledge	65
Consciousness and Its Behavior	70
The Essential Moments	74
Intellectual Reason	78
The Notion of Emptying and Filling	80
Insight and Intuition	82

Part Two

Actualization of the Spirit	87
Thoughts on Life and Living	93
Wisdom and Knowledge	97
Strength and Virtue of Understanding	99
The Certainty of Spirit	105
The Artist, Architect, Musician, and Poet	109
A Reasonable Explanation	111
Conception and Expression of Ideas	114
Confidence of Thought	120
A New Dawn for Philosophy	133
Notes from the Pen of a Philosopher	138
Another Thought	146
A Philosophical Examination of the Nature of Knowledge	152
A Higher Realm of Thinking	159
Subject and Objectivity of Knowledge	169
The Qualities of Thought	174
Our Expanding Horizon	183

Part Three

A Deeper Thought	193
The Philosopher	199
On Meditations of Ideas	208
On Sentiment and Recognition of Knowledge	217
Knowledge of Heart and Mind	228
Recollections of a Philosopher	239
A Philosophy of Man	250
A Fairy Tale or an Acute Observation	261
An Evolution of Thought	263

Understanding the Intelligence of a Philosopher	276
The Claims of Philosophy in its Own Domain	281
The Freestyle Philosopher	288

Part Four

Creative Thinking: A Supplement to Knowledge	293
Reflections and Meditations	298
Learning as a Skill and Art Form	313
Study and Reflection as a Way of Life	318
Exercising the Mind	331
Greater Thoughts On Knowledge	343

Concluding Thoughts and Reflections   355

Afterthoughts: Looking Back   383

Foreword

Scott Martin Locke is a self-described "laborer in thought." Having spent years in study, he is a man driven by a seemingly insatiable desire for knowledge. Yet he is not satisfied with simply learning for its own sake. He reflects, contemplates, and yearns for wisdom to arise from the words he digests. He "thinks about his own thinking," thereby pondering the nature of consciousness itself. He utilizes his learning to reflect upon his own life experience and to strive for self-improvement. In this final part of his trilogy, one that began with *An Adventure in Learning* and continued with *The Basis of Elemental Thoughts*, Locke stretches himself further, moving beyond his own questioning and search for self-discovery to highlight the importance of sharing one's thoughts, knowledge, and wisdom with others. For Locke is not only a philosopher — he is a humanist.

His goals are not small ones. For him, it is "our necessary duty to transform and improve humanity through our own learning and pass knowledge to one another as a means to improve the condition of all of civilization." *We Pass Knowledge to One Another* is a call not only for seeking but for sharing. It appears that during his years of study and contemplation Locke had an epiphany. Yes, he has relentlessly driven himself to achieve self-enlightenment through learning and reflection. Yet now he seems to have decided that knowledge for knowledge's sake is simply not enough. He has come to understand that only through the "passing of knowledge to one another" can we be true brothers and sisters in this human endeavor. He realizes that only through sharing with each other can we rise above and beyond our toils and troubles and move forward — together. This is the ultimate point of *We Pass Knowledge to One Another*. It is a message that resonates loudly, attracts one's attention, and, most importantly, deserves to be shared.

—Dean Lee Polk

Author's Notes

This collection of thoughts and observations began as research and evolved into a pleasure of learning and communicating that found knowledge, inspiration, and revelation. I suppose I've been carried away with the majesty of knowledge itself. For a long time I was consumed with thoughts but had hesitated in expressing them; but one day many years ago, I began to write.

This is the third book continuing *An Adventure in Learning*, and establishing *The New Basis of Elemental Thoughts* for myself, consummating in this deliberation with *We Pass Knowledge to One Another*.

Though we find many faults in our previous thoughts, the improvement of the mind comes with a well-contemplated series of Ideas and Notions, bound to the work of a philosopher sage, bard of humanity.

In spite of all that has been written, we take aim at its utility in an evolving understanding and improved capability of reasoning. As we develop our resources and advance in wisdom we must keep to the path of understanding that is unique to the individual in each of us.

I write not of what we ought to know, nor of what is known, but of our relationship with intelligence of the mind and spirit.

I think I've clearly perceived what I've found from experience and study, from conceiving and calculating theory, and from observing my own increased awareness of nature and of our own consciousness, which our mind perceives through its own dialogue and in the quiet silence of thinking.

When I freely express my own opinion and theory I leave myself open to judgment, but that's just fine with me. Philosophy is the discovery of wisdom and its conversation with others and within our own creative intelligence. When the mind is set to take aim at a target-thought, it observes what surrounds it and the conditions that affect it. Then it focuses our attention and tries to hit the mark.

Your mind is an instrument, a tool. It is there to be used for a specific task, and when completed it is due a measure of rest and repose. Because you are identified with your mind, you drive your sense of self from the content and activity it produces.

The present moment is all that matters. The past and future are content to be beside themselves with carefree thoughts.

Enlightenment means rising above thought to the creative impulse of insight. This work can be described as a rich treasure of luminous truths and reflections that are deep as the oceans and vast as the distances between the stars.

One must not forget the differences that meanings have upon the different ages throughout history. At any point in time, as far back as one can remember makes up one's own life; but each generation as well can project their thoughts into the future. Most important for each generation, however, is the here and now in which we live our own lives.

Observation is the notice that we take of all occurrences in human life, whether they are sensible or intellectual. It is the variety of ideas that come to our attention that enlighten our observations. Observations include both means of sensation and reflection. Observation demands the utility of the resources of the mind.

Reading is the means or method of acquiring knowledge that parallels discourse. The arts of reading and writing are an infinite advantage to our passing of knowledge from one to another and accumulating wisdom from this found knowledge and experience we discover in life.

Conversation as well as meditation improves the mind. From meditation and reflection we establish the general principles of our knowledge and come to our own wisdom. This work is made up of a variety of remarks collected from my own observations and from my life experience. Through reading, conversation, and experience in the pursuit of knowledge we can observe ourselves learning and experiencing an evolution in our own understanding.

This work has been composed during different times of day, night, and season, and has been considerably assisted by the knowledge passed to me from previous ages in history. As we live, we learn. Plants are fashioned by cultivation — man by education and experience.

The sentiments of mind differ in severity; some arise through pleasure and leisure, others through hardship and coarse labor. We are born weak and need strength; helpless, we need aid; foolish, we need reason. All that we lack at birth we gain through experience and education.

I have been sufficiently satisfied with the theme and content of this study. The subject is almost endless and has qualities that have been discussed through all ages of time; yet through time I have found an appropriate end to this work from my own labor.

The pursuit of improving our condition in life is necessary not only to our survival but to our own mental security. The quest for truth is one of the never-ending stories we share with the rites of passage through the time of our life.

To the rising generation there is much to be said, and just as much to be learned and discovered. The method of our quest leads to the same end — the increase in knowledge and wisdom. Our efforts may bring us within sight of the goal, but fortune must favor us if we are to reach it.

In the natural order we all are equal, and our common calling is that of maturity. Those of us who can best endure the good and evil of life are the best educated. We begin to learn when we begin to live; our education begins with ourselves. Our first teacher is nature. Our second is society. Though we seem alone in this world in our individuality, we are not; our life is surrounded by something greater than our self — it is society. When we consider the fleeting nature of human affairs and the restless and uneasy spirit of our times, we must advance in life by the use of our senses, our minds, and all our faculties, recognizing our own spirit and the spirit that is greater than ourselves, the world, and the universe.

It appears our necessary duty to transform and improve humanity through our own learning and pass knowledge to one another as a means to improve the condition of all of civilization. Good judgment comes from found wisdom and right reasoning that knowledge affords to us as an inestimable advantage.

We must fix our memory on what we learn and practice the art of applying it to our individual lives. When we read good authors we learn the best, the most labored and inspired, and the most refined sentiments of those wise and learned ones who came before us.

In free and friendly conversation our intellectual powers are more animated, and our spirit acts with vigor in the quest and pursuit of unknown truths. The important matter is to keep an open mind, free from suggestion, until we can reflect on what has been passed to us with a certain degree of sureness and certainty.

It is in meditation and study that the transference of the notions and sentiments of others joins with our own ideas and becomes a more complete, but never perfected, knowledge. It seems that there is always something more that can be added to what we already know.

It is the variables of wisdom that denote their difference. It is our judgment of others' opinions and convictions that, by reasoning, becomes our own property. Our acquired knowledge becomes our wisdom. Our reasoning of this newfound wisdom becomes our judgment.

What increases the proficiency of our judgment is the passing of knowledge to one another, which is the theme and subject of this work. This passing of knowledge is meant for our own improvement and for the improvement of others which we carry with us through our life experience.

It is hardly possible for a thinking man to gain experiences or observations without making some short reflections upon them. The enlargement of our knowledge and understanding should be consistent and necessary in the design of our lifestyle to promote the highest achievement we are capable of: the improvement of ourselves and of others from newfound wisdom. We can only grow and mature from the experience found accumulating knowledge.

I have endeavored to take up my pen to share what has come to my attention. What is practicable is to write thoughts. As for the want of details, my task may remain in part undone; yet, the readers may yield to their imagination to fill in what I have missed. For the want of education our guide will come from instinct. The insight I will provide is from my own enlightenment.

I know that in the evolution of this work I will keep to my own vision and abide by my own requirements.

A healthy imagination goes in stride with a good education in the advancement of our ability to learn and comprehend the reliability of our understanding. As you read this book you will see how generous I have been with myself applying what I have learned in the past to my new learning. Understanding comes with long patience, enduring over time the newness of thought and Idea.

One must endeavor therefore to derive improvement of the mind from every experience which occurs in human life. In every moment, seize every opportunity to increase your knowledge. Be in the habit of useful thinking to your own advantage and survival. Let each circumstance, condition, and opportunity lead you to utilize the resourcefulness and faculties of the mind to the best of your ability. Keep your mind as free as possible from prejudice of opinion. Busy your own curiosity with the increase in knowledge of spiritual things as well as things of the world. This will increase the worth and value of your judgments.

Whatever you learn will be your treasure; if it is useful in your life, count it part of your intellectual genius. It is the enlargement of your treasures of knowledge that leads to the improvement of your power of reasoning and logic and the growth of your skill in rational analysis of the truths you find through your study, contemplation, and life experience.

What increases our awareness of the spirit is enlightenment and personal revelation. Spirit is the self of the actual consciousness. Spirit is the immovable and irreducible basis and the starting point of every creature and thing. Spirit is the self-supporting, absolutely real, ultimate entity that gives us the ability to have awareness of not only our own consciousness but of the universe that surrounds our existence.

From our learning and experience, and from the passing of knowledge to one another, we learn great and small things having the most significance. Spirit is thus consciousness in general, which contains sense-certainty, perception, and understanding. Spirit is our intelligence that utilizes its resources to the fullest potential.

This is a story of discovery and exploration of our intelligent spirit, which comes to know knowledge as its own wisdom and the wisdom of others that we learn from.

By pursuing the study of books, you will not only enlarge your treasures of knowledge but also improve your reasoning powers by proper reflection and contemplation of this intellectual nourishment. You must allow time for thought after the passing of knowledge comes your way.

This thought and thinking is like the sun and rain that brings growth to the Earth. Books are never to be judged merely by their subject and theme, but by the justness of the author's sentiment, the beauty of their manner, and the strength of the expression of reason that appears in them. Let us remind ourselves that style is one thing and content is another. The refinement of expression comes with practice and experimentation.

I can only say, in my own defense, that this work took me years of study, contemplation, and reflection on the subject of knowledge and wisdom. After the creation of a massive compilation of notes, I went back to the beginning — after I found a suitable ending — and started typing from these hand-written pages of wisdom and knowledge from which I had found insight and enlightenment.

We are born capable of learning; but knowing nothing, perceiving everything around us without understanding, we are purely reflex without knowledge or will.

However little you may have thought about the order and development of our knowledge, you cannot deny that we learn from experience and from others. Each of us progresses according to our own level of genius.

No one could dare say how far a human can grow in intelligence. We know not what nature allows us to be when we apply ourselves to study and the accumulation of wisdom. I know how much I have already done, but how much more I can achieve depends upon my motivation and ambition.

A man's education begins at birth; before he can speak or understand he is becoming a learning creature. If all human knowledge were divided into two parts, one common to all and the other peculiar to the learned, the latter would seem very small compared with the former. In the dawn of life, when memory and imagination have not yet begun to function, the child only attends to what affects its senses. As the child grows, it learns from the passing of knowledge to one another as well as from experience, and develops its own peculiar wisdom.

As you venture into the ocean of knowledge and survey the riches of others' minds, believe that it is possible to learn something from everyone and from every event that happens and apply your learning to your condition and the situation of your life experience. Remember that there are connections between notions and ideas that may not be strictly expressed and that you must therefore infer. What has come into this world is a vast increase in knowledge, bringing us a whole new treasure-house of facts and nuggets of previous wisdom. We have increased the relativity of man's beliefs about himself and about the world he lives in as part of a universe, and we seem to have an increasing awareness of this universe in proportion to its size and composition. We are living in the dawn of a new age of technology and discovery, where probabilities become real possibilities.

The question comes forward: What is it that binds us to the Ancient and Exalted amid mankind? Many a thought sublime and great comes to our mortal mind. Over and over again we ask: Why have you kept away my Lord? But all the time you were here in my mind, provoking certainty and truth as to your being near.

The destiny of great eras has passed, and those who know of them remember as another goes their way, with time both at our back and at our doorstep. Where there's a destiny there must have been a beginning. The design transgresses beyond what humanity can create with skillful minds unknowingly divinely ordained.

The question is how much you want to know about your true nature, which perhaps remains a real mystery even to yourself. We find the answer in the paradigm of assumptions, concepts, and practices that constitutes a way of viewing reality for the community that shares them. One conclusion that can be made is that truth comes on different levels, and each truth yields different results at each level according to the properties of that level.

What we find is that truth is the same everywhere and for everyone but comes with a variety of replicas on a smaller scale than the original. Truth, then, becomes the plaything of individual subjectivity.

The world as creation never actually is but acts as if it is always becoming. It is only the temporary here and now that our senses react to, seeking some kind of permanence remaining without essential change, on a continual infinite progression. One has to become a reasoner and distinguisher, not only as an observer of oneself but as an active participant in the world in which one exists.

It is your stream of thinking that carries you with it. It wants to draw your attention in completely. If you take your thoughts too seriously, you become trapped in a conceptual prison, either from your own making or from the dogma and convictions of others, without realizing that how you interpret becomes a judgment and is susceptible to human error and mistaken reasoning.

It is the idea of understanding that we are given thought to. All that we know we do not understand. Our knowledge comes from different sources. Our wisdom comes from the mind. It takes little steps — small ones, hardly noticeable — to make the journey seem like forever.

Not all things at once does the Highest intend. It takes time and patience to endure the trials Earth brings to mankind. Though one accrues much wisdom, never is there enough to be right all the time. To err is human. To learn from our mistakes gives rise to opportunity to re-think and make amends. If not for knowledge learned from experience, and passed to us, we would have no direction at all.

From experience we learn nature's ways and take heed from the lessons we learn, thereby increasing our own wisdom. The theme is a series of well thought of and defined ideas and notions of the most common and ordinary surface conclusions we can conjure; but within the explanations of our questions and inquiries, and the solutions we come up with, there is a deeper meaning to life than we can explain.

The elements of nature and the ancient laws of earth have a constancy of truth about them that cannot be denied. There is a yearning that seeks the unbound, the things that make us wonder. Revealing comes the morning and inspiring comes the sunset. The earth and all the planets are kept in motion by some unknown force; perhaps it is the same force that inspires one's thoughts of this never-ending creation. Perhaps there was no beginning but that it always was, implying that there is no end as well. The reality of it all is that quite possibly we are deceived by the illusion that what we think reality is may very well not be the whole and complete truth. The wind goes where it wills, and the river takes its rough course over the rocks but suffers no harm. We people prepare ourselves for contentment and satisfaction by enlightening ourselves with knowledge passed to us along the stages of our maturity.

This work is a philosophical examination of thought and wisdom, and the knowledge both are entangled with. This requires an artillery of thinking and words to express a newly considered thought or the remembrance of something previously thought. The challenging combat is an exploration in the recovery of lost ideas and the search and seizure of re-defined truths without being distracted from other worldly considerations.

Maxims and reflections in our thinking and stylized rhetoric of prose form bring to the page observations of things we once thought or are given to think about in our life. Yielding to reason, our thoughts carry us on a journey of discovery, and in the process of learning we accumulate knowledge and raise our own wisdom to new heights. Enlightenment takes work and comes shining through the darkness of ignorance like the morning dawn, ushering us into a day where we can be certain, in our intelligence, of what we know, or thought we knew but were not sure.

We live in an age where we rely on verification, but some things we just have to take upon faith and belief, perhaps with a slight degree of doubt due to our incomplete understanding. I think the important matter involving the theme of this work was to capture the thought, find its relevance, and explore what meaning I could draw from it.

The more that I studied and reflected, the sequence of evolution in my awareness became worthy of exploring the varieties of meaning that ideas and notions have from an infinite source of interpretations.

The fact that we pass knowledge to one another is a concept not only of necessity, but of a kind of measurement that gets more specific with age and technological advancement. In the evolution of human achievement we have progressed from word of mouth stories, as well as tales and ballads in song, to written books scribed by hand with the labor of dedicated people, to the use of the printing press, which expanded the availability of knowledge to society and civilization as a whole. With the evolution of knowledge also came the transcribing of works into different languages, which enabled the passing of knowledge to others around the world.

Knowledge of man is hard to acquire, but the wisdom of man is immediately noticeable in his revelation and actualization of that knowledge, which makes him an intelligent creature. The reason truth is so hard to explain is because no formula which expresses clearly the thought of one generation can convey the same meaning to the generation which follows. For this reason we pass knowledge to one another and continue in our interpretation throughout the ages.

What we know from experience depends on the age in which we live. Experience, or real knowledge, is different than book learning. A well-seasoned traveler learns of different people in their own natural social and cultural domain. From observing and studying different people we can learn about ourselves.

After reading many a thousand pages one can truly appreciate the reminiscing thought of Aristotle in his metaphysics: "All men naturally desire knowledge." The "I want to know" part of our spirit confirms this, so we naturally pass knowledge to one another from necessity.

—*Scott Martin Locke*
December 2013

Prologue

Let us first and foremost acknowledge that it is the philosophical and theological ideas which inflame the mind, stir up emotion, and excite passion, bringing society and its people to where we are today. The complexities of the imagination and accompanying thought-provoking ideas are primary forces which further our knowledge and understanding.

I've taken a probing look into the reality of mind and all that accompanies our intelligence and mental resources. I have attempted to resolve and answer questions and opinions in various degrees, but some things which are really unexplainable remain mysterious.

Compassion and compromise serve to resolve the stalemate that our philosophical, theological, and metaphysical notions bring to our attention. As we pursue our own interests, it is interesting to note that we admit mistakes, thereby uncovering truths that we search for about life. Every view we come to terms with is challenged from all sides. Our reliance on credit due from knowledge throughout the ages is invaluable. The past speaks for itself and brings itself into our contemporary world.

We come to much learning from our own experience, but we should not rule out the consequence of learning from all the literature written in history for our own well-being and the expanded wisdom for which it was written in the first place. Writers write for contemporary and future generations. John Milton once wrote, "As books are given to the world from writers' hearts, their information becomes free for those who give thought to it, in the public domain."

In retrospect, it seems clear that passing knowledge to one another in honest, tried, and true ways conveys wisdom which has led civilization to higher states in each succeeding generation. Knowledge and wisdom speak to us from that still voice inside, and we listen, become enlightened, and have inspiring revelations of the most ordinary and supernatural things. Still, there is more to be known than we already have knowledge of.

As we pass knowledge to one another this newfound wisdom comes to us in all forms. Books, we find, are like new acquaintances. Once we become familiar with particular ones that seem agreeable to our disposition, we cherish them and consider their contents with deep thought and emotion. The fulfillment of our inner reality comes from the wisdom we find in our total experience from life itself. Actual reality keeps concealed within itself this other reality we call consciousness, which brings us true and clear knowledge about ourselves and the world we live in.

As a philosopher and theologian, I have made bold and new discoveries through my studies as ancient as antiquity itself. I have discovered a kind of mysticism so astonishing and seductive that it raises to an articulated level matters not otherwise accessible by the usual avenues of understanding, reason, and religion. Should anyone who believes in a great and fantastic spirit have enough courage and vigor to study it without being overwhelmed, they would know in themselves and in the world a great and mysterious power that is clearly beyond our comprehension. Yet in some way our attraction to it grows with an intensity compared to the emotion it brings to us from our reasonable certainty in what we believe to be part of our same reality inward as it is outward.

Today, we have progressed to the point where the questions we ask divide us. We have become entangled in conflicts over competing revelations, dogmatic purity, and divine duty. Those with insight can already hear the sounds of the shattering of ideology invented from ages long since past our own time. Being eager to embrace the future, we are re-creating our own ideals and ideology of life. It is an unnerving tale, one that raises profound questions about the fragility of our modern outlook. We must measure the challenge and face it, deciding how to respond. So I've prepared this work to set the stride towards achieving a new wisdom, with the clarity and all the certainty our potential capabilities will allow us.

Many theories have been proposed, especially by those suspicious of the religious impulse inherent in our nature. Theology and philosophy are, after all, a set of reasons people give themselves for the way things are and the way they ought to be. The way things could be is still only a dream that one must pursue for oneself.

Imagine human beings who first became aware of themselves in a world not of their own making. Their world has unknown origins and behaves in a regular fashion, so they wonder why that is. The cosmic order of things must have been created for some purpose still to be discovered in each of their own particular lives.

This is a magnificent picture that allows for great imagination and significant observation through thought. The subject now has evolved with a dramatic change: from nature and creation to our all-consuming beliefs and faith. It is a revolutionary and dramatic construction of our human intelligence.

We have such a great capacity that is yet to be fulfilled, and the excellence of the world is still to be discovered. Our natural state is overwhelmed with anxiety, only to be relieved by sleep. We come to separate our own ideas centered on theology by creating a new and enriched philosophy from knowledge passed to us and found through study and reflection centered on previous and contemporary conditions of humanity, and from the thinking we do about ourselves.

It is a familiar story known personally to everyone: we let the world go as it is and focus our attention on elevating ourselves, as much inwardly as we do outwardly, to new spiritual and metaphysical heights within the capacity of our intelligence.

When a question is important, we want an answer, but often there are no answers to be found except through random chance and a certain amount of creative speculation. The mind decides in one way or another, despite itself, and prefers to be mistaken to believing nothing at all. Consider just how often reality is overtaken by a steady state of life seeming like a dream.

Anyone writing a creative work knows that you open up, yielding yourself, and the book talks to you and builds itself through your hesitant thought and deliberate concentration. Inspiration comes from many sources, from the unconscious to one's experience to being conscious of the power the mind gains from the wealth of written and oral traditions.

The stages of human development are the same today as they were in ancient times. If one even considers antiquity when our Neanderthal ancestors were living, or when some rare species of human form was living off in some distant nebula, we all are really the same, though our individuality causes some slight variations.

As a child you are brought up in a world of discipline and are dependent on others. As an adult you are a self-responsible authority, yet still you are dependent on others in some way or another.

As you live you learn of life and come to the knowledge that you will some day pass on into another world. That other world is just a thought in your own mind. We learn about the passage of life by living our own, which un-shells the elemental idea of guiding you towards your own inward self and yielding to it.

As we learn to apply our knowledge to our particular life, individuality and action constitute the principle of individualism in general — a principle which in its pure universality is called inner divine law — opening us up to the knowledge of our own consciousness.

Looking within to our inner light is the only way to cope and deal with what life has to offer. The answers are not outside ourselves; they are concealed in the depths of our hearts, where the mind connects with the spirit and the spirit connects with the soul. We need to believe in something to orient ourselves to the world.

This is a story of that reflection that shadows our existence with all its own brilliance and magnificence, where a connection is made from wisdom and knowledge passed to us through study and personal introspection.

What we really need to do is to take a step closer to understanding the world we live in. By doing so we come to know and understand ourselves and our relations to others, increasing our conscious wisdom while addressing the recovery of who we really are.

This is a story that addresses the recovery of knowledge of ourselves, so that we can understand in a better way not only ourselves but others as well, who we learn from and pass knowledge to.

This is a story of a compelling vision that provokes thought of the prospect of understanding the individual living in a highly technical and secular age where personal beliefs, inspired by genuine inspiration, are confronted with the persistent endurance of our modern rituals for survival.

Even as we are buffeted by social pressures, high fantasies, and the political intoxication of our super-rich bureaucrats, we must find our own way through philosophy and theology to adapt to the demands from not only modern life but also our own personal intellectual curiosity.

Today there are still voices calling from the wilderness and urban centers to challenge the wisdom of past ages and their subtle interpretations in our contemporary and modern culture. The attempt to broaden the horizon of our thought continues through the renewal of compelling philosophical and theological reasoning within each of our own traditions, securing our fundamental liberties of thought and providing for our basic welfare while leaving our spiritual destinies in our own hands and within our own abilities of mind.

Following the general theme of enlightenment, each of us has the responsibility of educating our own mind and spirit. In doing so, we can further the advancement of civilization and humanity to which we belong.

So we pass knowledge to one another and increase our own potential capabilities of thought and action.

Part One

In the Beginning: We Pass Knowledge to One Another

The more a thing is invisible, the more it astounds the mind to wonder and amuses our intelligent soul. And then while solitude and stillness stir the mind, what you thought could only be a dream was really this inner reality brought to enlightenment. Your thoughts constrained, but loosened insight recalled a better moment of understanding.

This is a work of reflection and inspiration together, adorned with other excellencies the mind can fabricate; from our own knowledge and knowledge passed along to us we contemplate and try to make some sense of it all. "To what avail?" we say, so that we can relax in our own distilled comprehension.

The subject is elevating and amusing, now more ready to awake in each of us the potential enthusiasm for the procurement of knowledge and wisdom, which in turn can help us along in this journey we call life. Through my studies and reflection upon what I've found I have met with enormous variety and beauty in thinking beyond compare.

What this work does to me is to excite and answer the moods one goes through in the course of the process of thought and invention. The memories we retain, the influx of new information, and the consideration we give to both — we reach out to capture our potential and come to terms with the mystery life holds us to.

This work has more than didactic principles at heart; it is meant for enjoyment and discovery of the adventure in learning and what that learning means to us personally and individually.

In this work I've discovered not merely surface observations. To a reasonable mind invisible notions and ideas become visible and impassioned expressions of what knowledge becomes, including its causes and our awareness of the influences all around us. The hidden mechanisms that bring the rainbow to our eye also bring influences to our reasoning and further excite our intelligence as our own wisdom evolves, matures, and develops; the unknown becomes known, alluring us to more exciting investigations and evaluations.

The more extended our reason is, and the more able to grapple with the past wisdom we've accessed in our mind, the greater still are these discoveries which make our wisdom earn its keep in the treasured resources of our own intelligence.

Superficial changes are always possible, but real transformation depends upon whether we can become present enough to dissolve the future and disconnect with the past, making living in the present the most important option to us. If it were not for our sleep the mind would be overwhelmed by its own curiosity of the present moment in the majesty of the part of eternity we call the here and now.

As we explore all the mind-created layers of complexity, the one simple notion of questioning fact and fiction leads us to think more of the magnificent simplicity of the real reality we seem to know so closely from our own life experience.

Everything and everyone are in some way connected. This connection is made deep within our own thinking. Contentment is such a difficult place to reach because we are always trying to get somewhere other than where we are. Our own curiosity reaches out for fulfillment with anticipated expectations. We focus ourselves on becoming, achieving, and attaining what is within our own abilities. If we could only find satisfaction and contentment along the way we could stop ourselves from turning more pages, but our inner divinity keeps us reaching out for the ideal we create for ourselves.

In the moments when this ideal is found, we may feel awe and admiration for our own achievements. When the excitement of fulfillment passes, we reach out for the continual "more" with yet another "dawn" and a better understanding within ourselves.

The human race has lifted itself through millions of years from a semi-intelligent barbaric state into a state of high intelligence surrounded by materialistic wealth and technological inventions. Our civilization and the societies that surround our own have become so peculiarly advanced that moral and intellectual enlightenment have reached a new and bold norm for humanity.

The whole is like each single moment — a self-estranged reality. It breaks up into two spheres: in one kingdom self-consciousness is actually both the self and its objective, and in another we have the kingdom of pure consciousness, which being beyond forever has no actual present, but exists for faith and is a matter for belief.

The thought-constituted universality of the spiritual world over the world of natural reality becomes another true reality of itself.

The individuality that cultivates itself and the development of that individuality becomes the realization of a universal self-consciousness in which we belong to the world and know the world as it is in our present here and now moment of the thought of both, existing between the two.

We people like soldiers must find our place in society. We are destined to be a collective and not just an individual among the many. We've gone from crossing vast lands by foot, wagons, and machines to being been propelled into the sky and as well into space, even to the moon and beyond with technological machines that brought us visions of the heavens and distant places in our universe.

Through this sequence of ideas each individual may rise to an eventual everlasting scale of their own activities and enterprise. The underlying idea here is our belief in human evolution by the passing of knowledge to one another asserted in several climactic points of view. When you rise up in your ability to consider life and recognize your own identity, emotion comes to your intelligence, revealing new self-discovery that occupies great places in your mental world.

Curiously enough the emotional shock of finding out about yourself enables you to see more clearly what was always there except that before you cared less to know your own potential capabilities. Our gracious sovereign knows our destiny, but still we have to find our own by the life we lead and by the thoughts we think, even if not spoken aloud but silently to ourselves. Through knowledge we come to a profound and genuine expression of our own ideals. Life goes on just the same, but our point of view changes with our wisdom.

What is presumed or conjectured to be considered a truth or principle once removed from any tense has a singularity all its own and can be sensed, to the highest degree, as a pure and absolute condition of eternity. The idea of knowledge drives our curiosity and draws our attention, and that knowledge leads us either facts or to fantasy.

We are drawn from tale and fable to the similarity of truth or to an actual truth. We are as well drawn from myth to legend in the same way. Our mind naturally leads us on by its own power of curiosity. The concluding factor rests in our own imagination from the knowledge and wisdom others have given to us. As we discover what reality really means to us, we cultivate the thought and bring it to its principal form. Once we become familiar with a certain truth we can find similarities and appearances of that same truth which are just across the threshold of believing.

Through theory and speculation we are driven to one opinion or to another from the foundation of elemental thoughts we've created for our own individual understanding and reasonable comprehension.

What is of concern here is simply the method we use to explain, though a straightforward logical derivation of an event or phenomena may seem simplistic. Essentially our own metaphysical explanation has a certain validity because of the ways and means we've brought our own comprehension to measurable conclusions.

This work is an attempt to show that we can postulate a very small number of assumptions and utilize them to explain a very large spectrum of phenomena. Common sense is not so common and is the highest praise we give to a chain of seemingly logical conclusions.

One needs the courage to face inconsistencies and a conviction to develop a belief that the world does make sense — that it is logical and somewhat reasonable to understand. The passing of knowledge to one another continues the theme of learning and its adventure in discovering its actual simplicity, which is perplexing to the complications we make of it from within our own intelligence.

After all, what we are looking through is the distorted and disguised truth that we've always heard about and occasionally thought of. The clarification of myth and tale brings allegory and metaphor to a comparative elucidation not so immediately apparent in the parallels drawn from them. We must find our own way through the labyrinth of emotional overtones the mind brings to us from the activity to which it gives us awareness. The thought of a perennially peaceful life in tune with the thought of an infinite reality is not far off the course we pursue increasing our knowledge. The seeking of knowledge is an honorable way of dealing with the tension and anxiety that comes along with the rites of passage in our life. Our world of ambition, ideal, and achievement brings us to surpass mediocrity.

Often in the solitude of a secluded place, or in my room, my sanctuary from the world, I contemplated the grandeur and magnificence of my own inner reality and of the natural reality that surrounds me. The more I thought of the theme this work represents, the more determined I became to ensure its completion. My notes were ready from another year of study and concentrated reflection, and I had passed a mid-point and found a suitable conclusion. So I began the labor of typing out my notes which evolved into this draft of my story. I persisted tenaciously in my endeavor and felt a genuine sense of accomplishment.

I read avidly, my developing mind eager for satisfactory replies to the questions which on occasion crop up as the result of my own survey of the narrow world we all seem to live in. In spite of the phenomenal increase in knowledge over the past recent centuries there are still certain questions that defy any reasonable explanation.

Only after many years was I able to locate the source of the bewildering phenomena and trace it to a marvelous spiritual intelligence natural to people, which is both illuminating and mystifying in the paradoxical enigma of retaining found knowledge and turning it into personal wisdom.

The achievements of science had brought astounding possibilities within the reach of man, possibilities no less amazing than the miracle of transcendental experiences periodically vouchsafed to specially constituted individuals seeking knowledge of an extraordinary kind.

The truth is one certain sureness that comes in various forms and mental representations passed along by civilization throughout the ages. Throughout the inhabited world the metaphysical unknown has been described by tales and legends arising in inspiration from our own human intelligence.

The human spirit is carried forward through time and with time, through the course of human events, uncovering along the way what has been kept concealed from our investigation with our intelligent perception and by its revealing or opening-up of our imagination. It is our personal obligation and responsibility to hear the call of the adventure in learning and beckon it to come closer for our own inspection and contemplation. Knowledge is nothing without someone to think about it and pass it along as we find out what we do and find some relevance and importance to it.

As one thinks logically and consistently about the world, certain relationships can be discovered and our thinking evolves the more we learn about them. Understanding of our world is not something to be pursued for its own sake; knowledge should be pursued to make our world better and to make life more fulfilling.

We need to have courage to face the inconsistencies we find between what we see and deduce and the way things come to be. As we challenge the basic assumptions we seem to know we can better understand our world and the principles that govern it.

We get from today's knowledge to tomorrow's knowledge by challenging what we seem to know today and what is coming to be from the new conclusions we make by the discovery our investigating and exploration leads us to. Just as the developments of past generations led us to where we are, the projections we make today lead us to tomorrow.

As we live we cannot deny our experience. Our imagination creates in us another reality just as sensual as the physical world. The experience of mind-related matters constitutes the other reality our investigation yields us to. The unexplainable is a justified experience we have no defense for, yet its reality is just as obvious in our mind as is our sense perception, though on a different level of thought. That world we think of inside our mind is an inner experience that has a rationality and sanctioned justifiability.

Even as I am conscious of my own experience in a greater world than my own its singular reality cannot as well be denied. Though it is full of emotion, we sense that emotion just as we do everything else in the material world. What is important here is not how things actually are but how we think about them, including their worth and value. We must consider what is more than probability but their possibility.

What we do have are elementary concepts of understanding. The things we seem to know are the basics of life and their comprehension comes reduced to its own simplistic form for all of us understand on each of our own levels and with our own abilities.

What we have in our intuition is thought that has been processed and about which we can come to conclusions without difficulty, because these concepts of intuition are inherent in our humanness.

The appearances which reality impresses on us are true, just as our inner reality, but we must be aware that appearances of truth are not the same as actual truth and can be deceiving.

The reality we perceive is an object of sensation which has magnitude — that is, a degree of heightened importance on our reason and ability to conceive what we seem to have an understanding of.

What one must consider and take into account in one's thoughts is that there are three categories in the status of things: first is the possibility of things, second is the actuality of them, and third is the necessity of their actual existence. If we can relate these properties to even our spirit and soul, we have there a basis to believe in the possibility of a Higher Power of the divine.

It is important to remember that there are two classes of things in this world: first there are those that can be grasped by sense perception, and secondly those that are grasped by the intellect alone. We must consider all things in an intelligible and sensible way. There is a distinction between thinking and knowing which one must give further consideration to.

Quite possibly it is this bringing of the inner experience into the outer experience life offers us that is an important aspect of knowledge itself. Wisdom is knowing the difference and acquiring a taste for the truth as we find it in both the inner and outer experiences.

The road to enlightenment is arduous and tedious. The mental exertion of concentration is a strenuous activity. The real issue is how to integrate these experiences, how to live with them, and how to keep them from overwhelming the internal mind with revelation and the external reality with fantasy. It is our ability to translate them into awareness and our ability to ground them with the human condition we find ourselves living in.

It is an undeniable fact that the quest of the unknown is as unmistakable a feature of ancient civilizations as it is now in our modern day and age. This is a story of that awakening in me as it has happened so often in others.

The evolution of man in actual fact signifies the evolution of our consciousness existing deep in the human mind, fed by a higher form of vital energy permeating the whole personality of an individual, an energy that belongs more to heaven than to earth.

With this one notion in mind one is more inclined to believe that passing knowledge to one another has more importance than we would ordinarily be given to understand. In being human we are conscious of what we think just as we are conscious of ourselves both physically and emotionally. Through the utility of our intellect we, through our creative imagination and by our sense of reason and logic, come to determinations and judgments of natural things and morals and determine our own ethics and convictions on such matters.

Our sensibility gives us grounds for employing, in transcendental reflection, the concept of thinking of our own thoughts in an intelligent and creative manner. Any method that we use must come from our own preference in a regular way or from procedures and techniques of a particular discipline or field of knowledge.

The world in which we live is a sum of the appearances things give to our senses and the ground of thought we give to the inner working of our own intelligent mind. Bearing in mind the stupendous extent of the universe, the conception of the Creator becomes so staggering that it is utterly beyond the capacity of the human mind, yet we still imagine possibilities beyond compare.

The developed capacity of the one who labors in thought rises above the sense-bound human intellect to apprehend a certain principle of the Creator's immeasurable qualities. There is no known method by which the intelligence of a normal person can overstep the boundaries set to it by nature, yet we still try.

Even though we are sharpened and improved with applications of all sorts to accommodate more information and assimilate more facts, with the exception of certain gifted and eccentric individuals few have come to know God who is ultimately unknowable.

An ordinary man in a humble walk of life, burdened with responsibilities just like any other, I never allowed the mountain of despondency to bring me down further than a level from which I would be capable of rising up, one in which the bottom seemed in sight but still remained out of reach. This forms an inevitable corollary to the struggle for existence and the strides we take for our own survival.

We cannot get away from a contradiction in our own make-up;

we must make an effort to reconcile it. The greatest probability of fulfillment still admits an element of doubt; that is why what you hope for is always surprising when it really happens. It could be truly didactic if we could learn as much as we are taught, but as it seems, each of us have our own level of understanding. Comprehension comes to each of us from our own abilities.

An idea is something eternal and unique. Like the spirit, there are many ideas, but only one spirit of God. It is not correct to use this term in the plural. Only one idea can surface in the mind at a time. Everything that enters our awareness and that we can talk about is no more than the manifestation of an idea; we explain and express concepts, and to that extent an idea itself becomes a concept. Our knowledge is only a conglomeration of ideas, of concepts in the mind, but our wisdom is the consolidation of our knowledge.

The spirit, like air, is spread out all through nature and appears as a whole organized world within many others and surrounding them and interacting with them as a concept, in principle, to science. Spirit acts the same as air does in our environment and is a force of dissolution independent and self-existent without any other force necessary for its natural being, because it is self-fulfilling.

Its self-containment is the same quality of self-completeness of the whole, in its own entirety and enduring into its own unity. It is critically important to nature and at the same time has its own criterion which judgments and decisions can be formed about.

As a real force and power in the world and in living things, its own simplicity is fathomable and comprehensible. It gives itself to its own understanding. It is phenomenal and is at the beginning of universal when seen as an element that sustains life. The spirit is just like air and has a weight and measure of its own.

In the connection with a transcendental theology, we ask, first, whether there is anything distinct from the world, which contains the ground of the order of the world and its connection in accordance with universal laws. The answer is that there must be therefore some transcendental ground of that which is thinkable only by pure understanding which takes place within our own mind in thought and reflection. The spirit is something real; it draws its own existence from the thought we give to it and finds its place in the universal because of its immediate validity and acknowledgement of its presence and permanence in the world as we come to know it.

What we need to do is to be able to grasp the underlying reality of the world experience by purely intellectual means. We can find the means to experience our inner and outer world by more than just the use of our senses; we can experience it intellectually with our natural ability of creative thinking and thought-provoking imagination.

Throughout the ages the dialogue about thought and about non-empirical objects has been widely discussed; though its affirmation has been accepted, the metaphysical notions about thought and the realm of mind are still a subject of great debate. The inner experience is just as important as the experience we bring from the natural world outside ourselves, yet still our thoughts wander aimlessly.

Transcendental metaphysics is as much of an intrinsically worthy object of philosophical investigation as the possibility of knowledge itself. So we pass knowledge to one another through debate and by dialogue in addition to the ambitious speculation and logical revelation from the inner working of our own mind.

The essential bridge that leads the world into our mind is built from our thoughts and requires our intellect for its structure and grounding. Though the world exists by itself, and outside ourselves, what we make of it comes totally from within.

Reason produces concepts of its own, distinct from those of understanding. These are transcendental ideas or the notions of reason known similarly as creative thought or the thinking of contemplation and reflection upon itself. Reason has its own stock of innate ideas; these resources of the mind supply us with the spirit to endure and survive the trials and tribulations that life brings to the threshold of our existence.

My experience with the natural sciences is like that of a man who gets up early and then in the dusky light of dawn impatiently awaits the early brightness of the sky, with all its splendor and color, yet is blinded, in a way, when the sun actually appears, bringing with it a new day full of anticipation and reflection of expectation for what the mobius spiral of the endless cycle of nature reveals.

Our world and our knowledge of it invite a metaphysical explanation that perhaps from the mind's indulgence in study and reflection brings about a unity that cannot be denied. Real existences rather than mere logical relations between concepts transgress the limits of experience and advance us towards completeness of our understanding and how we came to that understanding.

What we do is to project images of what we think we know and have an understanding of into the void beyond experience and associate thought with real knowledge.

When the moon appears at the horizon the illusion of its grandeur is much greater then when it is high in the sky. Just the same, when our thoughts perceive the grandeur of notions and ideas at the horizon in our mind, once thoroughly considered the appearance from different views takes on the truth of reality as we come to know it on our own terms.

Concrete actual conscious life has within it both principles, and the distinction between its forms falls solely within its own nature, from inside the relation of itself to the reality that we conceive. A conscious life which finds itself at one with them has the attribute of nobility. These principles regard what is in accord with itself and find that it has there its own nature pure and simple and stands in the position of actually rendering obedient service in its interests, as well as that of inner reverence towards it.

Through this process of thought the universal becomes united and bound up with existence in general. By thus shaping its life in accordance with what is universal, it acquires a reverence for itself and gets reverence from others giving and receiving knowledge unconditionally.

The result of this action binding indissolubly together the essential reality and self is to produce a twofold actuality — a self that is truly actualized and a state of power whose authority is accepted as a true and useful purpose. It has an idea of conformity with an essential nature and is acknowledged and accepted because of its inherent reality.

Dealing with the unknown is a magical experience. What becomes revealed from its concealment is a wonder itself. The adventure is always and everywhere a passage beyond the veil of the known into the unknown.

The powers that watch at the boundary are real and to deal with them is risky; yet for anyone with competence and courage the danger fades and revelation becomes more than just imagination.

The spiritual world is to be reckoned with and not to be denied. It surrounds us and finds its own way into our ordinary lifestyles. This knowledge of the transcendental is independent of experience; it comes to our experience as an idea in the motion of our mind's thinking experience. Even this, however, can never be final; it is the transcendental illusion that continually entraps reason and will always call for correction.

Our judgments are interconnected; giving unity to knowledge is the job of reason, just as understanding works on the manifold of sensibility substantially. At the base of pure reason, we begin by considering the origin of the concept and idea of God. Knowledge of this type, though it has a common ground throughout the history of civilization, leads one to wonder how this idea came about. The challenge comes; thinking of our own mind, the possibility of a greater cosmological mind becomes intuitively curious. Just the thought requires a certain imagination and ingenuity.

The mystique of the transcendental is helpful because the mind feels at home with the images it creates and seems to be remembering something already known to it.

All things are in process, rising and returning in the mobius cycle of nature. Seeking tranquility is like moving towards destiny. To move forward destiny is like eternity. To know eternity is enlightenment. Knowing eternity allows one to comprehend; comprehension makes one broad-minded. The breadth of vision brings nobility, and this nobility is like knowing there is a heaven within our own mind.

The irony, of course, lies in the fact that, while one is enchanted with enlightenment, the quest for illumination can be deceiving.

The state of enlightenment only makes us more certain that there is so much more that we do not know and must experience for ourselves along destiny's path towards eternity. Every object of cognition can be considered in terms of the concept of probability. Rational theology, like all transcendental metaphysics, expresses reason's search for an idea of the highest mind, the ideal being that we call Creator.

The one with the original mind we call the Holy Spirit gives reason to our own spirit as well as to the idea and notion of heart and soul. They are necessarily intimately related. Somehow and in some way we must account for our own mystical and spiritual experiences.

As we search for reason our own creative intelligence supplies us with a foundation and basis for what we believe and hope for. Our finite mortality seeks the means for substantiating the immortality of spirit and soul for our own well-being and emotional security. The possibility of an ideal Higher Power navigates its way through each of us in our very own terms of being and existence.

The source of possibility is the ideal of pure reason; the intellect in all its magnificence and grandeur considers the whole picture while focusing on each individual part. It is this notion that provides the core of our concept of the entity or being we have given the name of Creator, God the Almighty Maker, or Architect of all.

I think this is a genuine rational theology, a way and means of reaching a metaphysical philosophy. From this possibility we achieve the highest ground and degree of reality within our own understanding.

What one must consider at this point is there being an Architect rather than a Creator, now called "Great Inventor."

The Great Inventor seems most appropriate to reform a system of thinking; within this same consideration one ought to be concerned with the model rather than the idea. If the premise of an Architect is taken into account, we come to a reasonable conclusion that nature works its way through design rather than providence, which allows for a greater view of composing the world rather than simply bringing it into view, both conceiving and perceiving it simultaneously in eternity.

The implications of this view bring unity to theology and to naturalism, and hence a wider range of acceptability among our contemporary philosophers and humans' ability to converse in dialogue on a subject so renowned and equilaterally universal as We Passing Knowledge to One Another, distinguishing it as a work of revelation through study and thought of those studies that bring comprehension and understanding to our own reality. Though one cannot deny providence, one must at the same time be open-minded to other perspectives that include nature equally within the realm of the divine.

By the means of this notion an idea comes to mind that God's own spirit finds necessarily a dominant role, perhaps just because of the implications the word brings to life, in nature and in the inner mind, the evolution that includes us in the quantum idea of universe and brings nature into the same spirit of autonomy as does an ordinary human bring the spirit of autonomy to his own level of existence.

Could it be that nature has been given the spirit of compensation along with that same universal spirit we all now seem to acknowledge? Our rites of passage do go by noticed as the continuum envelops our own universe. As we become legends in time there is a principle that considers with the human motif of "some day you are going to pay." So you can pay it forward or pay as your ingenuity allows, keeping an opening in your mind to accumulate newly gathered knowledge and responding appropriately with a sense of rationality and logic.

Forms and conceptions that the mind and its essential qualities can comprehend and make judgments on are arranged in such a way to suggest a truth or openness beyond resolution; yet depending on the one who labors in thought, this resolution comes to agreement with one's self-made personal beliefs and convictions.

Briefly formulated, the universal doctrine teaches that all things and beings, and the universal structures of nature's visible world, are the effects of a ubiquitous power out of which arise curious characteristics which must ultimately dissolve into creative imagination. The vital essence of the spiritual world is that same power of our own. Philosophy and theology are the things of the mind that make our reality what it is. This is something deeply personal that each of us at some time in our lives has to come to terms with. The occasions are real and the situations of events are sure and certain. We should never give up on God, because God never gives up on us. There is a mutual and reciprocal relationship there, in our mind and in the spiritual sense of our intellect.

The life of the spirit is something to be cherished, and though it is only a symbol to move and awaken us in the morning light of the dawn of our intellect, it calls us past its own presence to a still mightier power: God's own Holy Spirit.

We are simultaneously caught in a thought-bewildering sublime paradox, the kingdom of God within, yet without even an end or a beginning; but our awareness comes along with time during the course of events in our rites of passage and can be found in the beginning of the unconscious to the surface of our consciousness.

Experience cannot present us with an object adequate to the concept of God or the Holy Spirit, the mind of God, and no principle of inference can bridge the gap; yet the part of the Holy Trinity in the form of Jesus brings us closer to an understanding, even of our own spirit and soul that the intellect gives us wisdom and knowledge of.

The spirit of nature is the closest representation of our own spirit with the will to survive, endure living, and make the best of it that we can. Our inherent and innate quality of persistence and endurance, and that power of endurance, is encountered with an unwavering passion, one full of emotion that presents itself with chance and opportunity. The concept of God is intrinsically coherent and rationally necessary to our own stability and well-being. It is the transcendental origin of the concept as old as antiquity itself. It is not immune to criticism and is certainly open to be challenged.

This view is not obligatory yet A basic philosophical proposition that comes to mind is that our knowledge is adequate enough to get by; though being sick with mediocrity, our curiosity remains strong enough to supplement what it is that we think we already know. But the surprising thing is, when chance meets with opportunity and reason makes logical ideas and notions, we become familiar with ourselves and find a comfort which is one of those never-forgotten things that keeps us witty.

Though the nature of things provides insoluble problems, our quest for knowledge continues unceasingly. Our drive to break through the limits of perception lies in our ability to conceive and use our faculty of imagination in a constructive way.

What we need is a way of contemplating experience as an idea or thought that determines, rather than transgresses, the bounds of achievement and does not confuse these bounds with the natural limits of reality.

It was the end of December already, headed right towards the New Year, mid-winter yet bearable to a degree. What concerns the intelligible world shares a common situation. To get along with what we've got and control our needs — utopia would have been a nice place if it all worked out. We create our own world from within outwards.

Our own theoretical faculties must determine these concepts by their own power still within our understanding. Just beyond is a mighty land where the mind reaches its own ideal in the role it fulfills, gaining repose and a sense of comfort within itself.

Euphoria lures repose and stillness full with a quiet mind. Writing is almost a noble tradition and art that spans eons of history. Communicated with the voice of language, thought takes on many forms. Generatively it is protocol issues that guide us through life.

The call of mankind to preserve words that have emotion behind them is writing's most useful ideal. So we have remembrance to lay up for each generation's literary amusement with the thinking about thinking.

Sick with mediocrity, trying our learning becomes our own genius. At its height, writing becomes crucial to the generations to come and relevant even to our own.

I think it all comes down to how you think and why you do it as you do. So with this thought in mind this study has become a real story about thought, idea, and notion; as we pass knowledge to one another, we do as well pass it on to our own mind from both inside and from our relationship with the world.

From here we proceed through our understanding and rationalizing our very own way of thinking and continue in our adventure in learning about how we think and the ways and means open to our abilities, luring us to the conclusions that we come to.

Beyond its application transcendental idealism coupled with metaphysics acts as a grounding foundation for the reality we perceive and conceive deep within our brain's powers of moving thoughts along with the passage of time. These theories strive to relieve theoretical reasoning of its conflicts in a multidimensional way.

Even a stopped clock shows the right time twice a day. Life goes on just the same but different somehow, and the choice is ours to make of it just what we can. Through our own rational psychology, our chief motive is to secure our thinking against the danger of misconception and illusion. We continue in our quest for more and greater knowledge.

To think of ourselves outside reality in a possible experience of unknown conception is the ground for our faith and belief and gives us reason for hope through moral and ethical behavior within a civilized society.

What we do is to think ourselves beyond experience in the world of reality into the world of mind, spirit, and soul. As thought gives way to wonder, we need to concern ourselves with the relationships concepts have with one another and their interaction in our intelligent mind without regard for emotion.

Foundations for Noumenal Reason

We are question-begging beings; the answers we seek are everywhere, even within our own mind, waiting to be revealed from their concealment. We must decide for ourselves whether their appearance is real or just an illusion further begging confirmation through our reason.

The cognition of our inner experience precedes that of the outer experience that comes to us from the world around us, which our mind interprets by its nature.

Once we recognize the existence of our own being we come to terms with the physical world and then try to explain our own spiritual world. The exploration of both occurs simultaneously and on the same plane by the faculty of our imaginative and intelligent mind.

It is our noumenal reason, or that which we perceive by thought; that reason makes clear to us our ability to conceive notions and ideas. The matrix of destiny is bound up in the mobius cycle of nature. The world of human life is now the problem. Survival is the immediate answer, but it is more than mere survival; we have to come to terms with our own thoughts in order to endure any anxiety we cause for ourselves from our own thinking or from the thoughts passed to us from others.

Saint Thomas Aquinas declares, "The name of being wise is reserved to him alone whose consideration is about the end of the universe, an end that is also the beginning of the universe."

One of the most curious principles of theology, metaphysics, and philosophy is the notion of a beginning at the end. It creates for itself an enigmatic paradox, considering eternity as something that has neither end nor beginning, where both are in the same place in the current of time.

The forms go forth powerfully, but inevitably reach their heights, break from a sublime awakening, and return to physical reality. True being, meanwhile, is not in the shapes our mind conceives, but in the dreamer. As in a dream, the images have a variety of ranges from the sublime to the incredible, creating in the mind an absolute reason for comprehension and understanding.

The world-generating spirit of the Creator passes into the manifold of earthly experience through a transforming medium — the mother of the world. She is a personification of the primal element named in the second verse of Genesis, where we read that "the spirit of God moved upon the face of the waters." More abstractly she is the lure that moved the Creator to the act of creation. It is the spirit of God that acted in God's own mind, making reality of a dream.

Here idealism and realism find their own differences. It is how we consider things that brings fulfillment to the answers we find. We can eliminate the notion that our knowledge is subject to limitations. For those who labor in thought, what we can know is a vast area still yet to be explored, and not denied just because we have no knowledge or understanding of it and its properties.

One must realize that the unknown is greater than the known, from the necessity of the grandeur of the universe we are part of. Our knowledge is not subject to limitations; only our ability and willingness to learn prevent us from discovering what can be known. Even if we do not understand what we know we can still attempt a certain level of comprehension according to our understanding and reason inherent in our intelligent nature.

What we need to do is to make theoretical philosophy into a practical philosophy an ordinary user can come to terms with in their relative way of conceiving and understanding. What we are looking for is a practical way of understanding the peculiarities of life, including the concepts of spirit, nature, and God — God the architect, an ideal entity, though in thought quite possibly something more real than we can conceive.

What we do on many occasions is to view the same objects from two different points of view. It is our perspective that makes the difference. On the one hand, in connection with experience, and on the other as objects which are merely thought of. This is the notion of a twofold manner of conceiving things, which we do regularly in the course of our own existence.

The degree of reality in our mind is just as relevant as the physical reality that surrounds us. In the grandeur of the whole picture, the inner and outer world our life encounters has just as much importance because nature made it that way. A life without an emotional response would be no life at all. It is our emotions that give life its flavor.

In any writing, just like thinking, you pay attention to theme, content, and style. You discover along the way astonishments and features that make you wonder with enthusiastic curiosity, which engages the senses to further exploration.

Intellectual intuition answers our questions, by allowing what we perceive and conceive to be intuitable. Sensible intuition allows itself to be extended through the imagination over all possibilities. What is on the edge of experience can be known, but what is on the far side we can only give thought to with conjecture. Experience has bounds but does not bound itself, as shown by the notion that thought extends beyond the confines of our own intelligence.

Knowledge is just a shape, a form, of our perspective of it. The human perspective itself fixes upon itself and the world in which we live. Though we are in search for the grounds of reality, metaphysical knowledge becomes at once a deep need of human reason to find firm footing somewhere beyond the limits of experience. From the point of view of meaningful human activity, the world and universe are greater than we can either conceive or comprehend, though our understanding remains within our reasoning ability.

Because the idea of transcendental freedom lies ready, pre-prepared by theoretical reason, we are fully entitled to regard our moral and self consciousness as an expression of reason's capacity for self-determination. By the power and use of our will, inherent in our nature, we justify and vindicate our judgment uniquely from inferring through the use of deduction and logic. Noumenal reality is, as conceived by theoretical reason, the realm of the unconditioned super-sensible that gives satisfaction to our own intellect.

By rational necessity we come to know the person of God not only as an ideal, but as, by practical reason, the architect of our intuition of all that is possible within our imagination. Without that belief in the mighty power of the one we call God, ethics and morality would not be possible. Just as well the concept of justice would have no plausible ground as its foundation.

The sensible side of humanity is not an illusion but is essential to its reality. Sensibly derived motivation cannot be denied, because of the conviction we have of our own consciousness of our conscience.

Reason is thereby called upon to supply some set of theoretical judgments which will rationalize the hope which is presupposed by the concepts and notions of spirit and soul, and in the one we call Almighty God. The existence of God and eternity, including the concept of infinity, reveal their rational necessity for a future world that is not so far off from our own — really just on the other side of the mind. To deny this would be illogical and impractical consistent with our present interpretation of the doctrine written in as many cultures as there are within our own civilization on the scale of humanity as a whole, even throughout the ages that history has been written.

As we explore our own mind the variety of considerations we are given to assures us that our creative intelligence is constantly at work, bringing us to new and higher evaluations of our own capabilities.

Reason finds itself constrained to assume an intelligible world, under the authority of a wise architect and spirit who is both the guide of nature to which we belong and the arbiter in the conscience of humans with themselves and their counterparts of which civilization is made complete and whole. Without the invisible spiritual world to console our thoughts and assure us of our beliefs, the idea and notion might as well be an empty figment of our imagination. But it is more than that and has substantial qualities accompanied by a system of divinely administered rewards and sanctions, on the strict condition that we regard them as rational faith with inward obligation necessary to fulfill what theology enjoins with philosophy.

As we go about our learning every challenge is actually a disguised opportunity. At every stage in the unfolding of our understanding we find a freedom, a satisfaction of accumulating new treasures of wisdom. Our mind is empowered to think of reality as the physical reality; though the one who labors in thought knows that the reality within our mind is just as real and can go beyond and surpass the physical reality into some curious and mysterious realm of spiritual inspiration and revelation about the higher forms of nature, still included in nature but of a higher form than the ordinary.

To reconnect to this deeper reality is natural and only requires a certain amount of genuine thought. One must not only think about the intense but act on it as inspiration as if it were more than just a means of entertainment but as a thrill one encounters as one goes about learning. I write to be read, to create something that other people will read, care about, and enjoy.

I took a short walk today in mid-winter's fresh coolness and enjoyed seeing the blue sky with some light clouds scattered about. I enjoyed the feeling that I had found connecting with the earth while it revolved about the sun in the universe. I found myself in the luxury of connecting my inner with the real outer. The experience motivated me to continue in my studies and writing.

Happiness depends on conditions in the real world that include both the inner and outer experience. If you are happy and want to be happier you should redefine what you expect happiness to be. Seen from a higher perspective, conditions have their own worth of positivity.

In the meantime what we have to do is to accept what is and contend with what is beyond our control. It is this mind-enhancing experience that gives us a certain security in our own thinking. The present moment is a great relief when things are going our way, but when things do not seem to be going our way we must find a path through the past and future to reconnect with the moment where all things find their place, both in time and in our intelligent mind with its own abilities and capacities.

Life is strange and wonderful at the same time. What makes us curious about it is not how things happen but the eternal why. Whoever or whatever enters our field of consciousness has an effect on us, and how we deal with these conditions makes the difference in our life. As long as you are in the physical dimension you are connected with the collective human psyche, but what is more important is how you connect to yourself. Through allowing the "isness" of all things, a deeper dimension underneath the surface of reality, communicating with your own inner stillness, still remains one of the important factors of living a full and sincere life.

Your physical energy is also subject to cycles, just as everything else in nature. Understanding your own peaks and lows is a factor we must not deny. All conditions are highly unstable and in constant flux. One must be able to understand that through these cycles our emotions act the same way, and though they are explainable they are not always understandable.

Nothing is what it seems to be. The world you create and see through your mind may seem like a very imperfect place, which it is, but still we make our own sense of it. You become the light of your own world.

The conflict of reason with faith is now superseded; matters of faith having been brought within the scope of reason become an expression of the inner self, deeper than the intellect.

Practical reason could not require theoretical reason to assure the existence of something that is judged only possible yet probable due to the inherent nature of the faculty of our intellect.

Reason generates contradiction and is driven to go beyond them. Reason's capacity to overcome, guaranteed by its awareness of its own discord, compels it to produce new concepts in which former contradictions are resolved. This is, in part, the evolution of an increasingly complex and comprehensive philosophy of rationality evoked from the human condition for those who labor in thought of ideas and notions within and beyond experience.

Intellectual Necessity

What we need to do is to find a way from within to explore the outer world and the depths of our own being. Within the realm of enlightenment we stand to be corrected and define our intellectual horizon, one that we possess singularly and individually while completing ourselves in the whole human experience civilization offers us.

We must question ourselves whether existence precedes essence or essence acquires a new dimension with existence. Yet to be considered is the destiny essence comes from and proceeds to. It must be that the failure of human thinking leaves out the possible because the mind brings reality to our thought so easily.

There is room enough for the imagination to make its way through our thoughts into our real intelligence that includes our creativity. We are thinking creatures. Our imagination roams freely through the depths of our knowledge and beyond into the probable and possible. This is our intellectual necessity that comes with the will to live and learn and struggles to survive along the way.

There are gaps between the demands of the mind for confirmation and the expectations of what we find to be true, even without that confirmation we all look for in exploring truth and validity.

If you have lived long enough, you know how the mind identifies its wisdom and connects its knowledge to it. This is purely an inner phenomenon from the actions of the mind at work. It is thought in the process of thinking about itself and what grounds it. There is something inside you that remains unaffected by the transient circumstances that make up your life situation; that is your eternal spirit in your consciousness.

Those who run themselves on mind energy, which is still the vast majority of Earth's population, remain unaware of the existence of spiritual energy. This energy belongs to a different order of reality and is empowering by the way it creates in a person a different world than exists in those without that awareness. It is a silent but intense presence that makes us aware of our own consciousness and spirit.

What still remains to be said could perhaps be of some guidance where one thoughtfully attends to the dimension of truth which governs the essence of our existence and being. Metaphysics is a storehouse full of treasure for thought and reflection.

What cannot be explained we try to do; what can be explained needs to be thoughtfully reasoned. One thing that I've noticed is that we get very temperamental and tenacious with our thinking. Open-mindedness is an essential quality for the one who labors in thought.

We may not transform reality or humanity, but we may transform ourselves. And if we do, we might just change the world a bit in doing so. In the process, we must, in our creative stewardship, trust in the self-disciplined elegance of the mind seeking its potential ability.

Practically speaking, we must make the complex simple and make the simple easier to understand. Life throws a whole lot at us at once; I wonder just how many people in the drama of life realize their own connectedness with each other and the world. I put myself in my books, in my writing, because that's all I know. It's an opportunity for me to realize and recognize my own strengths and weakness.

The human mind is a mass of associations, more poetic even than actually thought. There must be a reason if we could only imagine that far into ourselves. Our thinking attends to relationships of thought and matter. It tries to find the right words for expression within the traditional forms of language, but comes out through music as well. It is through language that our thoughts become representational in their meanings designated to them; music does the same.

There is more to thought than just thinking, and there is more to words than just their meaning. Just the same there is more to reading than words. It is the thought-provoking words that lead our thinking in thought. What we are seeking is the true meaning of belongingness, the feeling for humanity as we are part of and not apart from. This is the spirit of humanity and the same spirit we carry in our being, because we know that we are part of something bigger than ourselves.

Essentially we circle around ourselves through our individuality, while belonging to a well-organized society where culture and tradition keep us united yet keep our separateness bonded with integrity. Not only do we have community, but as well we have nationalism; and then there is the internationalism that brings humanity together. It is a historical collectivism that binds humanity to our planet.

Though we are part of a greater world than our own, we often find ourselves alone and isolated either by chance or by choice. The fundamental intellectual necessity is our belonging that is exposed from our alienation. It is something each of us has to find for ourselves in the rites of passage through our existence.

What we are left with is the residue of humanity, which is the distilled self we find in contemplation and reflection, thinking curiously about the world we live in and our own personal life within that world in a universe greater than we could even imagine.

What is concealed in our thinking is the step back, indulging in a special sort of philosophical inquiry that lets thinking enter into questioning rather than engaging in dialogue upon a specific subject. Things that really matter find a way of presenting themselves to us at an opportune time when we are ready to think about them in an open-minded way, considering both sides of a possibility or principle.

We must judge for ourselves the road we are to follow by trying one or another, by blazing a new road never before traveled, or by taking one less traveled except by those few who know its possibilities.

Experience is something we can all value, especially the man who is old and has time to think, to reflect; he has the confident, comfortable feeling that no one can rob him of. The one who labors in thought is the same; no one can take away that person's notions and ideas of what seems real. Who can take away from me the secret joy of knowing what I do by my unremitting attentive work, with such amazing discoveries that I've made through my own adventure in learning and from the passing of knowledge to one another? The questions you pose help to clarify the way thinking evolves, from theory to fact and from imagination to reality. The same thinking that leads insight compels us to adjust our perspective to take into account the grandeur of the whole picture. The panorama has many beautiful sights, but there is always at least one that captures our attention and compels us to wonder about it more than any other.

We should not settle for misinterpretation when we know better. Compelled by reflection upon a thought, the path of thinking most suitable is a natural reinterpretation of the most common elements of the basis of our elemental thoughts. What could be more valid and logical while accepting existence as life? But the denial that is irresponsible and destructive to the human element is renouncing life beyond what we already know as limited and finite. There must be more to it than can be explained.

Prevailing opinion is always filled with contradiction; but there is more and it can't be proved so why even try to deny it. Concealed in doctrine is more than fantasy; but we must overcome our differences.

We must be discursive thinkers traveling to conclusions through reason rather than by intuition. We must articulate and use clear expressive thoughts, evaluating our wording to get the message that we thought we wanted to portray across to the reader from our writer's mind. We must as well find in our imagination a logic that fits into the common laws of nature as we know it.

This is just one of the notions of intellectual necessity that promotes our well-being and ability to survive in an illogical and unresponsive world where everyone looks after themselves and has the least compassion for another human as could be required by simple moral and ethical social norms. It is not only our ability to survive but our ability to reach out and pass knowledge to one another, along with giving a helping hand when either chance or opportunity rises to the occasion. The world we live in is more than just intriguing and complex; it is a world where each of us must find our place and in that place find comfort and repose.

There are two very real realities we exist with simultaneously: ideas in the mind, and objects in the external world. We cannot deny that the external world exists without us, because it was there before we were and will still be here after us; but it is in our mind that we conceive and perceive it, and interpret what we find from both realities.

Philosophy does not make decisions, people do; but philosophy opens up the debate and dialogue people encounter in their decision-making process. Philosophy does not decide for or against something; it only expands the thought into parts and considers them both in their parts and in the whole. Perhaps this is the beauty of philosophy?

It is the thinking we do that points us towards the truth in our discovery and exploration of it, which surpasses the limits and boundaries and overcomes the obstacles of thought in the way of finding what the real truth is. We surmount and transcend the real and perceive the unknown with our intelligent curiosity. The descent back into thought is more arduous than the ascent, which brings us to thought itself.

The hidden perplexity of man soars immeasurably to great heights. The greatest care must be fostered in how we think and not just why. As our thinking becomes more disciplined, the parameters of our thoughts approach boundaries of known limits, but only cross the threshold in our imagination.

The atmosphere that surrounds the thinker is ordinary and common, yet what is inside the thinker's mind is eccentric and reaches towards the ideal. Some thought to be pondered over captures our attention without release until we reach some stage of involvement with it that brings us peace of mind in our comprehension and understanding.

There is a type of thinking more rigorous than the conceptual.

It is thinking without regard for words, a pure thought that consists of wonder and amusement and resides in our creativity consciously. This is the basis of our intellectual necessity. It is a thinking of a sort that requires contemplation and reflection on the idea as much as on the concept of that idea.

The one who labors in thought needs to be practical and theoretical in the thoughts that come upon his own mind. It comes to pass that before distinction there is a common ground that we all use as common knowledge. Our knowledge works in a circular motion; we are presented with an idea and proceed to discover and explore the notions that evoked the very same idea.

Thinking towers above action, not through the grandeur of its achievement or as a consequence of its effects but through the humility of its inconsequential accomplishment.

Thinking is an adventure, not only as a search and inquiry of knowledge to increase our personal wisdom but as something that brings the humanness out of our being. Thinking is the one thing that is bound to the necessity of our intellect.

Thinking brings us into recollection just as it brings us further into our imagination. Thinking is the arbiter of our spirit which decides the destiny of our character.

When we look back on our life we really only see it as something piecemeal, because our omissions always surface first in our mind and dominate our achievements. Every true insight is part of a sequence and leads to finding revelation in that sequence, which is the search and discovery of knowledge and wisdom. Nature has given us a chessboard and all the pieces to play the game of life. How we move the pieces is up to us, even though we may not understand the consequences of our moves.

What is really most extraordinary is when a person finds that there is an ultimate source for most phenomena; the classical borders between our inner and outer worlds have filters that can be interchanged with our mindset. New possibilities are opened up with each new setting we change in the functioning of our patterns of thought.

One senses, or possibly even realizes, that this new makeshift way of thinking opens new doors and windows to one's perception that one could have never before thought possible. The result is a more active and progressive way of thinking.

Facient Interpretation

What causes or brings about something intangible is thought. What is incapable of being perceived by the senses can be known by the mind and conceived by it through what we have come to know as the abilities of the mind from intelligent necessity; and as well it becomes facient, bringing out reasonable notions of thought.

It is our instinct to be thoughtful creatures and to use our abilities integral to possessing everything essential and entire to ensure our completeness as humans. What is in the light of the fundamental conceptions we arrive at depends upon just how far our conceptions can reach through the known into the unknown.

We must stretch out our mind beyond its natural limits to come up with new and bold insight into what we already seem to know and discover further in our knowledge the things and qualities we may have missed along the way of our exploration.

What needs to be done therefore is to create new ways of posing questions and, above all, hold out in the questionable for a more reasonable answer. A story once was told about a traveler in ancient times who was a friend of Socrates. He found Socrates on the street lecturing to people who gathered around him. The friend approached Socrates and said to him, "Are you still standing there saying the same thing about the same thing?" Socrates replied, "That I am." The traveler said, "You who are so smart never say the same thing about the same thing," and pleasantly walked on.

As we bring out our interpretation of things our attention is drawn from the beginning of thought about the thought's inertia to how the mind curiously leads itself on with its own momentum.

Newton explained every "body" or "thing" continues in its state of rest or uniform motion unless it is compelled to change that state by some force impressed upon it. Just the same is our thinking which stays the same until forces act upon it to compel its change. We think as we do until we are given options to think differently in the light of newly acquired knowledge, which becomes a step forward in our wisdom.

As to things whose purpose of existence is obscure and things whose existence is visibly beneficial, which do you decide to be works of chance and which are of design? There must be some correlation between one and the other. Could it be that whether the universe was made by chance or design is a question each of us must answer for ourselves. When one examines things in this way the obvious reaction is that within the freedom of choice our mind can oblige that same autonomous power given to us just as is our will. If I were to be worth anything at all it would be only the value I give to my thoughts.

When our thinking has changed we can say we have learned something, which in turn brings out a better interpretation and thereby a better understanding. With this in mind it can be said that we have had an increase in knowledge and have broadened the foundation from which the necessity of our intelligence is built.

From our learning and the increase in our knowledge, our experience of the world, both the inner and outer, becomes fuller. It is a principle of nature universally received by all. All great insights and discoveries are not only thought by many, but by those who give their imagination time to wonder.

There are two kinds of knowledge: knowledge of what occurs from out of itself and knowledge of what is produced. The first is a type we have of known things, and the second is something we learn of things' properties. The second type we are given to think further about; the first is something we only consider. The knowledge we have of ourselves is produced and comes from the faculties of our mind. Through both we discover what we really know and as well realize what we think we know. The possibilities are infinite and endless in both directions.

What is required for a change in thinking is a change in the mode of approach, a new perspective of the view, along with the achievement of a new manner of thought. Though we may observe the same facts, they can be interpreted differently making the same event visible in many and various different ways.

We do this with our life experience depending on the position and status we hold to in our society. At different levels of the social realm we see the same things differently. Things show themselves only in their relations conceived in the mind. We need not be ruled by traditional opinions; we, each of us, can determine for ourselves what we want to believe.

Thus, to think in the mind is that giving ourselves a cognition about the determination of things concerning the objects before us, and what thoughts we have collected in our mind, we should pursue the questions, not what others have thought, or what we ourselves conjecture, but what we can clearly and insightfully intuit, or deduce, with steps of certainty. For in no other way is knowledge arrived at but by our own basis for the conclusions we come to.

Questioning builds a way. The way is one of thinking. In the process of thinking we bring forth thoughts and notions of ideas that we conceptualize and perceive in our mind. We are challenged with our thoughts, determining the real from the illusion that imagination brings forth beyond any evidence or verification. Through contemplation we can think about our own thoughts and determine their value and worth. As we pass from one thought to the next the challenge becomes keeping one's concentration from breaking up by the constant interruptions that come from the outside world and from within. The thinker only responds to what is addressed to him or her or what he or she brings to thought from the depths of the mind's hidden resources. We are an ordering sort of creature; we prioritize things and thoughts by their apparent need to our wellbeing or by the emotional value they evoke. Sometimes we choose to remember and sometimes we choose to forget. Our memories just fade; but our thoughts leap into our life, and then we do with them what we will from our own rationalization and logic.

If one considers the probable, there are three terms which could describe the outcome: certain, possible, and impossible. Every probability has a reliable term that yields to a reasonable conclusion.

It's the meanings that we are after, and what is essential to the meanings is a significant interpretation of them. Through our thoughts we create what seems real in our own mind. The mind is a powerful tool that needs to be trained in a significant way to make our understanding reasonable. The inner connections we make between thoughts give them their own existence, self-evident from the logical inference we make from them. We use probability only in default of certainty. What we can be sure of is that there will always be a day after today even if we are not here to perceive its existence.

For the most part I see that human beings differ from one another by nature and attentiveness. It is the direction to which we focus our mind that makes the difference. If you begin by instructing yourself then you will receive instruction from others, showing that the passing of knowledge to one another becomes a necessity of nature itself.

Man, born to be a creature of reason, nevertheless needs much education. Every individual must think in their own way and in their way always find a truth or a kind of truth. But we must keep a check on ourselves that we do not go out-of-bounds of our natural ability to reason and must continue in our education to understand the conclusions that we come to terms with.

Though we safeguard our own originality, we must accept through learning that our interpretation of others becomes original thought in itself that we acquire in the accumulation of our own knowledge.

The mind comes to itself as it gazes into the world around it as actual reality; but from the other side, it gazes into itself, and the object of its view is a region beyond the world into the world of itself. Self-existence is an actual reality, just as is the reality of the physical world which we live in. Since the mind apprehends what is substantial, it combines what it knows, or seems to know, and, truly grasping its accumulated knowledge, finds a general recognition of the truth it has been searching for with a significance it values and gives worth to.

Logic and Simplicity

The solutions of logic must be simple, since they set the standard for the idea and ideal of simplicity so that our intelligent mind can comprehend what it determines understandable. What we think a definite answer is may, perhaps, be incomplete because of the possibility of some unknown knowledge. We are arid, but still we pursue that knowledge to increase the potential of our wisdom.

Logic must look after itself and is responsible for its own simplicity. Though it is human to make the simple complicated we must find our way back to the origin of simplicity. Though the labyrinth is a perplexing matter, as we follow the route of all causes simplicity becomes self-evident.

When we construct our individual systems of thought there must be a logical connection within the coherent reality that affects our existence. The common factor that makes life logical and simple is its unfailing gravity, which leads our senses to the common ground of sound reason and logical analysis. From the standpoint of human necessity life must have a logical foundation even though it is not readily apparent. Here then we rely on our inherent intelligence to find some kind of sense of it all in our own reasoning ability.

The question here is: Can the thoughts and philosophy of a person go beyond their pursuits? The answer is that one thing unique about wisdom is that it cannot be inherited but must be acquired. A man's success should not be judged by the wealth he has, except for his own treasury of knowledge, but to the extent he is at peace with himself.

The success of our achievement depends on the intensity of our desire to learn and our ability to comprehend what we learn. Wisdom comes from these choices — to desire learning or not.

The task at hand is to understand ourselves before we can understand others. The world is just a reflection of ourselves; what we feel outwardly stems from the emotions we hold inwardly. We may not yet realize that this understanding is within our reach. It is the thoughts we carry that we keep when we are awake and bring with us in our sleep.

He who is able to apply knowledge is intelligent, but he who is able to assimilate it is wise. For self-realization we require clarity of mind. The clearer our thoughts, the better our concept is of the spirit within our own mind and of the world. Do not underestimate a child, for all their abilities have yet to be realized, and do not overestimate an adult because as well their abilities are still evolving.

Logic is all-embracing and mirrors the world. Connections are all throughout and find their way to appear from their concealment. Only because things are connected can we discover the logic in their connections from their basic structure in simplicity. Once broken down into simple parts, the whole can be logically discovered and made to agree with reality as it seems to be from our interpretation and understanding of it.

Through contemplation we find the means for expression; though limited by our understanding of language there are words, upon their discovery, for expressing what we think. It's the words and their meanings that make the world intelligible to us. The more words that become familiar to us the greater the world becomes, because then all of its subtleties become expressible in each of our forms of language.

We have to determine for ourselves what appears to be true or false. It is our considerations that make alterations in our construction of the world. The experience that we need in order to understand logic comes with our maturing and the perspective we choose to see the world from. While logic depends upon experience, it is experience that makes logic possible.

Logic is prior to every experience. It is a necessity which nature extends to us so that we may know and make sense of nature. If we are to find our way and play a constructive role in the dialogue of our times, we need to understand the theoretical foundations of current and past convictions to apply to our contemporary concerns and open ourselves to alternate views that arouse our thinking.

There are two types of knowledge that concern us: general things which are universals, and particular things which have an identity of their own. The logic and simplicity of a thought and notion like this could, perhaps, fulfill some inner need we have to distinguish things.

This work is not only concerned with the knowledge that has been accumulating throughout the ages but with its implications on our own thoughts. There are certain traditional questions which people of a thoughtful nature have always been asking. Is humanity, in particular, realizing its most promising achievement, destined to carry life to a higher level than has yet appeared? Or is humanity stagnated for reasons that civilization has become the way it is, because of social and cultural differences we all can recognize? One conclusion is that economic factors now play an important role in our living, despite all the knowledge we have gained.

The simple logic one comes to is this: one must bear in mind one's own convictions and also take into account the considerations and conclusions of contemporary and past thinkers.

From where does our knowledge come? It comes from study and experience, from which one is led to contemplation and reflection. Everything is an extension of what comes from both inside and outside our head. Life couldn't be real if it were not for our interpretation of it. Though both realities are convincing it is our certain way of thinking that flavors and colors life.

While considering the little points of interest we must not forego considering the grandeur of the big picture. It is the logic and simplicity of our thoughts that we must surmount in face of all the complexities that come to our attention, and the relations they bring forth to our imagination. Thinking is one thing, expression is another. Language creates the means to form a coherent union between thought and expression.

Our concern for care in expression keeps the mind at ease and relieves us of the tension for communicating with the use of words that language provides through our intelligent faculties of the mind.

We use language as a means for thought, which is the highest and most essential necessity. If we cannot communicate with ourselves we cannot communicate with others. Just as well, if we cannot understand ourselves then how can we understand others. It is one of those enigmatic problems that humanity must face one individual at a time. You have to learn to recognize your own depth. You won't know anything of it until you start exploring and considering all the possibilities that await you in your search and discovery. It is the invisible means of support that the mind realizes when it becomes aware of its own potential. It's all part of nature's simplicity and becomes a logical necessity as well.

The time must come on its own, being somehow tethered to providence. Let those who reckon the depth understand first what they are seeking for. The depth has been preserved in the heart and soul. That loosened mind finds its own way, both into and out of the depth.

It does not make war upon itself but looks for the celebration of that royal unity. It is only a temporary moment. The mind sees many things but understands few. We depend on others; no one can bear this life on their own.

Measure demands that coarseness exists; the road is rough, not smooth, and there are trials to be conquered. Like in a fairytale the conqueror always returns home, only wiser from the experience. By our own reason and logic we find our way through the complexity, and the simplicity becomes readily apparent. It's nature's way of teaching; it's that simple.

A simplistic logic one could come up with convincing thought and expression is that it would not be possible in a way without language. Communication skills become essential to pass knowledge to one another. When I go toward the door that leads to my perception, the door approaches me at the same rate which I come nearer to it. Once at the threshold of the door we have the choice to alter our perspective; from the mind we can perceive what is really there or we can conceive what seems to be there. The qualities of reality still remain in our mind.

Elements of Thought

What should concern us as humans is the question of whether thoughts come to us or do we lead ourselves to the thoughts that occupy our attention until the time when they pass and distraction takes over. What is a most provoking thought is the element of thoughtlessness — the failure of remembrance in which we choose deliberately not to think about experiences which we've encountered.

We can only draw from what is already in our head and in our imagination. What we put into our head becomes available to us through remembrance and our intelligence. We are intelligent creatures who think. It is the having of pictures, words, and symbols; it is the ideas and notions in our mind that we think about. It is something we experience and bring to experience, too.

The brooding, the pondering, is the meditation and contemplation that we do which provokes thought and brings it to the surface so we can think about it in our waking hours and even in our sleep.

Thinking is the calculating, reckoning, and problem solving we do in the reverie of our casual daily routine of our waking hours, our existence. We come to know what it means to think when we ourselves are given to thought. If our goal is to be successful, we must be ready to learn new processes of thinking. This is essential to our activity of being human.

Memory is the gathering of thought. It holds to what impressions we have gained through experience and imagination. It is the gift of thinking back given we are inclined towards it. Only when we are so inclined toward what in itself is to be thought are we capable of giving thought to the grandeur of the whole picture, to the universe we belong to and the whole experience it provides for us.

We learn to think by giving heed to whatever addresses our attention and thereby becomes essential for us to give thought to at the moment; this interpretation is what life is, just another thought.

For those who desire to learn there are stepping stones along the way that one must challenge and overcome in achieving greater knowledge and wisdom.

Memory safely keeps concealed within it that to which thoughts must first be given as to everything that unfolds at any given time, appealing to us as what has being and has been being. Memory, the mother of muses, is the source of all our knowledge and keeps wisdom by its side to be used and applied as needed.

Surely, as long as we take the view that logic gives us insight into what thinking is, we shall never be able to think how much prose and poetry rests on thinking back, with science and technology mostly taking our thoughts forward. Most surely, though, the here and now is really what matters and makes the most difference in our life.

We are the people of today. Of course there are generational overlaps, but with the passing of knowledge to one another we can overcome time and discover who we really are. We are a special breed of people caught between mythology and technology. We must always remember that the people of the future will have different dreams than our own.

It is the elements of our thoughts that give us a reference to not only who we are but where in time we are. What is important here is our reference. Where we go from here depends on our knowledge and wisdom. The matter of thinking is always confounding — all the more in proportion as we try to keep clear of prejudice from our own convictions, despite some generally accepted doctrine gained from the ages before us. Though this is confining we must be open to the wide terrain ahead of us and surmount those boundaries, pushing the outside of the envelope of past and contemporary thought to new limits.

The beginning and the end greatly deceive us. Full of foreknowledge, heaven opens itself to us in our mind. There is a stirring in our spirit that awakens in us an awareness that we are on a mission, on a journey, to find understanding in the elements of our thoughts. We must be guided on this journey lest with our own mind we leave the road which would have taken us to our goal. The mighty powers of our mind take hold of the destiny we make for ourselves and shape it with the elements of our thoughts.

We create relationships in the mind where each seems to lift the other up into a higher realm of thought than once conceived. One part of these relationships is contended by the other and then both find relevancies and create a whole new, bolder, conception. Humankind's common desire is for a more stable center, and the assurance of mastery leads us on to further knowledge within the elements of our thoughts. The steady advance in our knowledge is a most suitable end. This goal is a shared and common concern for a humanity that is always searching for new ways to verify truth with a certain amount of sureness.

In the examination of familiar things we come to unfamiliar conclusions that make not only our thoughts, but the words expressing them, contorted, leaving us with mixed emotion and a contented conviction leading us on deeper into thought and reflection of both our initial and final conclusions.

Because of man's openness to new and unfound knowledge, its presentation and explanation give it its worth and value by how someone can use it and its applications. The beginning and end of philosophy is the same; the revealing dialogue is its ultimate use.

What clouds the light of wisdom is the knowledge we do not possess, and the knowledge we have may be filled with misconceptions and error. To these concerns we must find a middle ground that surrounds the light of wisdom with truth and logical reason.

Simplicity of the mind comes from simplicity of the heart. There is an essential and necessary mutual relationship here. We are not asking ourselves too much to compromise, both for the sake of reason and compassion for wisdom.

The work of our Creator does not allow anything to perish without a struggle to survive. The will to live is a very powerful force. The means by which each of us struggles is only the preparation for the reward to come that precedes and precludes our achievements. This idea has been discussed and explained in philosophy and theology throughout the ages.

Knowledge breaks through truth and falls on the pure being of our consciousness. Knowledge allows us only as much as we can understand and comprehend. There is in our intellectual spirit something very secret and hidden deep within its core that allows the power of reason to come forth, enabling us to appreciate the concepts of metaphysical philosophy to take form and be known and understood.

The imaginative conception of reality no longer being limited by likeness to the things we can see or touch allows us much more room for wider and more abstract views, because reality is more unknown than known. What we are doing now is redefining reality, encompassing the unknown and bringing it closer for us to inspect and consider its parts with the dignity they deserve revealing them from their concealment.

Behind the world of physics, scientists given to philosophizing surmise that there is another world. This other is the spiritual world and the world of mind in which the mind circles around itself with intense concentration on the reality about which we know so little.

Evolution, in other words, is coming to be regarded as a creative process, continually engaged in bringing to birth something new so at any moment that there is more then before — an expanding universe in all directions.

The cumulative effect of our discoveries and the increase in our knowledge allows for our reason and logic to open up to us a new formulation of a theory of the universe in which our own personal worlds exist. The explanation of all that has happened now includes the possibilities of what can and is probable to happen.

The first dim light of dawn must share the name of sunlight with the rays of full midday. Just as higher levels of life emerge, so does the knowledge that they are higher and are merely a stage in a process which will involve the emergence of levels that are still yet higher. Our consciousness has no limits, but our awareness does, just because we are human and what is conceived is not always perceived.

We are, then, in this view required to think of life as a force or principle, at first unconscious or possessing only a latent germ of consciousness, seeking to realize not only higher power, but a more conscious realization for powers to naturally grow proportionally greater. The path of evolution is littered with the debris of mistakes and mutations of the truth that fade with the evolution of higher species or with the few who realize that there is more to life than it seems.

Existence by its very nature must be a process of struggle and endeavor. No one said it would be easy, and it doesn't say anywhere that it would. We get carried away with our expectations and anticipations. Our own thoughts carry us away into our imagination. By this means development is achieved, represented by the effort of an individual to jump from one level to another — a higher one.

At each stage assimilation and natural selection occurs, promoting the further development of a species more adapted to change through time from opportunity and random chance. To pass beyond life we must first pass through it, enduring the struggle for survival and overcoming it with the steadfastness of our own wisdom to get us through.

The reservoir of life, enriched by our daily experiences, a more intense consciousness, and an enlarged power of understanding turns the stream of life into a river of actualizing our potential. We may learn from the mistakes of others, but we change only from realizing our own.

There is usually a story of struggle behind every story of success. The chances of success improve with every attempt. We must control our thoughts but not our minds, for in the mind our imagination runs deep.

Intelligence and Survival

The instincts are the prime movers of all human activity; by the will or impulsive force of some instinct every train of thought is born along towards its goal and end. All the complex intellectual apparatus of the most highly developed mind is but the instrument by which impulses seek out their satisfaction. Reason, in fact, is a mere tool of instinct and of the will. It is instinct which determines the occasions of reason's operation, and its function is limited to discovering means for satisfying the will that employs it.

The inner life, it is increasingly being realized, may be more important than the outer, and the strife between conflicting elements can be envisioned and experienced by those engaged in living it. Our survival depends on how we interact with ourselves and others and come to logical and reasonable conclusions to the conflicting exceptions that occur within us in the intervals of peace and anxiety.

Perhaps there is a hero in each of us and our life evokes its character. It is safer to depend on what we realize than to depend on what we only seem to know. The light of a lantern illuminates many pictures of life, yet it all comes from one flame — our mind. The grandeur of the whole picture must not be forgotten even though it comes from that single flame. This is essential to our intellectual survival.

The fundamental principle of intellectual survival is the answering of questions that aid and assist our existence through mind and matter. Logic is part of nature and is prior to all existence, just as the world existed before any human inhabited it. The limitations of my language may limit my explainable world, but just because sometimes I can find no words does not deny my own possibilities. In any case, what I can conceive goes beyond my own perception.

When an answer cannot be put into words, neither can the question. There is no riddle; doubt or certainty can exist only when questions and answers have words to express them. What is mystical and transcendental may have words to express the notion or idea, but sometimes there are no expressions to either answer the question or explain the answer one seeks.

The human element is what makes this world so extraordinary. The human imagination creates for us new and bold concepts for knowledge to mature and aid in our survival. It is our imagination and knowledge that gives us the skills we call wisdom to move forward with our will in one direction or another. There is no turning back, only looking and remembering back.

The future is open to all the possibilities we can imagine. Don't underestimate your own wisdom. You are smarter than you think; your intelligence surpasses your own expectations of yourself. Only in the halls of experience and the infamous school of hard knocks do we surprise ourselves and excel. Sometimes it is not entirely possible to express an idea fully; so in its description the parts must do as much as the whole. In like measure nature shows its parts and from them we consider and ponder the grandeur of the whole picture.

Granted that every will is a will to something, and has an objective and a purpose in its willing, we ask of the world: What is this ultimate desire, the goal of ambition? The answer is that through life, the life of any thing or creature, we have the will to live and survive by the intelligence we are endowed with or accumulate through rigorous study and contemplation of matters within our understanding and beyond.

The will, as a thing in itself, constitutes the true inner and indestructible nature of a person's spirit; yet also an unconscious quality takes hold of our being and aligns itself with our heart and soul. It serves the purpose of self-preserving. It is a phenomenon of nature that even nature itself consequently has an essential and necessary quality of a very difficult nature to explain. Life would not be without either spirit or will. They work reciprocally. One reinforces the other, and both act conditionally upon each other.

When you look at your own life, who could have thought this is what you could have expected. Surprises do happen. The unexpected is always just around the next corner, and if per chance there are no corners then just down the road life jumps out at you and says "here I am."

What is of concern here is our sphere of knowledge, which is just how far we can stretch our wisdom to not just get by but, perhaps, even a little more than that. There are two things that knowledge depends upon. The first interprets; the second is that, although known things exist in reality, the idea of them requires a knower with a reasonable intelligence to understand what is being interpreted. Although we have self-consciousness of ourselves existing, the real knower is our spirit within our intelligence that holds all our wisdom, because wisdom gives meaning to what we think.

This notion is philosophy in its depths and heights as known throughout the ages by those who labor in thought, expressing theory and opinion upon that which they seem to have an acquaintance with in their own genius. Our survival depends on our intelligence. Our intelligence, independent of our knowledge, which we have accumulated with our age and experience, associates with nature the true determinant of our character. There are two kinds of people in this world: those who really know and those who just think they know.

Our character is as well dependent on our will to excel and to achieve what seems to have importance in our particular life. Our life is the total sum of our qualities, abilities, and willingness to learn; yet we must also not prejudice ourselves when we seem to think that we know something even though verification and certainty have a subtle doubt in the forethought of our thinking.

Survival in the 21st century will be a challenge like no other. Perhaps we are too smart for our own good? Perhaps more people ought to recognize they really need to learn more instead of being content with mediocrity. I believe people ought to excel as much as their will would allow. We were born hunters for satisfaction, and we will die hunters for contentment. Though our routine daily experiments only yield explanation of theory and speculation, they consistently fall apart under the scrutiny of our verification for certainty; but some things we cannot be sure of and in the end yield only to our intellectual imagination.

Language and Expression of the Will

What is important here is how we come to the conclusions that we do, how we interpret those conclusions, and how, through language, we use and take apart these expressions in further understanding of them. What happens in our interpretation and understanding is the tracing of origin and erasure of misconceptions from our increase in knowledge, gaining a new wisdom with each event. This initiating of understanding, in our own ways, becomes our language and expression of our will.

What happens in this process is a strategy of philosophizing about concepts, notions, and the variability of ideas of thought. It is bringing them into the open from their concealment for relevant discussion and consideration, for investigating and verifiability of their consideration, which may be worthwhile even at all.

We must ask ourselves to change the habits of mind we have been so accustomed to and consider the way things seem to be, and are, in a new light without emotion; by the facts alone we find with our language skills in the expression of the will to know and learn. It is expression that is the means of knowing what we have comprehended.

Language is the only thing that limits our expression, so we should do our most to learn the words we need to relate what seems to be in our thoughts of what we conceive and perceive. It is our creative imagination that surpasses language in that it develops its own concepts without the use of language through images and symbols assigned to particular concepts and notions in the mind. Once you know that you can know more, your will drives you to excel.

Ideas are creations; they are creatures of the intellect and are very close to concepts which the imagination expands upon and the intellect gives logic and reason to. Whatever is the object of the understanding that we have is what we think about, create images of, and make symbols for so that we can pass knowledge to one another.

At each phase and era in history, philosophers expand, take

apart, and develop an increased awareness to the understanding that we seem to have of a particular idea, notion, or concept.

As we explore our own mind we can recognize the enduring aspect of the truth and separate it from its temporal applications. That is the action of the will. It's not the first cause, but a higher cause. It's the prime mover of the universe. It's in you; you just have to go in there and find it.

What you will to believe is all you know, unless you are open enough to receive knowledge passed to you from others with a certain amount of positivity that leads beyond doubt to possibilities.

You go into the labyrinth of your mind, and go so far you realize things about yourself that you always knew but couldn't express or want to believe. An inspiration comes to you as revelation and awakens your spirit to a new reality — a spiritual reality that always existed but you wouldn't accept because for some reason you were not ready. But when the time comes, you open yourself to the reality of truth.

If we are ever going to give a gift to the world it has to come from our own experience and fulfillment of our own potentialities. So I write in the hope that someone may gain something from my own experience, not just a thought of remembrance of who they thought I was, but a thought of who I really am from the insight I found by my own exploration of my inner world and the outer world that surrounds my own.

The notions of what we think borrow from their heritage the resources necessary for their own construction and re-construction to come to a more complete and fulfilling description of the knowledge we accumulate with our experience romancing life with conceptions and concepts, some of which we are not familiar with but act as if we seem to know something of, either by insight or by actual comprehension of the expression of them within our own understanding.

Knowledge is not a systematic tracking down of a truth that is hidden but may be found through study and reflection. It is rather the field of what can be known and expanded upon. Though knowledge is filled with nostalgia, it has a certain contemporary newness added to it through time in accordance with the ongoing creation of history.

A philosopher-artist is one who labors in thought as a discipline which finds its own importance when language finds its way into thinking and is expressed as a way, or style, of life. What's going on here, from the philosopher-artist's point of view, is an economic phenomenon using the concepts of interpretation, perspective, and evaluation of life with the language of expression as a liberation and departure for a fuller explanation of life then before known.

This knowing is the discovery of new knowledge passed from one to another, which becomes in turn a newfound wisdom to be wondered about and expressed for generations to come.

What comes to mind now is the value we put on truth, or the similarities to what we find as something like the truth. At first we have an image of what we think, and then we find similarities in the differences of our thoughts. The end result is an inequality in the parts from the whole. The process of discovery is itself an adventure in learning.

If one is always bound by one's interpretation, or perspective, where can one find room for differences? It is in the opening up and dialogue language affords to us through the expression and will to know, and know more, as we grow old and even older. We must not forget that the differences of views only add to the meanings we give to things bringing out the very truth we are seeking.

I suddenly woke up as from a dream, conscious of my new insight into a philosophical knowledge that bordered on the metaphysical. I had now enough understanding to know what the real truth was from its similarities. Discovering the origins of language and its use becomes exponential when dealing with the subtleties of words and their associated meanings. I realized that life can be explained.

Like sleep we must afford ourselves time for stillness to contemplate what we've come to realize as conclusions in our own ways. We have to allow ourselves to remember back and dream forward;

it's all part of the nature of life. To do this is to empower the will to express itself and come to terms with its own wisdom.

The idea was to sublimate life into a spiritual plane of existence. It is to accept reality as it is and go beyond it in your mind. There was an essential requirement to this gift of the spirit that one should have a gentle heart receptive to revelation and inspiration. The powerful impulse of the will is a fundamental impulse that nature endowed us with so that we could think and act with some kind of responsibility to our conscience, whether we know it or not. It is the conscience that is the keeper of the will, and it is our spirit that empowers our will to thought and action.

It is important, though, human as we are, to not forego or desist from the quest for as much knowledge as possible to enable us to survive as easily as possible; and that means working smart, not just working at the struggle before us. I maintain that it is wise to reiterate without being redundant that we explore meanings so that we are not deceived by misconceptions that language often implies from our not being familiar with the details some meanings imply in their usage, which is the knowing of a truth from its apparent similarities.

There is more to reading than just the interpretation of the mentioned words, bringing to mind thoughts of them. It is the words' relationship to the mind, and the emotional factor, that is important here — considering how words are used and the intent of their usage in the context they are used.

The command of language always makes a thought more clear, but due to our limited vocabulary the meaning we extract is not always the intended meaning; so we must read into the words and bring out the thought once conceived and now perceived.

The relationship between the writer and reader is not only the writer's command of language but the reader's command of creative interpretation and a certain qualitative distribution of the reader's concepts, allowing for openness to a new and higher understanding. What the writer does is to bring the unknown world into the open clearing of the reader's creative imagination through thought and inventive conceptual creativity.

The knowable is within our reach; all that we have to do is to reach out and grab hold. Then understanding takes a little more effort in comprehending what we've learned. What seems important here is the phenomenological structure of our gained knowledge and the autonomy of its meaning with regard to our own cognitive capacity. We must have some sort of familiarity with what we seek to know in order to find it amongst the vast amount of knowledge at our disposal, within the resources and treasures that contain the wisdom of the ages.

Definitions of movements of thought are always contingent and provisional. The question here is whether philosophical notions have privilege. The answer is yes, because in the general use of philosophy one explores the grandeur of all that is in the world and in some metaphysical way belongs to the world.

It is important not only that we find the knowledge that we seek, but that we uncover the interpretation that suits the truth best, in face of any opposition that may arise, while still being open enough to conversation of alternative views of the same object of thought.

It is not only the text that has some superficial importance; it is what that text brings to mind, how it is interpreted and understood, that advances our wisdom along life's journey. Even philosophy as literature has an appealing aura because it stimulates the mind into thinking beyond itself.

The knowledge of the philosopher places him among the dreamers, because the more you know the more you are likely to be part of the dream itself; the reality of life suspends us in a temporal dream that is only a fragment of the eternal.

The least gifted man can be complete if he keeps within the limits of his capacities. Yet still he dreams, of wonders out of his reach, but reaches for them he does and strives for excellence, raising his own determination for a better insight, unless he is satisfied with not knowing the whole truth and has come to terms with his own mediocrity.

A Theoretical Matrix of Patterns of Thought

If we can raise ourselves from the knowledge of particular things to that of Ideas, we can pass beyond sufficient reason into the realm of pure thought, and discover the notions of spirit and will as analogous to that of Idea.

By its origin and nature Idea, subject to the law of causality, becomes the starting point of knowledge; thereby all knowledge has grounds for sufficient reason by starting from Idea and passing into what is to be known from that particular Idea. The notion of an Idea coming to thought, and as the starting point for knowledge, makes innumerable connections and has just as many relationships with other thoughts in the mind, bringing knowledge to the state of wisdom.

All these relations and connections with the mind create the theoretical matrix of the patterns of thought and the process of thinking, including the utility of the imagination.

Raised by the power of the mind, a person relinquishes the usual way of looking at things and considers "what" instead of just how, why, where, and when. One then takes possession of one's own consciousness of a thought, in relation to an idea, and becomes immersed entirely in this capacity. With quiet contemplation the perceiver and perception become one. The matrix becomes complete.

The mind is eternal in so far as it understands the aspect of eternity. I considered just how there could be infinity without eternity, both being contingent on finiteness and mortality. In its own capacity the mind becomes infinite from its ability and capacity for imagination beyond the limits of the known, further delimiting the mind's potential in the realm of probability and possibilities of the unknown and metaphysical.

Only those people who are both clever and active in thought, clear about their own capacities, and can use their abilities will really get on in this world. But the spirit of the day threatens them in every way, and nothing is more important than to make them realize early enough the direction in which they should steer their will with the exception of the increase in knowledge, thereby increasing their own wisdom about worldly things and about spiritual matters as well.

Consider the thought and Idea of the clouds in a clear sky with a gentle breeze. When the clouds move, the shapes which these clouds form are not essential, but accidental, to them. These clouds are made of vapor that expands and contracts and are affected by the wind, driven along, spreading out and torn apart. This is their nature, such as is definition and meaning in the matrix of the patterns of our thoughts.

The mind works just the same — taking thoughts, moving them along, reshaping them and both increasing and decreasing their content with the activity of the mind at work.

We do this creative activity with the matrix of thinking, perfectly malleable and liquid, developing the thought as it solidifies within the logic and reason inherent in the quality of our own matrix, the labyrinth of the process of thought.

The mind cannot be still so long, as there are thoughts within it. Thoughts are a part of nature that makes us human. This quality can be improved through the proper use of its utility. What is not a self-born thought is something intuitive and comes from the treasury of the mind by the resources it holds in its depths.

The solution to all problems is the clarity of thought which comes from our own evolved wisdom. When we are not able to see the whole picture we see only the parts, and conceiving and perceiving misrepresents the whole. A truth may vary in its own depths. The truth is too simple and obvious once it is realized, which makes the matrix seem more complicated than it really is.

The development of an Idea, the unfolding and reconfiguring the mind does with notion and idea is a many-sided phenomenon that is particular to our intelligence and personal abilities to imagine and conceive a thought in the mind. This concept is at the heart of the matrix, and its notion is a quality of our mind's capacity. This same notion gives us our wisdom as we seek out knowledge and new ideas through thought and contemplation of both the known and of the unknown.

In the manifold forms of human life and the unceasing flux of events, the philosopher will consider permanent and essential only the idea in which the will to life has its fullest objectivity, seeking out knowledge for its own sake of making one wise, and showing its different aspects in the capacities, the passions, the achievements, and the errors we make pursuing the excellencies of the human race in its greatest form — the actuality of the idea of the ideal being.

The cosmic rhythm can be experienced throughout the universe if only one would find the special and certain awareness of it within one's own mind. Consciousness is an inherent and actual quality of nature itself. In nature everything is created with help from others; so just as well, in the matrix we pass and receive knowledge to and from one another.

There is one common source that is the infinite ground of human knowledge: experience and study. It is the essential part of the matrix of thought. It is the infinite supply of Ideas and notions the mind is capable of producing from either the known world or from the creative imagination. This is the foundation of the matrix of thought.

The mind essentially draws its ideas from the known world as we explore it and also from our own thoughts about what we think of. We reconfigure our interpretations as we draw on the supply of information and revelation that comes to our attention and awareness. This method can be compared to a line extending horizontally and another vertically indefinitely in all directions conceivable from our own center outward and back inward into our own center.

The matrix of thought projects ideally and ultimately through space and time of the present here and now, considering that the past and future are only conceptions the mind produces from memory and from imagination. It is the point of origin, the essential quality of the utility of the mind that we rely on to be secure and certain and that gives us a firm foundation for our beliefs and faith.

The matrix of thought essentially is a sphere collapsing into itself and reforming into another sphere with different qualities than from which it began at its origin. It is only through contemplation that ideas are understood and comprehended enough to express in a language that enables conversation and debate. The nature of genius has pre-eminent capacity for such contemplation. We recognize our own thoughts and consider them in dedicated reflection. Genius is the capacity to maintain oneself in the state of pure perception, leaving one's own interests and entirely divesting oneself as to remain free from distraction, concentrating on the thought of the idea set in motion by the capacity of our intelligence.

Imagination has rightly been recognized as an essential element of genius, but it is the motivation and ambition, the drive to excel, that brings out the genius in each of us. It is the imagination that extends the horizon far beyond the limits of our actual personal experience, enabling us to construct the rest of the picture from the will to think of idea and thought.

In the matrix of thought actual objects are almost always very imperfect copies of the Idea which shows itself in them. Therefore the person of genius requires imagination in order to see in things not what nature has actually fashioned, but what could not be found in nature because of the qualities inherent in nature itself.

In this way, imagination accompanies genius, and is indeed its prerequisite. We must assume therefore there exists in all people the potential for accumulated knowledge, wisdom, and genius. It's all part of the matrix of patterns of thought. This power of knowing and recognizing the importance of notion and idea, in the field of knowledge and wisdom, envelops the entire matrix of thought.

Through our learning from either experience or opportunity and study, whether voluntary or unintentional, we lead ourselves on in our excellence of appreciating what is known and what can be known through the journey life brings us on and in our quest for finding out what the actual truth consists of creating our genius.

Within the matrix of the patterns of thought aesthetic pleasure is one and the same, whether it is elicited by a thought or by some object our thought is given attention to.

The deeper part of the matrix of thought is recognizing the inner nature of things apart from their relations and understanding that the inner person is actually greater than the real external world a human is enveloped in.

If we lose ourselves in contemplation of the infinite greatness of the universe in space and time, meditating on the millennia of years that have passed and are yet to come, or if the night sky actually brings before our eyes countless words as does the clear blue of daylight, through the forces on our consciousness and the immensity of the universe we feel ourselves increasingly bound to the great spirit of nature, and the transient phenomena of will and idea rise to the immediate notion that our actual thoughts exceed our capabilities and soar towards our divine potential. This notion is part of the foundation of the matrix of our thoughts, which are in some way connected to the universal great spirit. With this perspective in mind we can intellectually see the greatness of the matrix of thought.

One moment consumes the next. We actually live in the here and now, but always seem to be concerned with the past and future. The best we get from history is that it rouses our enthusiasm. The sign of a historical feeling for humanity is that, at the same time as we appreciate the merits and achievements of the present, we also take into account the merits of the past. The matrix is only a labyrinth of connections we make in the here and now with the past and with our future dreams, anticipations, and expectations.

We would know much more about things if we were not intent on discerning them too precisely. For surely it is the perspective we use to conceive and perceive that establishes the foundation for the matrix of the patterns of thoughts we use in our life experience.

The Aesthetic Feeling of Knowledge

The source of aesthetic satisfaction sometimes comes from the apprehension of a known idea, or from the seeking of new knowledge. Sometimes it comes from thinking of an Idea or having a Notion of some thought revealed to our conscious awareness of it. Sometimes it even comes from a thought that provokes an Idea that has new and decisive implications.

The essential notion of aesthetic pleasure of accumulating knowledge is beyond compare. The concrete actuality of spirit is directly present to itself, but to us, as humans, we only have an awareness of it, which remains but a belief as an inner principle that affects us all but never itself comes to light except in our creative imagination as a feeling and emotion that overwhelms us with insight and revelation to our intelligence.

Sometimes an idea or thought provokes an aesthetic feeling giving us a certain serenity or inner peace just from having knowledge and wisdom about a concept; new knowledge about it heightens our awareness, and attention concerning that concept we conceive from the passing of knowledge to one another.

No doubt thought remains in all actuality because it creates in us a sensuous and uncomprehended character giving it a remoteness to our outer life; but to our inner life thought brings insight and a lasting relation to our beliefs that essentially in ourselves keeps us rational creatures with our innate intelligence.

The aesthetic content knowledge brings us is not in the quantity but in the quality of knowledge we accumulate. The beauty of it all is that we are capable of feeling good about knowing something, which is different than just feeling good for some reason or another. People who think deeply and seriously have a roused enthusiasm about knowledge because of their nature concerning finding the truth and searching the world and themselves for genius.

If we are to listen to someone else's opinion we must first be positive in our own mind about what we think we know and what we do know, even with our intelligent creativity.

One of the constituent parts of an aesthetic feeling is the emotion it brings about. Objectively aesthetic contemplation is a matter that resides predominately in the significance and content of the thought and idea itself, and what meaning it has to the one who is given thought to it.

It follows that for our understanding and aesthetic enjoyment of a work or thought, or idea, we must have some grounding knowledge of it first to consider, or else our imagination would run free without bounds or limits.

The dynamic forces that act upon our emotions come from our accumulated knowledge and certain wisdom we have and can be explained only by the reason we develop on the subject under consideration.

The amount of arbitrary antagonism has a tendency to sway our feelings and affect our emotions towards a subject, whether it is a thought or something else. But where there is doubt there is questioning, and questioning is the basis of finding out what we don't know or verifying what we do. It supports our beliefs and gives our convictions firm ground.

Consequently the significance and necessity of our knowledge gives gravity to the appropriateness of our judgment and wisdom. The truth is that the consistency and weight of our treasury of knowledge in thought and idea, and in notion as well, give truth a great and bold significance in the aesthetic pleasure of just knowing.

The symmetry and special relationship knowledge has to aesthetics determines the worth and value of our considerations and thinking.

No individual and no action or thought can be without significance; in everyone and through everything the Idea one thinks about unfolds gradually and comes to the surface for our inspection and interpretation. We first ought to reflect on our inward properties and then, after finding significance there, reflect on the outward things of the world to find in them their significance, which brings us pleasure, logic, and reason for their appreciation in aesthetic terms of our knowledge and individual wisdom.

The outward significance is the importance of something related to the actual world. The inward significance is important because of its depth of insight into what we consider the thought of the ideal true intelligence we've been endowed with, which gives us this sense of appreciation for what we are, and also for what we can become — the ideal of all significances put together.

It is human to perceive what seems dear to us because it has some significant importance. We seek not only knowledge of ourselves and of the world but of what has significant importance.

We long for knowledge and understanding of what was kept secret as though by nature's design. Some things we can pass along to one another; other things we must learn on our own. Nocturnally we forge through our sleep and while awake we struggle for survival and wisdom.

Every day molds us into what we will become while ancient erudition lures us into the great depths of thought and consideration. We amuse ourselves with trifling matters, but what is most important is that we amuse ourselves with the aesthetic pleasure of learning and knowledge to increase our own wisdom, understanding, and genius.

The ideal would to be to perfect our logic and reason over every thought we could conceive. It is nature's imprint on us that cries out for significance and meaning; so we go our own separate ways seeking answers and imagining the outcome of events while looking for chance and opportunity to find our own satisfaction.

The ideal considered as an idea may be defined as an adequate representative of the concept and is always an object of perception, although we may have a pre-conceived notion of it. The mind is like a container filled with objects, and no more can be taken out than what was put in either by learning or by the Almighty Spirit. So in search for knowledge we must fill our mind with as much significant information and thoughts as we can, thereby increasing the treasury of wisdom and genius to be drawn from in reserve.

Because an idea remains an object of our conception and perception it instinctively works like an impression stored in the intelligence of the mind.

Ideas belong to no particular age, though concepts do. It is the spirit of humanity that brings them out through selected individuals who are given to labor in thought. No great perfection in a work of art is required for what it is intended. It may as well be just the creator's expression of some inner emotion seeking release. It is enough that we should see what the thing is perhaps meant to be in our own creative imagination.

As soon as this has been discovered the mind is led away to a concept enveloped by the original thought or idea that presented itself to the mind's awareness. Those inclined to consider the artist's intention may be aroused by the final creation, disregarding any original intention by the creator-artist.

The artist is the mirror of all mankind and brings to humanity his or her own consciousness and being of the era and age in which one lives with all that makes up the aesthetic pleasure that is derived from the composition of the work.

The nature of mankind consists in this: human beings have a will and determination striving not only for survival, but deriving some aesthetic pleasure from life and finding gratification both inward and outward in their existence. We seek pleasure along the way to balance the hardship we endure, pursuing our survival knowing all along that everything in existence comes and goes, except for the spirit and soul of ourselves and of the Almighty Creator.

We all are artists in our own individual ways. We create from what the spirit in us allows and give back to humanity what we can. Philosophy is nothing but a relationship and reproduction of what we can express from our own point of view and from the impression we gain from our worldly experience. The world in concepts and notions of ideas is the equivalent to the notion that beauty is in the eyes of the beholder. Philosophy is just a means of expression of the nature held within the one who labors in thought and exercises the mind, even if one does not even know one is philosophizing.

Our Intelligible Character

Whatever the subject of our immediate inquiry we must adopt a contemplative attitude as we proceed from self-knowledge to knowledge of the world and of the universe. One must not forget that we live in our own little worlds that are surrounded by a much greater world.

Our world is the ground that our life existence supplies us. What we do with it is of our own making, but we can leave to the world more than when we entered it. This work is my third volume of philosophical suggestion that I am leaving, so that I can say I gave and took as well.

Just as our outer world is open for inspection and interpretation so is our inner world; but searching our inner world requires just a bit more concentration and considerable reflection. Before we can change the world we have to change ourselves, and that is in our intelligible character we've been endowed with.

I do not wonder where the present comes from, I know that much; but where we go from the here and now is my concern. Doctrine changes and our knowledge can be deceptive. Our quest is the seeking of a truth that can be verified with a certain amount of reliability. What we can be sure of is widely accepted, but the unknown remains mysterious. Day by day we are carried along with time into that certainty knowing that sureness is a highly speculative involvement with our intelligence.

When we express ourselves we must find a way to express and explain our thoughts laconically, that is, with as few words as possible, to get our intended meaning across to the one reading or listening in conversation or in literature.

Pure and simple, theory is no use except in that it makes us believe in the interconnection of phenomena. One who is content just to experience life and act accordingly has all the truth he needs. This is the wisdom of a child who grows up learning while experiencing life as it really is; beyond that a good imagination goes a long way.

To the mind all things have some significance, but there is always something that comes along that captures our attention and thoughts.

All men, women, and children carry within them the spirit of life and the will to live, struggling with the facts of life and the endurance to come to terms with reality in the presence of joy and pain, ecstasy and suffering; this spirit and will can allow them to live with a sense of curiosity and wonder and amusement of life itself when the moments come where they are given to thought of its great mystery.

Permanence and transience are only names we give to explain the things of life, but knowledge is immortal and comes to our individual lives like the wind and rain, like the passing clouds across the sky. The seasons pass and the phases of the moon continue everlasting only as far as we know them during our own life. Knowledge surpasses time because it is part of nature that is concealed and seeks to be revealed.

Inspiration and revelation come when with our curiosity and wonder we are given to thought of the things life holds in store for us in the treasury of life's resources. Those who willingly and gladly accept all the joy and hardship to which they are subject would stand firm and well-grounded on the enduring earth and would have nothing to fear.

Armed with the knowledge which has equipped them with intelligence they would be carried on the wings of time, certain that their life was just part of nature that ennobled their spirit to seek for and acquire more knowledge about themselves and the world to make their life more fulfilling and find satisfaction in knowing, even though they do not understand everything they seem to know.

In humans, the spirit, or will, can attain the full self-consciousness possible in the knowledge of its own nature; we mirror the world in our character by opportunity or chance knowing what we do. Some people are so enlightened with a high degree of knowledge they live their life in thought more so than in action. They are consumed with learning, and the world manifests itself in their degree of contemplation. Those so enlightened know themselves, their potential, and capabilities; studying and learning become an essential part of their character.

The primary character of humans is their will to live and the accumulation of knowledge, which is another primary enablement associated with our existence. If we add to that creativity, then even creatures as well are ennobled with this character.

The constant striving which constitutes the essence of the spirit or will establishes itself with an iron command to nourish it. What gives strength to this command is our inner nature of spirit and will that enables us to have faith and endure being creative as we can, moving along the way towards our destiny which we actually make for ourselves by our thoughts and actions — whether premeditated or copiously occupied with gaining knowledge so we can work smart while we toil and labor at our work.

Humans, as the highest known earthly embodiment of will and spirit, are in like measure of all beings the most necessitous of that spirit and will. We stand upon this earth to fend for ourselves with a thousand needs. The maintenance of this striving is threatened on all sides by dangers of different kinds, even from within our own minds. Cautiously we can escape by constant watchfulness as though our very existence depends on it. Here is where we find the determining intelligent character of human beings in all of our resourcefulness and creative ingenuity.

Every creature, knowingly or not, is a microcosm of the world. Consequently the world is a macrocosm of our inner self-fulfilling nature. As the world grows so do we. Nature itself which is truthful at all times gives humanity its knowledge straight from the source with direct certainty and also independently from reflection, showing itself to the inner being by the way of thought and imagination.

This knowledge is synonymous and indistinguishable from the spirit of the world that is within us as well. Though we are full of projections of the future and remembrances of the past, there is still so much to be learned that no one could search through the archives of history and find the least bit, notwithstanding the metaphysical and spiritual theory we've come to seem to know.

Experiencing Relationships of Knowledge

That we pass knowledge to one another is the greatest importance to humanity, because what is known can be expanded and re-interpreted from generation to generation, and then the whole of humanity benefits from a better reasoning leading to a fuller understanding. Our spirit will not be broken, because we strive for liberty as if it were some kind of work that our survival depended upon. The best and sweetest gains are the ones we work and toil for.

If knowledge were entirely suspended, the world would entirely disappear because we could not know it. It is within our spirit that the treasury of knowledge holds to being keen to ourselves and our surrounding world. We pass knowledge to one another so that we can have some kind of common ground with each other.

Through myths, tales, stories and common discourse we level ourselves so that each of us may know something of our past and share in a common dream of the future. The greatest height humanity can climb to is sharing in the wisdom we find from experience and revelation.

The mind plays tricks on us; we must be aware of what we think. The phenomenon of our inner nature is suspended when we bring it out into the open and share it with a common nature inherent in humanity as a whole; when we go out into the public domain we give up part of ourselves, diminishing our individuality and becoming part of the community that surrounds us and to which we belong. There is a common ground we all share in, and that is this earth.

However different the doctrines of different societies may be, we all share the common goal of inner and outer peace. Contentment is such a hard place to reach because we always seem to want more. If we could do with less or be satisfied with what we have, peace would be much easier to find. It's not concealed; but in a way it's all in a certain way of thinking and how we go about that thinking.

The gulf between intuitive and abstract knowledge is wide, but it can be closed by continuous contemplation and having an active relationship with philosophy in our life.

Intuitively we are conscious of philosophical truths, but to bring them to our conceptual awareness, to reflection and contemplation, is our moral and ethical obligation to our own spirit. The inner nature of holiness surpasses the wisdom of the philosopher and theologian and begs the individual for knowing and understanding.

Our wisdom lies in the knowledge that we seem to have come to terms with, within our own logic and reason, yet our sureness of what we seem to know brings us close to doubt because of what we don't know.

To reproduce the whole nature of the world abstractly, distinctly in concepts and ideas, and to lay it down in a treasury of history as a reflected image would be considered the beginning of philosophy.

A closer and more complete knowledge would allow us to associate the abstract wisdom of ethics and morals common to humanity into basic principles and the notions of ideas relevant to the discussion of metaphysics and abstract doctrines of theology in a philosophical way. Ethical prescripts given with this intention and by people inspired by it will show how old this viewpoint is, and can be found in the treasuries of religious wisdom around the world; but still we have to make our own choices and reflect on the culture and society to which we belong. So with these thoughts we give reasons for a need in people to consider the spirit within themselves and in the world.

There seems to be some basis in human nature that we are given to meditation on and contemplation of the metaphysical aspects of divinity. This divinity is the spirit of nature that instills in us and in the things of nature the will to live and the curiosity to know. Despite all the different doctrines found throughout the world in the cultures of humanity that dwell under the great umbrella of a great and Almighty spirit, there is a common element which all seem to convey: the individual is part of the whole yet the contemplation of the inner being of the individual is the same as the contemplation of the world and of the universe that holds our world in its depths. There seems to be so much agreement expressed among so many different people that the spirit is an essential part of our existence.

We are called upon with excellence, beyond mediocrity, to the ideal; *sapere aude*, dare to be wise, is an old and ancient saying that still holds true. Human nature has depths, obscurities, and complications which are extremely hard to illustrate and unravel. Yet we try to make some sense of it all in our own singular and individual ways of logic and reason, which give a certain sense of understanding to our own satisfaction.

Behind our life something else is hidden, more powerful than we can know. We can only reach for it, yet it is still known to us; but it is not tangible, only conceivable.

It is the great spirit, our will that strives for survival, and we find its likeness in nature, in the grey sky, in the blue sky, and in the night sky. We find it living on the earth in everything that grows. It is the great motivator that ensures freedom with knowledge and understanding, and with wisdom from experience. It creates its own experience with our awareness to it.

There is one consolation which we can be sure of, and that is even if we don't understand all we know, and when our life passes to another realm, the knowledge we pass to one another remains; and if perchance someone comes along and finds it, they too gain insight into their own genius.

There is nothing without a reason why it should be rather than not be, with only one exception: human nature. So many times we are led off course, but a reason is there, concealed in the road we travel, and it becomes revealed the further along we journey.

Sometimes we just cannot justify "why" but its leading implications bring us to the Architect of nature —a metaphysical phenomena. Why is just one of those concepts that was created for our intelligent imagination to consider while laboring in thought. As for virtues and ethics, one can only learn principles. Their application becomes an individual act of the will carried along by our inherent spirit. Life goes on and we journey beside time in our own space.

From our wisdom we come to judgments and decisions made and based on what we have learned on our own through experience and through teachers from whom we have accepted the passing of knowledge to one another. From our knowledge comes our wisdom, and through our wisdom ethics brings to mind the values we give worth to, demanding us to consider what we ought to think and do while questioning ourselves along the way.

It is our mind that thinks and we are our mind; we are our spirit with an intelligent soul, the heart of our spirit. Ethics addresses such questions about moral choices and exceptions to moral rules as to the extent of our ethical and moral responsibility.

By the inherent necessity of freewill and the right to choice by our own inner thoughts, the most we can learn is to moderate some of our choices and refrain from others, having learned by experience. This is our common wisdom we share in a domesticated society.

From our shared wisdom, we learn that cultural diversity and moral values depend on the social conditions of particular cultures, so that no moral belief can be absolutely true with the exception that we be at least as good to our neighbor as we are to ourselves and have a respectable relationship with the concept of the great spirit. One must be the final judge for oneself without any exception.

Elated in thought, I counted my own and have written what suits my own comfort. The sage consumed in thought knew his own and searched for more. As each atom was stirred, a prelude to something new arose, each combination of thought producing something more. The latent spirit arose like a phoenix and asked not why, but how, the universe is so agitated like it is.

Life rising to a higher tone in universal nature is shown. Resolve to exert that noble privilege to control desire and find contentment in what you have. Is happiness a crime? One asks why is it so hard to find when before you it was there all the time; and then is taken away as if it were a crime to possess. Your infant spirit grows, you feel a perfect change; what grace may yet shine forth from the etheral radiance that lends a hand to cope with life and all its challenges.

Only if we can get beyond thinking, and rise to pure thought, we can make it so there can be justification in claiming that there are objective metaphysical claims which have a certain truth at their core. The question here is can there be any universal claim to the ethical and logical reasoning in a civilized society. The answer must be one that can be correctly connected to its universal objective.

Apart from difficulties about the rational and properly considered, the matter here creates further difficulties concerning the value of truth or falsity of any metaphysical statement.

The individual must be the final judge of his or her own thoughts and actions, and no other arbiter need be involved except for one's own conscience.

Consciousness and Its Behavior

The behavior of consciousness, which we have now to consider, is so constituted that consciousness no longer merely perceives but is also conscious of its reflection into itself. Consciousness not only finds the truthful perceiving of an object but also contains the distinct moments of apprehension of the quality of the objects it perceives.

The attitude of skepticism and that of theoretical and practical idealism are inferior attitudes compared with that of pure insight and its expansion, which is enlightenment that is born of the substance of spirit and knows all reality, including both the inner and outer reality of ourselves and of the world we live in, surrounded by the vast expanse of the greater universe to which we belong.

The voices of fate cry out to meet you just where you are at the moment without any thought they arise. The ways of the wanderer are led by insight and determination to reach a goal still conceived but not perceived. Tempered by the existence of God, nature runs its course without hesitation.

A great beginning can come at any moment, always bringing with it some new response from knowledge passed to us and stored in the depths of our mind. Above all reflection is the ethereal majesty of the spirit that watches over everything and decides for itself what will be withheld from our knowing, yet still conceived in our imagination as intelligent human creatures.

The ancient knowledge of eras long since passed is in danger of being lost, because who today has the longing for thought of it; though its effects can still be felt through our limited knowing of what we seemed to have learned so little of.

Intelligence is the art of learning knowledge, remaining faithful to the sureness of our understanding. Still, there is so much to learn and just as much that needs to be explained to fulfill our rational and logical understanding within our own limited comprehension.

It is our comprehension that gives us our understanding whereby we find our own genius.

Consciousness in its behavior brings itself back into itself through contemplation and leads us deeper into wonder. The discovery of what it finds is revelation, which leads to further insight. There is a reasonable explanation for everything, but one has to search it out from its concealment in the treasuries of recorded history.

Consciousness is an object for understanding. It goes beyond reason into the unlimited resources of our intelligent and creative spirit, the part of the mind that thinks. Everything has a constant difference in relation to other things, but in the conscience there is one universal understanding that stands as principle in the unity of all things. It is the spirit of nature where our own spirit finds its home.

Within the moments of the mind's activity distinctions are made clear through the acquisition of knowledge whereby our wisdom becomes pure understanding of the utility of all things within the realm of the knowable through our intelligence.

We can see through this infinity of the spirit within our consciousness an imminent necessity where all the moments of the world of appearance are taken up into the inner world of the mind. Once achieved in this inner world of mind stability becomes a certain sacred moment relevant to the time it is given to thought.

This simple infinity taken as a notion of the mind becomes the simple essence of life, undisturbed and indifferent to everything and to every thought outside itself. The understanding one comes to, its explanation, is primarily only the description of what self-consciousness is. The reason why explaining affords so much self-satisfaction is because in explanation is where consciousness is, where our intellectual spirit keeps its life momentum.

So to speak of communicating with ourselves is just as important as communicating with others. Even as we pass knowledge to one another we enjoy the satisfaction of passing knowledge to ourselves through the thought of talking to ourselves without words but with pure thought alone.

The two extremes — the one, of the pure inner world, and the other that of the inner being, gazing into this pure inner world — are here now coincided with the intelligent spirit at the heart of our soul.

Thought, pure thought, is all that is left for meditation and contemplation. The more you really think about your own thinking, the certainty of it becomes surer, because you lose your doubt due to your increased knowledge, experience, and wisdom.

The truth about self-certainty is that you are actually conscious of what you think, but it is the how, now, that finds its importance.

The truth of self-certainty is that you are actually conscious of your own thoughts. It shows the power of the mind to understand itself collecting information, processing it, and interpreting it to our own satisfaction. This process of thinking about our own thoughts is an invaluable experience once realized and achieved.

The mode of understanding is plain and simple. It is a self-fulfilling of the will to thought; an action and achievement only possible through the resources and utility of the power of our mind. The certainty is to itself its own object of recognition. Life in the universal becomes the separating out of its individual parts and becomes life as a process; the ongoing act of creation. Upon this notion we perceive its differences and conceive its actual unity.

Life consists in its own self-developing nature in an enduring form, in a movement forward always towards its goal, simply preserving itself along the way. Any gain that might come to one's life is through experience and the acquiring of knowledge, thereby increasing one's own wisdom and intelligence and making life the more tolerable. The result of personal gain is that we pass knowledge to one another while securing a certain security in our own genius.

As a result of this notion a simple determination is that life itself points to something other than itself; it leads us to the significance of others and to a unity with nature's great spirit directly through its own discovery, not by chance, but by nature's own will to be known.

Humans have always been curious creatures, but as we explore the universe, in effect, we are exploring ourselves. Our destiny lies in just how much we can discover, and in our own time we come to an understanding of what we really are: curious creatures.

Let us search out some spiritual repose from the foundations of our own genius. From the winds of turbulence we strive to endure. Poverty and debt ruin our spirit, yet still we live and endure. The laws of maintaining our destiny are undisrupted in spite of events and occurrences in our life.

The division in our nature that occurs when our needs are not satisfied and our goals not achieved brings our faith and beliefs into doubt. We spend our life nourishing our heart accompanying the opinions of the most versatile minds.

With our manifold endeavors we lend skill to the mind that makes for a long life as it speeds our lingering existence. Out of a sense of perfecting our spirit, on earth and in heaven, if one is so inclined to believe, meeting fate by traces of the ancient discipline of laboring in thought, we find a recollection of original need and are glad to maintain ourselves in this temporary existence.

The spirit is a river that makes its own course and along its path we find a quiet entrance and swim in its majesty. Drawn downstream by its current we find an appropriate exit and remember our experience so that we can pass the knowledge we found to others.

The Essential Moments

The essential moments of one's life are the most thrilling and memorable and consist of recognizing the importance of feeling and emotion which come from the heart of our spirit. The consciousness of these feelings and emotions brings us to a realization of a universal spirit common to ourselves and nature which we call the essential spirit or the divine holy spirit.

Sometimes we have to learn what things can wait and what things have importance in the moment of decision. One who is content to experience life and act accordingly has all the truths they need. This is the wisdom of a growing child, which we all still are.

What is remote from us influences us by means of experiencing. In its usual form it becomes historical as it happens. A higher form, which is related to the imagination, is mythical. If we look behind this form for a third factor, for some further meaning, we find a metaphysical interpretation we recognize without any proof or verification and just take as it is.

Our immediate relation to this spirit is recognized through contemplation; it can be considered one essential moment in our life when a new found feeling and emotion arises in the consciousness of it, in the awareness of its presence. It is a profound realization that we are not alone in our aloneness. Not recognizing it is a cause for our alienation from ourselves and from the world in which we live.

This essential and necessary spirit extends itself into the great beyond, into the metaphysical world of the unexplainable, beyond further than anyone's imagination can conceive.

In the consideration of satisfaction as a fleeting feeling it becomes known that, once initiated, desire becomes a force upon the will, and in realizing that a specific desire can be fulfilled we become again dissatisfied with one achievement and actively search out for another. One after another these moments continue in a never-ending cycle, surrounded by our sleep where the imagination roams free and our creativity reaches its height.

The essential moment is this experience of wanting nothing more than time to think and ponder on the greatness of the world and of its spirit that flows through everything living — everything except those things made by man. Though our creative spirit leads us to art, it really isn't the work of art but the thought of it that moves us.

Through this rediscovery of ourselves, by ourselves, we realize that it is precisely in our thoughts where we have seemed to have an alienated existence. Through acquiring a true mind of our own, capable of logic and deduction, creative intuition combined with discipline, and intelligent thoughtfulness, we have our essential moments.

Everyone must realize this power from within for themselves. It is a completely individual experience that has a profound effect on one's own spirit in the thoughtful utility of the mind. It is one of the most essential moments one could have in one's life to experience thinking about one's own thoughts.

This revelation becomes awe-inspiring and an overwhelming emotional experience not to be forgotten as quickly as it was acquired. Yet it can be kept intact only through sincere contemplation and reflection. Self-consciousness now assumes a new shape and form. As result of its own pure movement it becomes aware of itself as essential being, a being which thinks and entitles itself to genius intrinsic within itself, in its essential nature realized in the moment of thought.

We make clear-cut pathways along the road to success and achievement. Our trail is easily marked by our footsteps like graffiti sprayed on walls; the artist has no boundaries, finding freedom of expression whereever chance and opportunity arise.

A work of art sends a message, but only in the mind of the viewer or reader does the artist's expression disclose meaning. Think just how often the artist is misconceived from the original thought in the artist's mind; but the work's value is recognized by all. Art is the creator's genius at work. Whether the artist's medium is tangible such as a painting or sculpture or some kind of written form, the real truth of the matter is the essential moment it was created and the essential moment it is viewed and interpreted.

In thinking, objects and thoughts become concepts with meaning. Some things we think about are notions; they are mental images, representations and conceptions. Other things we think about are ideas; they are products of our mental activity that potentially or actually exist. An ideal is a conception of something in its absolute perfection, a concept we strive for if we choose to excel. To excel is to do better, to strive for the achievement of the ideal.

Some things we think about are immediately recognizable though they have an ambiguous nature about them. Once we find an explicit expression, and an unreserved truth as to their actual nature, our acquiescence reposes the ideal essence of the truth held within our singular thoughts in combination with our contemplation about our own thoughts on the subject.

This distinction we make is a decision to judgment and reflects our inner genius by the utility of our creativity that is common to all, though we are rarely aware of our true nature as human beings.

In thinking I become in communion with myself and reserve any doubt about the matter for later consideration. These times are the essential moments of my life. I can think about my own thoughts while I think about the world. It's all a big wonder; we ponder and come to our own conclusions based on our wisdom and experience.

But though I am connected to the world, and am not alone, I sometimes have this feeling of alienation which brings out my resolved emotions which I dare to hold on to without any form of expression for some unfounded fear of complications with others' visions of how the world seems to be and how it really is. Perhaps the *way* we think plays a more important role in our mind than *how* we think. In thinking I become in communion with myself, which is for me my essential being. This is if I recognize my own spirit as a living entity and my activity in conceptual thinking is a movement within myself and that I am aware of the essential movement when I think of the world and myself as part of it and no less. If I do not make this recognition, then I am not only alienated from the world but from myself as well.

The principle is that conscience and consciousness are entities that think and have intelligent capacities that are essentially important to our nature and to the world's composure. Ideas in the mind become just as real as objects in the external world. We are thinking creatures; we think of ideas, notions, and concepts, and just as well we think of principles and theory. In our intelligence we are capable of genius, but not everyone uses their capabilities fully and are satisfied with mediocrity; but I choose to excel and move forward.

This thinking time we do with ourselves makes up the essential moments throughout our life long existence along the whole course of our journey through, and with, time.

Once finding the reality of the universal Spirit, and experiencing the spirit in your life as a reality, you become aware of a reconciliation of its individuality with the universal. Here you find a real experience of unity, finding the serenity it enables once you become aware of its peculiar power.

This accomplishment is pure satisfaction of desire and cannot be denied or negated by any other counter thinking. It is an immediate experience of our essential being at its height and is found in the depths of our inner thoughts.

Although consciousness has its own self-certainty, it really reflects this activity back into the pure universality of its concept, starting as an activity that is directed first inward and then progresses outward in all directions, becoming centered in the Ideal essence of the embodied form the concept allures to.

Intellectual Reason

There is a positive meaning we can find in the things and events life throws at us, yet still some cannot rule out the negative. The only option is just to dismiss it and get on with your life. Even so you can still in such a way find some positive meaning in the appearance of what seems negative.

Now that I have learned to embellish my language skills I can feel confident that I have divided my senses from the intellectual and emotional and have experienced my own genius. My own vision is endless, but some time in the future my end will come and only then this new reality we all conceive will appear as a new reality.

Up until now consciousness has been aware of itself at the expense of the world. But as reason, assured of itself, it finds peace and can endure because it is certain that it is itself reality.

Previously consciousness did not understand the world, or itself, but through describing it, and working on it, it discovers the world as its home for a transitory experience with no real permanence, understanding that the transitory experience reveals truth and presence.

Reason requires sympathetic impulse from outside the mind, in which first is to be found the multiplicity of sensations and ideas which it can determine and give reference to from inner thought.

Through reason, conscience makes its own observations and experiments in judgment and perception coming to its own conclusions. The conceiving becomes as real as the perception through our intelligent thinking powers even as they are affected by the emotional qualities of our specific nature. So we pass knowledge to one another in order that the activity of describing shall not come to an end.

When one thought has been described and explained to sufficient reason for understanding it passes on to another and remains continually looked for in the mind to complete its sufficient reason for a significant answer. We take existing thoughts, divide them and analyze them further, and move on with a bolder expression of any newfound wisdom. It is an insatiable instinct that can never run out of material to think about.

In the realm where the universal is undetermined, at the threshold where particularization approximates, an immense field is opened up from that instinct where it finds not only immeasurable wealth but the bounds of nature and of its own activity.

The properties of reason enable things to be intelligently apprehended. Our thought and cognition make it clear just how important it really is. Reason creates the independence for the spirit to conceive detachment from the generality while perceiving the boundary line of individuality in specific instances of thought and reflection. Reason plays the role of observer and rises to the occasion of what it is aware of; but it is also no less present as something actual and is not an external relation to anything other than itself as the essence of our intelligent spirit.

This actuality, in the mind, is itself a purposive activity; something in the process of our thinking that is immediate though independently hidden is a necessity of our sensing our own thoughts. What thought, through reason, arrives at is the action itself of thinking and obtains its feeling of itself in reflection and through contemplation.

There is a distinction here in our self-consciousness of what it actually is and what it seeks for. It distinguishes itself from itself by what is given thought to and the actual thinking about that thought.

The instinct of reason in its quest finds only reason itself and is the same as self-consciousness where its own satisfaction comes in the very process of thought itself. When one makes the attempt to empty their thoughts of content, an open space is created from the emptying which allows for more filling. How can the desire for filling be limited while the increase of emptying exists as a purposeful activity? When one desires creating a void where pure meditation can exist, the constant barrage of ideas must seek its end where the beginning of the increase starts.

The Notion of Emptying and Filling

The peculiar quality of magnitude is no simple matter. A notion arises of balance between increase and decrease. Just as well is the notion of emptying and filling. These things we do with our mind to increase its capacity for accumulating knowledge and to assimilate it to what we think we already know. Verifiability is still another subject, but we can be certain that there is always something more to find out about and learn. Understanding comes after the process of learning and comprehending what we have learned.

If one would start with a quantity in a container and increased the size of the container the amount, the quantity, in the original container would be the same in a larger container, although it would appear to be smaller. But if we decreased the size of the container it would appear as a larger amount.

This observation and its relation to the mind have similarities and differences that deserve the same respect. Though the mind does not increase, its capacity to think more may, and as this capacity increases room is made there for more but does not diminish what it already has in its intelligence.

The phenomenon occurs when one disregards the non-important and inessential to make way for what seems more important and essential. Those who labor in thought have a familiarity with this concept and use the ability to distinguish and reason for that purpose. To empty allows for more to be filled, but the importance lies in the quality and not the quantity of what we want our mind to be filled with. The significant matter here is the quality of our thoughts just as well as what we are given to thinking about and in our contemplation.

Here one must consider the differences in what is already given as truth and the validity of that truth in relation to its certainty, as well as the exploration and investigation of what makes up that truth together with the appearance of a given truth upon its validity.

What is already given in a notion can be developed as an idea and in a concept not requiring any truth about it, only the thought of it.

What is explored in the discovery of new qualities only adds to the certainty of the truth's validity. As the mind approaches its ability to recognize the worthiness of a thought one must eventually consider the substance of the thought and its credibility, all the while emptying and filling the mind with enticing and curious developments in the progression thinking takes us.

We must be careful what we fill our mind with; it affects the way we think and may lead to unnecessary distraction from the certain way of thinking we ought to be focusing on. Sometimes we must leave nature to do her work before we take over her business or interfere with her dealings which affect our routine daily life.

People must be allowed to grow on their own with the exception of proper nurturing. Although memory and reason are different faculties, the one does not really develop apart from the other.

When considering what we fill our mind with, we must consider images and ideas. An image when it is recalled may exist by itself in the mind, but every idea implies other ideas. When we image we merely perceive; when we reason we compare and labor in thought and in contemplation. Our mind is formed by symbols and language; thoughts take their color from ideas we find in knowledge and as well through experience. Reason alone is common to all. So in effect we should consider what we fill our mind with and discover for ourselves what should be emptied and discarded when it comes to understanding and expression.

We cannot arrive at knowledge through indolence, which only brings despair; one should try to excel to excellence through study and proper learning to get along in life without regret.

Insight and Intuition

Insight is the capacity to discern the true nature of a situation. It is the act or outcome of grasping the inward or hidden nature of things or of perceiving in an intuitive manner. Intuition is the act or faculty of knowing or sensing without the use of rational processes. It is knowledge gained by the use of this faculty that is not deducible but rather an impression made on one's mind similar to insight. We all have these qualities in common, although some possess them more than others. How we use these abilities may determine our destiny.

An insight into the nature of perceiving and conceiving is entirely within the ability of the mind and is brought to the surface of thinking by conditional and abstract thoughts of the real and spiritual nature of thought itself. To look at understanding and expression we must first reflect unconditionally upon the mind's determination of logic and reason.

The relation and mutual correlation of what the mind thinks is in how it thinks and how it goes about its ways in doing so. The transition between immediacy and temporality comes in the time actually spent laboring on the thought at hand. The significance and importance of what we think has a direct proportional relationship with our comprehension and understanding of the knowledge we receive from the world, by the knowledge passed to us through the expressions of others, and by our own reflection of our wisdom.

Within our thoughts our intelligent reasoning brings us to a certain understanding of generalities, which leads us on to greater thoughts of universalities. Just below these, those specifics and their qualities bring us to differences and similarities. By thinking of all of these concepts in their entirety we can see the whole picture, with its separate and individual parts that have their relationships coexisting on a common ground, first by sense perception and then by the sense of cognition, which is the ability of the mind to interpret and as well to understand what it has comprehended. Though we can be sure of things outside the mind we can, as well, have a certainty of things inside our mind too.

These things of the mind are our knowledge, no matter where it comes from. We can claim them as our own from our interpretation and assimilation, which eventually become ours wisdom which in turn becomes our genius. The qualitative element in our thoughts that comes from sense perceptions or cognitive conceiving determines the magnitude that our observations come to conclusions about. Whether these observations are internal in the mind or external in the world both have to deal with our determinations about them.

These determinations we make from our understanding have a mutual relationship with our insight and intuition of these notions, concepts, and ideas. Somehow or another everything has a relationship with everything else. We are all interconnected in one way or another.

We are surrounded with freedom and don't even realize the quantity and quality of that freedom. Freedom is everywhere, and we have not even to look for it because it is so apparent throughout nature. There is freedom in the moments we are given to thought. The most important freedom is our own freedom of the will; we can do what we please most times even without a second thought.

To understand the freedom of will in the mind our insight brings us to reason and understanding; with certainty I know, just how or why I do not. This freedom is one and the same no matter how many differences in its stream of life or what kind of mill that drives it. It is the gravity of our thoughts that brings relationships to the mind and representation to our reason; it is the instinct of our will to live and be content that gives us the endurance make of life what we have the motivation and ambition to do.

Somewhere deep within our mind where instinct dwells with our spirit, our will finds its place alongside reality and abstraction. It has a necessary relation to the differences from within itself, negotiating reality from fantasy in our logic and reason by the understanding we come to from the ability and capabilities of our own creative intelligence.

The instinct and insight we have from this ability form a cohesion from the magnitude of our thoughts to their gravity upon our consciousness of them. The connotations we bring to thoughts give them their value and worth, but it is in this notion that appearances can be deceiving and the actual truth and certainty needs to be discovered on our own.

The multiplicity of properties together constitutes the aspect of this cohesion. It's a long hard road we travel, yet we endure and exist from our own necessity while being creative about it along the way regarding chance and opportunity as part of nature's own peculiar qualities.

The transition from one thought to another, through contemplation, brings different results and conclusions. Our instinct leads us in one direction and our intelligent abstraction leads us in another. And still we pass knowledge to one another depending entirely on our connection to its validity in our own mind, and the proof discovered through doctrine, myth, and tale brings us to our own conclusions.

Instinct, in our nature, becomes the true universality as the inner essence of our being and is due all the dignity essential to our own nature as thinking creatures that are both emotional and analytic.

One must not only think of creatures and things as being individual; but the earth itself is an individual singular entity existing with and for the things and creatures that inhabit its surface, core, waters, and atmosphere. Being conscious of the whole picture we can observe the unity and connections of all the parts and their harmonious interplay.

Not only does insight bring us to reason, but experience and knowledge that we've accumulated and passed along to one another gives us our own sense of wisdom and genius. This freedom we find in instinct offers on all sides the beginnings of laws, traces of necessity, allusions to order and systems that we create both ingenious and plausible connections between reality of mind and natural reality.

Instinct comes from the intro-reflected simplicity of the thoughts that cross the mind and return to be once again considered.

From instinct spirit knows itself as spontaneously active; it follows its own inclinations and reasons by and for itself for the being to which it enables life and motivates that life towards self-preservation, the allurement of pleasure, and the avoidance of pain — including the will to know and a desire for understanding.

Individuality is what the world is. It is the world of our own that makes each of us seek the means for our own gain. The individual exists for him or her self. No one can actually be alone; we have this dependency on others we desire not to accept. Individuality is one of the essential necessities of our nature, but we long for acceptance and have the constant desire to belong. It is one of our intrinsic qualities of being human creatures with emotion and pure intelligent reason that distinguishes us from other creatures and beings, each of us existing on our own level.

Instinct is an activity of one's own actualization in spirit and consciousness of generalities and universalities. Specifics and particulars are activities of reason by logic and by the higher functions of our intelligence, provided we have a certain apprehension and understanding of them.

Within our own realm of existence and survival, by patient endurance, our individuality is infinitely determined and determinable. It is our inner possibility, and capacity by which our motivation and intention is regarded as true actuality from whatever limited resources we have developed in our maturity.

If we now look at the range of relationships as a whole, in which the self-conscious individuality can be observed to stand towards its outer aspects, there will be one left which has to still be made an object for observation: the external reality of things and the internal reality the mind creates for itself, both of which have a peculiar counterpart in spirit that makes spirit intelligible and reasonably understandable essentially and necessarily valid concepts.

From instinct nature gives its own ideas to the notions the mind can conceive. Not only is what we perceive important but also what we conceive, and what we think of has its own importance. We are responsible for our thoughts just as much as we are responsible for our actions when, and if, judgment actually becomes a reality.

As we pass knowledge to one another we should take into account not only our knowledge of human nature but our knowledge and wisdom of spiritual things, just as we pass along knowledge of the elements of the earth and heavens. Spiritual knowledge is most beneficial to rescuing our heart and emotions from our own anxiety caused either by the world or by our own certain way of thinking.

Our reason in the role of observer of the intellect apprehends, comprehends, and understands the spirit by instinct, and through our insight we become aware of its presence and acknowledge it with thought and reflection.

It directs our activities and seeks to proportion our emotions contingent upon the amount of reflectivity we give to our own being. Spirit alone is in its own self-necessity and becomes our guiding light and beacon to further our virtue and genius.

Spring has finally come and the days are getting longer. There is much time now at the end of the work day to find comfort in study and meditation on what we not only learn but on what we dream. This is the second spring time in the creation of this work. The first stage is writing; the second is typing. All along the way there is the reviewing and revising to find some satisfaction in expressing what was once idea and is now concept finding release.

Insight and reason have to work together, as do emotion and feeling. Just the same is reality and fantasy as they create the whole picture of our life and what could, perhaps, be beyond. We must use our intuition to the best of our ability to benefit ourselves enduring our own survival and existence.

– II –

Part Two

Actualization of the Spirit

Instinct tells us of the immediate reality of the spirit of the world and of ourselves through nature and through our own nature. It is the essence of our being, gives reasoning to our life, and gives substance to our body, to the world, and to the nature of both. It gives meaning to our intelligence so that we can have some understanding of what we are giving thought to.

Self-consciousness found the spirit to be like itself, and spirit found itself to be like a thing with the ability to apprehend and to be aware of itself through the capabilities and abilities of the mind. Spirit found itself in nature as it does in one's own existence. It found this world from among all the stars and planets in the universe to share with the earth's creatures and things a remarkable and impressive wonder we can all be given thought to.

Spirit passes over sense-certainty from reason and understanding of its independence towards its own freedom expressed in thought, in creatures, and even further in nature by the elements of sun, rain, wind, and snow and through growth, development, and decay. It finds its freedom in the seasons and in the changing universe that we find our habitat within.

Phenomenology is a philosophy or method of inquiry based on the premise that reality consists of objects and events as they are perceived or understood in human consciousness and not of anything independent of human consciousness. Even if only one person believes in something the possibility that it exists is very real.

Phenomenalism is a doctrine that precepts and concepts constitute the sole objects of knowledge, with the objects of perception and the nature of the mind itself remaining unknowable; yet there is a certain amount of knowing we can have of ourselves and of the world around us by intuition and instinct of our own existence and the existence of the world in which we live. Theory pure and simple is no use except in that it makes us believe in the interconnection of phenomena. By application everything abstract is brought within the capacity of human reason.

By comparison the spirit of nature and the spirit of creatures are like creation and in a constant state of becoming. Our own evolution is a continual process, just like the evolution of the world and universe. Everything grows, but things just get old while everything else gets older. The natural state of this becoming is shown in its evolution and development, and in its growth and decay. There is an exception: things of the mind are created and stored in our memory, and we remember or just choose to forget; they never get old.

In the deep workings of our mind we can realize that our own spirit takes itself to be actual in another consciousness, that of the universal spirit which exists as an element of our own, standing in and beside this greater universal essence and substance of life itself, even beyond life as we know it, into the realm of the metaphysical infiniteness of the life we will experience after our physical life here on earth has ceased.

This ethical substance, taken in its abstract universality, is only principle in the form of thought which the mind apprehends and understands through its own instinctive intelligence.

Spirit is, at first, immediate; but existing immediately, it is separate and individual. It is the practical consciousness which steps into its own world, finding it already given as a positive reflection of itself in the mind's thought process. It holds that the unity is implicitly already present, and that this agreement of itself with the world already exists, comparing our thoughts against one another.

Enlightenment is pure insight. Pure insight, in its simplicity, is effective realization. Being as well that its parts dispose themselves at will in the simple element of its thought, and subsist there, letting them hold on only as its inherent nature independent from all other aspects of the mind consider and reflect upon themselves the ideas being made aware in our conscious thinking of them. There is an unbroken interfusion created in the mind between thought and our utility of intelligent thinking.

The communication that acts silently in the mind and our creative curiosity in the mind is an essential necessity to our nature. Our memory alone preserves our thoughts and in turn creates new connections to the notions and ideas we have already conceived and understood. This silent steady working of the mind makes its connection with our intelligent spirit, and we come to realize that our insight and revelations are part of our own genius.

Self-consciousness, which is at first only the notion of Spirit, enters on the path it finds, in existing, with the characteristic of holding itself to be a particular spirit, an essential being, then aims through the means of patient endurance of survival to give itself as a particular individual and to enjoy its individuality in freedom and cherishing that idea autonomously in the rites of passage through life and beyond life itself into the unknown realm of a metaphysical future for the human spirit and soul.

The ordinary that we have knowledge of, the way of the world we already know, when looked at more closely goes on existing and begins a pattern of phenomenal excitement and personal amusement, while we seek for pleasure and enjoyment in the midst of our personal pain and anguish over events and reoccurring thoughts.

Reality rests on distinctions which are purely nominal. We find truths and give them names and try to preserve them while defining them further, investigating their actual validity and relevance, their appearance provoking evidences to the senses and mind which need further investigation and thought reflection. This is a natural trait in the Adventure in Learning in which we involve ourselves throughout our life.

We mustn't scorn thinking that proceeds by the way of analogies. Analogy has the advantage of not closing doors or in fact aiming at any ultimate solution; it is the kind of inductive thinking with a preconceived purpose in view and in working towards it sweeps both falsehood and truth along with it. What is remote from us influences the imagination, and if we look for some further meaning it is then transformed into the realm of metaphysics we can only find congenial.

We should concern ourselves with the Ideals that we let go and the ineffectual words which lift up the heart but leave reason unsatisfied. We are forever changing the form of our Ideals to meet with our specific needs that create for us some kind of satisfaction.

The spirit through its conflicts learns by experience and brings the wisdom we gain to its height, but not its final one, because it understands now the infinite and the notion of eternity which in our life we pass through to the other side where the unknown only becomes known once we have reached that destination. Our imagination creates for itself an Ideal that brings satisfaction and understanding to our intelligent reasoning powers through the utility of our natural capacity for intelligently considering possibilities.

As we come in contact with our true self we learn about our qualities, both the good ones and our faults, and bring them into our thoughtful consideration. When we try to change our inner self we begin to change the world. It all starts within the mind, and extends outward to the world we live in and create for ourselves. Though the external world has already been created for us, it is our internal world that interprets both.

In its learning it finds the way of the world is actually not that bad, but in our confusion we seem to misinterpret the world we find both inside and outside ourselves. It is only our interpretation that is the great arbiter of the relations we have with ourselves and the real world we live in.

The act of individuality, all that it does, is its own self an end; the employment of its powers and what gives them life realizes its own positive attraction to endurance and survival and to its own well-being. What makes our individuality is the essence of our spirit and our intrinsic nature, which is the beginning, means, and end of our self through our conscience, the center of our heart and spirit, which brings us to our awareness of our consciousness and as well to our consciousness of the spirit that nature holds to in both the world and in the universe.

What seems to be a given reality is only our original nature which has merely the illusory appearance of what we seem to be; but there is more to ourselves and to the world than we think. Through the actualization of our spirit we find our nature and talent to raise ourselves up, by our intelligence, as a means and power, to realize our fullest potential that rests in our capabilities we learn from knowledge passed to one another and by the experience we have with the world.

In the actualization of our spirit what happens to us is just a simple transference of ourselves from the night of possibility into the daylight of the present reality, a reality that cannot be denied. It brings us into the significance of our actual being, into the realization and actualization of our spirit — who we really are deep under the shell we cover ourselves with, defending ourselves as a means for survival in this drama of a world we exist in.

If one is virtuous and wise, what more can they lack? Is there anything more satisfying than the realization of the Great Spirit and actualizing in the mind its presence? We have to do more than just be aware; we have to use the abilities awareness endows us with. It equips us and supplies us with particular talents that we have an obligation to use to our fullest potential.

Our spirit grows from within our mind, and its realization and actualization become revelation and our genius. Where the river of the spirit flows, it knows its destination; all we must do is to follow the rippling current, and in the midst of our attraction it lures us to our own end in the ocean of thought.

The river of the spirit is just the means to our own satisfaction from its necessity in nature. The lines of life are various and diverse; they merge and cease at no one's command but the Almighty

Spirit's — the arbiter of all. With harmonies we find the eternal peace and repose we all seek. Like the light of day that shines on humankind all things various and obscure gather in the knowledge deeply granted to the mind as it is as well to our own original spirit.

Thoughts on Life and Living

One can consider how they develop an idea of themselves and through that same idea observe themselves evolving from potential and possibilities to actuality. It is the interfusion of individuality and being that makes the whole person we see ourselves to be.

It is the interfusion of our character that brings the mind's intellect closer to the heart's emotions. Consciousness gives reality to itself through the thoughts we think and by the dreams we dream. This consciousness that our spirit realizes comprehends the world as a unity of our inner thought with the physical world. On a metaphysical level of thought our consciousness of the possibilities that doctrine has taught us allows us even more creativity with our logic and reason endowed to our intellect.

Our original nature has only an ideal existence in contrast to the actuality of what is, to what was, and to what could be. Our becoming has the quality of being perishable in that we, along with nature, especially in the course of the seasons, have new growth, states of dormancy, and evolve through the phases in our development that comes with age and life.

Like most things, creatures have their morning, midday, and then the evening in the rites of passage through life just as nature does, only to return again to morning in a different realm than where they started from which completes the circle and consistent cycle of reality as we have come to know it to be.

The entirety of our inner moments of thought are surpassed only by the environment in which we live and by the distractions we bring to ourselves from the moment of the mind's own powers of intelligence. Within our own powers our emotion and spirit leads us in willing and achieving, as well as considering the means we use to achieve a goal or end that our motivation and ambition bring us to.

Whether through thought or action our own mind is contingent upon the knowledge we accumulate and the formidable use of our wisdom and genius from that knowledge and as well by its application.

We can be certain that in life we pass knowledge to one another and build upon what we seem to know by further exploration and from the closer inspection of that knowledge. Our understanding comes after we apprehend and comprehend our knowledge by reasoning to the best of our ability from the capabilities within our potential and inherent ability, or aptitude for learning. We strive to excel.

For all our existence we sigh, but not of grief because we know that is true. Before the agony, the spirit grows. It forgets and it remembers. It laughs and it cries. It tastes the good life and the bad just as well; just it is so. There must be praised some certainty in all that we believe. And our faith keeps us strong in our weakness.

And that is true after perpetual defeat. No one would surrender; we fight for our survival without regret. What drives us forth is this spirit that gives us our nature. Nature is like that and made it so we could find it in ourselves and in the world. No genius is born; we all have some learning to do.

Our skills are various and diverse; to each their own responsibility builds defense and empowers us. Our perpetual defeat makes us rise up against the unknown powers of the world and mind.

What's never known is the safest treasure nature will not release. All else can be found in the wisdom we call knowledge. Sense-certainty and perception acquire their significance through self-consciousness and through it alone. The mind finalizes all decisions through reason and logic and comes to its understanding from its awareness our mind actualizes in being conscious of its own activity and accumulated knowledge along with the instinctive nature our spirit provides. What more reason does one find seeking out this spirit we acknowledge?

The subject proposed is inscribed in our mind and has its affects in the various parts of nature, ascending from the lower to the higher and mixed with digressions arising from the subject. Its influence on inanimate matter, what grows from the earth, creatures, and lastly on every man, woman and child is noticed and made to be aware of by nature's own design.

Our spirit is consciousness that is intelligent and that reasons. This reason gives the spirit its ethical and logical essence that has an actual existence. Spirit is aware of truth and makes distinctions between the appearance of truth and the actual truth itself.

Our mind apprehends its own spirit and gives it its significance. It is through the power of the mind that we become aware of our own insight and instinct which is our enlightenment and our wisdom.

Knowledge and wisdom are connected and have an immediate relationship with the spirit and mind. This natural relationship is as much spiritual as is mental in that it is solely in the mind, and each affects the other with their character and specific qualities.

With innocence and meditation we ponder on the passage of time and seasons, all the while growing in the wealth of new found knowledge. Trembling with satisfaction, we recognize the changing times as nature shakes off one season and rouses another. The shifting winds play with our mind. The expansive atmosphere is full of life and vivifying soul that animates and enlivens life throughout the universe.

We ask the heavens to be gracious on those who labor for life. For those left in despair and despondency we ask the same and more, for those with the greatest need are controlled more by desire than by passion. It is nature's swift and sweeping hand that sometimes goes unnoticed, far-diffused throughout the land and in the recesses of our individual mind's resources.

Hushed in short suspense, in silence, we wait with anticipation and expectation, impatient to demand. What will be, will be, with the exception of our own will to succeed; from nature's inborn motivation we cultivate our own ambition.

The most significant thing that can happen to you are the brief periods during which you are conscious without thoughts already occurring spontaneously that shift your awareness from thinking of the presence of the spirit to that unclouded persistence of thought about some of the things in life that don't really matter.

The acquisition and maintenance of our wisdom is directly connected by the passing of knowledge to one another and affects our life and the living of it. Music has the same effect on us; it reaches into our inner depths and soothes the soul of the listener with solemn and impressive passion. Because each of us has our individual qualities, our likes and dislikes do not compromise our own character but may have an effect on others. For that reason we should calculate what affects our own disposition has on others.

Sometimes we have to compromise ourselves, but that is where our decision-making process brings out our true wisdom. Our judgments have to be clear and direct towards the goal we perceive — towards the destination we sojourn to once we stop and view our world before it passes us by.

We discover differences and gradations, successive stages that pass imperceptibly from one degree to another, in the rites of passage we find ourselves going through. The projections of our thoughts that come from the mind find their way to the surface so that from what we conceive we can actually perceive with a true sort of definition and meaning. It is the spirit of our intelligence that brings us to the unity of thought that we quest for.

The whole is a stable equilibrium of all the parts, and each part is a spirit or idea at home within the whole. It does not seek any satisfaction outside itself, but finds satisfaction within itself because it is itself in this equilibrium with the grandeur of the whole, in concept. Spirit rises out of its unreality into actual existence, out of a state in which it is unknowing and unconscious into the realm of conscious spirit, intelligently known to us through the abilities of the mind to understand and know what it conceives. Though music has no actual words we can know its meaning through the composition relating the notes, melodies, harmonies, and tones produced in the work as if our own passions decide for us what the intent of the composition truly means to our own character.

Wisdom and Knowledge

Our ethical consciousness knows what it has to do, and has already decided whether to belong to divine or human law. The significance of our decisions rests solely in our own conscience. The activation of our will coincides with the realization of spirit in our intelligence.

In the beginning of our recognition of consciousness, we are for ourselves and protect our own survival and those of our close, significant relatives. As we mature we are for the other and self-sacrificing becomes a way of life. We surrender ourselves to the fact that significant others are at the heart of our own being.

We recognize that others are essential and necessary to our own survival and well-being. Our inner worth is this determination of our interaction with others. We pass knowledge to one another with our love and caring, with our wisdom and experience. No one was meant to be alone, so we were given others and the spirit to live with besides having to live with only ourselves.

Spirit's relation or intrinsic nature becomes a reflection into ourselves through which we can acquire our spiritual being, an essential part of our lively existence. Meditation on this notion brings out its implicitness in the nature of the consciousness we explore through life and our growing maturity.

It is from our knowledge and wisdom that truly universal concepts become united with existence in general. This is necessary and essential to our consciousness, on both sides of reality, the personal and the worldly. We are not alienated from the world, though it seems so at times, but immersed in existence with our life and thought. We continue living as we do, all the while setting our will in motion. It is our thought that is the cardinal essence of our simple inner being. It is our thoughts that make the world into consciousness, which is a step over and beyond self-consciousness itself, beyond the threshold of reality into the reality of a metaphysical dimension we explore from deep within our own mind. It is our thoughts that form the relationships we designate to the world and to ourselves in which we give our thoughts to.

It is thought in its own account that makes wisdom possible. As we accumulate knowledge, and assimilate it to our own, we become entirely more thoughtful about our own thinking. The notion of belief and faith is nothing more than the actual world raised into a state of universality.

In thought we confront our own reality, making sense of what we can, while being indifferent to what we can not. This not knowing in our reality raises our curiosity and keeps us interested in learning and discovery, while encountering our own thoughts with a certain diversity of significance and importance.

Isn't it a curious thing how people can be so naive with their limited knowledge and self-proclaimed wisdom? It is through experience and understanding that we come to critical judgments and make our decisions that determine our destiny.

It is in the remote tranquil realm of thought, when we are not disturbed by the world or by our own thoughts, that we bring reality to the heights of insight of spirit and actualization of its intrinsic essence in our humanness.

Genius, talent, and our special abilities have to be nurtured and brought to the surface from deep within, all the while realizing and actualizing our aptitude and talent for learning all that we are capable of and our hidden potential capabilities. Everyone has these gifts, but few can evoke them from their creative inner nature. Those who do are the ones who labor in thought and realize, actualize, their own creativity not only of thought, but in action as well.

The communication of insight and enlightenment, in the possession of our own wisdom, we pass knowledge to one another from its own necessity that everyone shares in some sort of common knowledge. It is our inner motivation and outer ambition that drive our will and spirit through the extremes and mediocrities we develop early in life and bring with us throughout our middle age and into our later years, whereby we actually determine a real and true cause for our destiny and where we bring ourselves to in this life.

Strength and Virtue of Understanding

The liberty we give to thought, in a world of objective thought, is our faith and belief in what we understand to be true and certain of. In our thoughts the communication between mind and spirit is unimpeded, direct, and constant. We know ourselves like no other.

We must be aware at all times of deception and illusion. One who knows the truth can stretch it, though not beyond recognition, beyond its limits and still make it seem like the real truth. Our creative process allows us this achievement; though it is not a thoughtful consequence of sincere reasoning, it may suit a given purpose.

It is our wisdom of discernment and apprehension and an aptitude for learning that gives reason to our thoughts in judgment, with discretion as a sole basis of our elemental thoughts.

Pure thought posited within itself is an object of our essence. It is partially what we are made up of, considering that without our mind we are just body. It is the idea of spirit and thought that gives us our substance and ability to carryon as intelligent human creatures. This intrinsic being of thought, this nature we possess, is more than empty form; it is matter beyond form abstractly and metaphysically thought of with our creative intelligence that our mind enables through its utility and aptitude for learning and expression. It is something presented to our consciousness that we are aware of. Not only are we aware of ourselves and of our own thinking, we are aware of the world and know that there are things happening in the world and in the universe that surrounds our world.

We have this sense-certainty which gives us our strength of mind and is the true virtue of our understanding. We mustn't scorn thinking that proceeds by the way of analogies. Analogy has the advantage of not closing doors or in fact aiming at any ultimate solution — the kind of inductive thinking, on the other hand, which has preconceived purposes that sweeps both truth and falsehood along with it. We should remember that it is the certain way of thinking that gets us through the days and nights of our life.

One must consider further just how faith and belief lead to experiences of enlightenment. It is through study and contemplation, and by the passing of knowledge to one another, that this enlightenment and insight come.

These moments are pure thought. The knowing we come to is grounds for our convictions and serves as a basis for our elemental thoughts. Pure thought is posited within itself as an object of essence, in the believing consciousness intrinsic in our spirit and mind.

The sense-certainty we have comes from our aptitude for learning, apprehending, and understanding of what we know, which is our wisdom. The ground of knowledge is the conscious universal, and in its truth is absolute spirit which, in abstract concepts, moves the mind to thought and wonder. One of these concepts is that of conscience and spirit which only the mind can fathom.

In this realization, the moment that is essential seems to belong to faith and have the character of something external to insight, yet internal in the faculties of our concentrated thinking. The strength we have in faith, in its certainty, is an unsophisticated relationship to its object in thought and our reflection upon it. This consciousness is the self-mediating ground of its knowledge.

Understanding is beside the point; just the recognizing that there is strength and virtue in believing what we have faith in is the important matter. We come to terms with our own understanding and interpretation, yet enlightenment lets itself be known and understood from our own certain way of thinking that gives us satisfaction.

Enlightenment finds a reasonable relationship with what is understood and previously known to the degree each of us are capable of achieving. It encounters its own wisdom and pursues genius as a virtue for its own strength. What's next? What is the truth enlightenment has propagated? It interprets the determinateness it discovers in our own Adventure in Learning as knowledge is passed to us, enlarging our own Basis of Elemental Thoughts and giving some kind of soundness to our decisions and judgments.

Through our emotions and senses we grasp mentally concepts and notions of all sorts. We all have the capability to understand, but on our own terms. We are all in some way or another apprentice to life, all the while learning from experience and our own research into life's mysteries. As the concealed becomes revealed we grow in our own knowledge and wisdom.

Our mind reveals the relationships it explores in the unity of things as universals in their particulars. When we allow for a clearing in our mind it creates a vacuum, a state of emptiness, for more knowledge and wisdom to accumulate in the storehouse of our mental resources. Thereby from this emptying and filling we increase our own potential genius, and come to a newer and bolder understanding of that we think we already know.

Reason and pure insight are certainly not empty, but full of conceptions, notions, ideas, and creative imagination. Our mind is an intelligent machine. Machines fail just like people do, but there is a fix for most things. To reconfigure our thinking is one. To adjust our perspective is another. To eliminate prejudice and bias is still another. Our continued maintenance is necessary and essential.

Understanding our limitations, we can strive towards overcoming them and approach the horizon fixing ourselves on a point and reaching the goal before looking past it into another new horizon and crossing the threshold of the new splendor of the grandeur of it all.

This singular thought has its own importance. We must have a sense of achievement that gives us the strength and satisfaction to move on and continue with our journey through time, progressing with history along each moment we are allowed to participate in. No one knows when they will be called away, so we ought to make the best use of our time while we are here on this planet we call earth. In that moment of achievement we find virtue and dignity within ourselves that give us an increased strength coming from our perseverance and endurance of all the previous moments chance and opportunity have availed us to. The step beyond the here and now ultimately starts with its origin.

Enlightenment merely presents faith with its own thoughts which faith unconsciously lets fall apart, but which enlightenment brings together. Enlightenment shows itself to faith to be pure insight, because it sees the whole from the parts and views the panorama without paradox in a paradigm way.

Enlightenment corrects our insight and presents to our thoughts ideas that give sureness and certainty to our beliefs and faith in a rational and consistent way. Since consciousness is divided within itself having a beyond of the real world and a world that is altogether this side of the world beyond, there is also present in our sensuous existence a world of feeling and emotion that stands independent of the physical world. But who is to say that the metaphysical is not part of the real world — just that it is so difficult to know?

Enlightenment makes immediate to us newfound inner knowledge and spiritual knowledge which is self-authenticated. It regards the content and quality of our thoughts and gives them definition and worth. We must learn to leave people to the laws of nature without any hindrance, but never forget that under our conditions they must rise above these laws. Once we become used to living a hard life of existence it increases our pleasurable experiences.

A child serves his or her apprenticeship in courage and endurance as well as in other virtues; but you cannot teach children as adults. These are virtues by name alone; children must learn them unconsciously through experience in the real world that surrounds their inner world of mind and spirit.

Faith itself apprehends, grasps mentally, and becomes conscious of the absolute and the universal. Enlightenment only adds to our own understanding what we already seem to know from insight and revelation. Enlightenment does away with "thought-less" and brings us closer to "thought-more." From study and contemplation we come to enlightenment and comprehension with our aptitude for learning in our reasoning and consistent logical utility of our creative intelligence and in our thoughtful dreams.

There was a time when we danced and played without care. We were children then, but now that we're grown we have to face reality straight on and keep our ambition and motivation to survive, in spite of conditions and events we come to by chance or opportunity in our daily life.

Under the sky we live with our only arms for defense being our active mind and creative thought. We ask why and get no reply. We ask how and again get no reply. We ask when and the answer comes as a beacon in the night — when we use all of our abilities to the fullest striving for the Ideal. I hear, "Be content and learn to not want and be satisfied." Isn't that what contentment is? The possible usually becomes part of the reality we live with.

Enlightenment holds an irresistible authority over our insight and intuition because it brings to our awareness further, and greater, knowledge which leads to a better wisdom than we once had, thereby increasing our ability for decision making in our judgments and evolving opinion making without bias or prejudice equally and unequivocally.

Enlightenment wakes our slumbering consciousness and illuminates the metaphysical part of reality only our mind can fathom, that heavenly world, with ideas belonging to the realm of sense, and points out this finitude which faith cannot deny because of its irresistible charm.

It is through enlightenment that our intuition and insight go beyond the ordinary into the extraordinary and satisfies itself through its new found reason and sense of intelligence from that knowledge brought to our attention and awareness. Theory pure and simple is of no use except in that it makes us believe in the interconnection of phenomena, and gives to us a foundation, the ground for our own simple and complex thinking activity.

By application everything abstract is brought within the capacity of human reason, and this is how action and observation lead human reason to the power of abstraction and understanding of metaphysical things which only the mind can fathom from its utility. In our thinking we use analogy, which has the advantage of not closing the doors and windows of our perception.

We ought to be cautious and curious of what occupies our attention, seeing that the mind is master of tricks and illusion. Where our mind wanders it wonders as well. We should be cautious of what we think our needs are as compared to our wants and desires.

From an adept insight we find our priorities and become alert to our motivations and intensions. From reasßon we find and distinguish their differences of opinion that come from within our own mind.

Consciousness has found its notion in utility and usefulness; but it is partially still an object, and partially for that very reason still an end to be attained. It returns to itself through nature and spirit in the thought of it. Our mind is drawn to it, like a magnet, to consider itself and ponder in awe and wonder of its magnificence.

We as individuals must remind ourselves we are part of the extravagance and immensity of the grandeur of the whole picture and do not exist alone. Spirit comes before us as an absolute freedom in thought, being able to pass beyond the finite into the infinite. Its certainty of itself is the essence of all spiritual matter, as well as of the super-sensible world. Essence and actuality are consciousness' ability to know itself and our surrounding world, and all that it includes even far off into the depths of the universe. It is our logic that we use to explain reality. What we can explain we do with a certain enthusiasm; what we cannot explain we ought to pass over, yet we do not, try as we will with our creative intelligence.

The unexplainable keeps us enthralled and spellbound. We use the unexplainable as a sort of entertainment for the mind. It is the enterprise of the mind that keeps at this systematic activity. Our reason and logic lure us to do the explaining that we do, no matter how far off it is; yet our discovery and exploration bring us closer to the truth than ever before by our study and contemplation. What we do not know stirs the imagination of philosophers. We all seem to be alike because it is our innate curiosity that yields us to make some kind of reason out of every sort of experience, notion, and idea that comes to our mind's attention.

The Certainty of Spirit

Even a stopped clock gives the right time twice a day. There are various problems regarding language. First, what actually occurs in our mind when we use language with the intention of meaning something by it? We use language expressing thoughts to ourselves and to others. We ought to know what we mean when we are given to thought of something or some matter.

Second, what is the relation between words and the thought of them by which we have given meaning to — the reference to what the words imply and our understanding of their usage? The third issue regards the using of words in conjunction with phrases and sentences thoughts express, and the relation of one statement to another conveying an idea or notion we ought to learn about word's applications and the various layers of their meaning in relation to our thoughts of them.

The last is a logical question which is of our most concern, that our expressions have meaning we can understand with our own reasoning. In practice language is merely as precise as the words used to portray a thought we have in mind. Even as we talk to ourselves we talk the same to others. These make up the rules of philosophical grammar.

When speaking of metaphysical things, or even the clouds, sky, and things like a rainbow or an angel, we use words as we do philosophy to clarify our own thoughts and notions of them. Philosophy is an activity produced by the mind to discover logical connections between our thoughts and the ideas that provoked them to be thought. Ideas such as the spirit have a greater meaning than we can express, yet we do try to explain what we think we have knowledge of from our own insight and intuition of the matter of the subject.

So in a manner we pass knowledge to one another and in that way increase the basis of our elemental thoughts, and give greater value and worth, as well as meaning, to our own philosophy we create for ourselves. From this endeavor, using language as a describing factor we come to know the certainty of the spirit we hold to ourselves and to the greater world beyond ourselves.

Just as the realm of the real world passes over into the realm of faith and insight, so does absolute freedom leave its reality and pass over into another land of self-conscious spirit where in this surreal world freedom has the value of truth and self-certainty.

In the thought of this truth, spirit refreshes itself, in so far as it remains thought. The certainty comes from our wisdom and genius. The self-contained thought becomes known and understood where a sense of completeness of the whole, the grand picture of reality, permeates the mind without illusion or misconception. The truth becomes certain.

Substance becomes for spirit at first the universal will, and finally becomes the spirit's own possession. Here, then, knowledge appears at least to have become completely identical with its original truth; for its truth is this very knowledge that self-consciousness has gained mastery over in its own understanding.

Thus, for self-consciousness, its knowledge and wisdom become all that its substance is. Our immediate existence, present in meditation and contemplation, creates our own reality within all reality that is both physically and metaphysically possible.

Absolute essential being is not exhausted when determined as the simple essence of thought; it is all reality, and this reality is only knowledge, and is our wisdom and genius. It is absolutely free in that it knows its freedom from its own creative ability to conceive and imagine.

Conscience is the common element and has an enduring reality through all space and time because it is part of the infinite mind. Once recognized it is given the authority to regulate our ethical and moral freedom, distinguishing choice as a matter of decision and judgment based on our own knowledge and personal wisdom. Conscience knows that it has to choose between differences of opinion. The self-certain spirit rests in conscience and its real universality or its duty lies in its pure conviction of that duty — to choose and distinguish the significance of thought before action. What it reasons as truth it finds significant certainty in belief and faith.

Conscience, in the majesty of its elevation, puts whatever content it pleases into its knowing and willing. It is the moral genius which knows the inner voice of what it immediately knows to be a divine voice that quietly speaks to us; and we understand somehow.

In knowing this, conscience has an equally immediate knowledge of its existence and utility for which it has been placed within our mind. It is the divine creative power which in notion possesses the spontaneity of life through nature and spirit that brings us to contemplation, a self-reflective thought, of divinity; and in meditation of its own connection to that divinity we create our own philosophy of theology, grounding our faith and belief in what we consider true and the certainty of that truth.

The judging consciousness does not stop short at the aspect of duty, and its significance. Those who labor in thought know the condition and status of their own reality. We know our intention and motivation that leads us to action whether physical or in thought. Our reactions are of a different kind; they are filled with emotion rather than fact. We are subject to feelings and emotions that attach themselves to the heart rather than subjecting themselves to the power of the mind. The outer forces of the world are reflected to the inner aspect of our intelligence; and we consider both and weigh our own conclusions based on our wisdom and knowledge, both learned and that which was passed on to us through culture and society.

The notion of a super-sensible world is not far off from the creative and intelligent power of the mind. It is more probable than possible. We have created a knowledge of the reality beyond reality from its own necessity. That necessity is what holds the notion and concept of spirit together, binding our own to nature and all that nature holds, including the realm of reality beyond our own. In conscience, thought brings itself into subjection. In thinking and its specific notions, self-consciousness communes with its own self; and spirit is conceived as object with its own significance. Here the universal conjoins with the particular of our own reality.

The universal spirit that contains within itself all essence and actuality, its substance, is known by one's own conscience. It is one of the necessary essentials that make up a human's being. It is the regulator and arbiter of spirit as it is known and realized by one's own nature. There is indeed one spirit of both, but its awareness does not embrace both together. We know our own spirit and give it significance, but the greater spirit has to come to us. In revelation and by study we come to our own insight of it.

There is a common thread that leads us to the realization that all things and creatures are connected in some way. It is through this grand spirit that we find the unity we seek for.

What is thought of ceases to be something merely thought of; it becomes something that is part of our inner reality the mind puts forth in our thinking and dreams. This knowledge we think of that is part of our intelligence is what is passed to one another, and upon consideration of it we incorporate it into our own genius.

It is not only the thoughts we think of, but the thoughts themselves that make up all that we know and can imagine that is our wisdom. Where the spirit meets the concept of a metaphysical spirit, there we find ourselves and what we truly are and are becoming. Life does not stand still; we are part of an everlasting creation, a process that had a beginning but no end.

The outer world retreats into itself by the laws of nature and by the principles of physics, but the inner world creates for itself a metaphysical reality that cannot be denied. Through knowledge we come to our beliefs, convictions, and faith. When we find what seems to be the truth, we explore it, discover its subtleties and fine distinctions, and draw from it our personal intellectual wisdom, which we pass along to one another in songs and tales, and create a new mythology from contemporary thinking. To the mind, all this is not significant unless we have an acute awareness of the meaning of what we think and is memorable from the significance we give to it from what we have not overlooked in our own patterns of thought.

The Artist, Architect, Musician, and Poet

There is one thing all these characters have in common: the spirit of creativity at the forefront of their mind. There are more characters as well, in literature, in the performing arts, and in the ordinary day and life of a human being.

People like these bring their own spirit to the surface in their work; in effect, they pass their own knowledge and creativity to others from their own fulfillment, perhaps with no other intention. The representations they create bring us to realizations and actualize what they conceive for us to perceive.

The simple certainty of spirit within itself has a twofold meaning: it is a serene, stable existence and settled truth, but also an absolute unrest and passing-away of an unknown and uncertain order of a realm beyond knowing. We are all creators in some way. We do this with our thoughts and actions on a regular basis, creating our own world within the greater world. The human mind is a creation factory with unlimited resources. Here is absolute freedom. We are restricted only by our own limited creativity.

The poet can capture words that bring us inspiration and then we interpret those words as revelation. The accumulation of thought is contemplated by the philosopher and theologian; we all have this quality in our own way. All of us take part in the passing of knowledge to one another in some way or another, through our own special talents and abilities. Still the mystery of life remains, but it is our various explanations that give it a sense of order and regularity that we can base our beliefs and faith on with a sense of truth and certainty.

The mystical is not concealment of secret, or ignorance, but consists in the self knowing itself to be one with the divine of our own creation and revealed from our knowledge and learned wisdom.

Necessity is the spiritual reality in which everything returns. It is the home and the base of Elemental Thoughts and forms a sure foundation for those who labor in thought, for the philosopher and the theologian to reason from their understanding they gain from knowledge.

What self-consciousness beholds is that whatever assumes the form of essentiality over against it, and is dissolved in it — in its thinking — its own very existence, and its action, is at its mercy. It is the return of everything universal into the certainty of itself. This self-certainty is a state of spiritual well-being and of repose therein where peace becomes a state of mind and contentment actualized.

Though spirit may be real it is only imagined into existence. This imagining is the visionary dreaming which is brought into humanity through the mythical ideas of earlier times, but further and deeper into contemporary thought from those who abound in the intellectual creativity we are endowed with as creatures with active minds.

The immediate in-itself of spirit knows it and comprehends it. The immediate in-itself gives shape and meaning, value and worth, to its own self-consciousness and means nothing else than the actual world-spirit we all come to know at some time in our life. This same knowledge enters into and reacts to the thought of itself without delay or doubt. It has a certain sureness of its own truth. In its turn our consciousness of spirit appears as the belief of the world where spirit is immediately present, something we can be certain of, and passes beyond all the reality we know into a new and unknown reality which is part of nature itself we quest to discover.

The knowledge and the object of that knowledge are the same. What is comprehended can be conceptually determined. The significance of one's own insight is in its actualization and realization that what one conceives has a degree of probability and possibility. It unfolds and becomes revealed from its concealment and turns back into itself in thought and contemplation.

Enlightenment itself becomes pure insight, aware of itself, and is self-understanding as an absolute reality in the mind of the one who searches out the truth and finds it and all its similarities, distinguishing the content of revelation implicitly. Enlightenment declares and explains reality as the self-same truth we know from the insight we have into ourselves and into the physical world.

A Reasonable Explanation

What first started as imagination in the believer becomes the actual, and part of our very own reality. The element of thought is contained in the notion of the nature of the thought itself.

Our contemplation and meditation are still incomplete because if the unreconciled were to split into the here and beyond, what is physical would at the same time become spiritual — a surrealistic reality at most, and we all would sense the unrealistic as true reality.

Consequently, what happens in the thought state of the mind is the tracing-back, based on instinct and intuition from deep within, is our primitive and imperfect idea of what spirit is all about. We should not be confused with the origin of the notion and the notion itself. Spirit makes itself known only when we are ready to receive its inspiration and realize its actuality in our lively existence.

The simplicity of the notion remains. It is not complicated or unresponsive to our actual thinking of it. It knows when it is thought. Spirit is a conception and can be perceived only in the mind. Though our thoughts are real, they are part of nature itself which makes the possibility of conception possible.

When spirit is at first conceived of as substance in the element of pure thought, it is immediately simple. When one then is in consideration of this simple thought its abstractness complicates the notion and leads our imagination into the eternal essence which spirit holds to in the conjunction with nature that it essentially has.

The idea goes beyond the limitations of words and becomes an experience and emotion, because in its abstraction it finds its synthetic connection between thinking and understanding our own thoughts, as well as the thoughts we pass along to one another from history into the contemporary realm of pure thought from reason.

Nature must be transcended, especially from the standpoint which takes the moment of our mind through the course of creating a reality for spirit to be thought and conceived. The compulsion is instinctive to bring the sense of spirit to our own absolute reality. The inner element of belief and faith has not vanished but is realized.

Since spirit is essentially the simple self, this self is equally present in the world as it is in the mind. Spirit, in its immediate existence, is more than thought actualized; it is sense-consciousness moved through our reason and intelligence into the consciousness of our thoughts. What we think is the mobilization and utility of our mind to recognize the reality of spirit is actually the awareness that we give to its experience.

What happens with our knowledge, and the increase of it, is the grasping of the imaginative idea that reconciles the unknown and, through our intelligence, creates wisdom for itself, which is our understanding and comprehension of the idea itself.

This knowing that we come to is the inbreathing of the spirit, and we recognize it with the natural ability in our human intelligence. In this way spirit is self-knowing, and we understand this notion because we realize the essence of our own being through nature and through our own cognition. What moves itself is spirit and, what we will moves us to knowledge and the evolution of our own wisdom.

The knowing of which we are speaking is not knowing as pure comprehension; here, this knowing is to be indicated only in its process of coming to be. Knowledge is never complete, but is added to with the passing of knowledge to one another, where it is elaborated and expanded from discovery, inquiry, and its own exploration, seeking to come to terms with the truth and certainty we believe and have faith in, and its similarities and appearances of what seems to be truth.

These are the moments of which the reconciliation of spirit with its own consciousness is composed. It is not only the intuition of the divine, but the divine's intuition of itself. Truth is not only in itself completely identical with certainty but also has the shape of self-certainty, and the knowledge thereof brings us to the realization of the actuality of reality, including the realm beyond our knowledge of which we conceive and have a conception of through our creative intelligence and reasonable imagination.

Just like a lot of things in the universe, the shape, or form, that is most common is the circular or spherical pattern. The movement of the mind is that way as well. It returns into itself from where it presupposes its own beginning. We ought to understand nature in all its variety that is necessary for itself to fulfill its own existence just as we do. For our survival, just as nature's, there is a certain amount of enduring we must go through in our rites of passage.

Everything we know or have knowledge of must have come before us so it can be learned. Instinct can only give us just so much to go by. There was a before us just as there will be an after us; the circular pattern shows itself in all directions. As we grow and mature, so does our pattern of learning. There must be an explanation for everything that there is, so we are endowed with imagination as well as a reasonable intellect to figure these mysteries to a satisfactory conclusion; but there are still some things that evade answers. Perhaps nature made it that way to keep our curiosity on the move, and to keep the sense of wonder in us alive.

By application everything abstract is brought within the capacity of human reason, and this is how action and observation lead human reason to the power of abstraction. Metaphysics is the same; it leads us on in thought and the mystery remains.

Common sense is said to be the genius of mankind, but it shows its varieties in many different ways. Knowledge and learning only give it a broader base to draw its conclusions from. As I grow in knowledge and become increasingly familiar and attached to this newfound wisdom, the experience of thinking and thought takes on a special meaning, value, and worth. Though I am happy to accept this new base for my truth, the question remains as to how I can find out more about the needs that I have facing the mystery associated with the unknown, mysterious, and metaphysical that cannot be proved nor disputed among those who labor in thought.

Conception and Expression of Ideas

What we cannot speak of we ought to leave alone in silence and contemplate on the issue until such a time when the words come to us to express our thoughts in a clear and precise way. For doubt can exist only where a question exists, and an answer only where something can be said.

The sense of the world must lie outside the world. In the world everything is as it is, and everything happens as it does, and if this were not so there could be no conception or expression at all of the matter that the mind has to come to terms with.

The whole modern conception of the world is founded on the illusion that the so-called laws of nature are explanations of natural phenomena; but there is more to the world than is known, so we all ought to continue in our studies and contemplate them with conviction.

Finite actualities can, properly speaking, be taken just in the way people have a need for them. The infinite takes another course: it becomes a realm where possible and probable can only be expressed with imagination and speculation in the reasonable part of our mind.

With our senses we gather information about the outer world. With our mind we compile the information we have gathered and bring it to our intelligence to be reasoned and interpreted. With our mind we create a world underlying and supporting that outer world. From our interpretation we bring ourselves to developing a particular philosophy suitable to our own character and disposition.

Within the mind our creative imagination is put to good use through its utility in contemplation, and we wonder about it, the way things seem to be, passing above and beyond reality into a surreality all our own, from the mind's utility and capacity to effectively use thought to express what the mind has brought itself to.

The miracle comes when language and word evolve to express not only to the world our ideas and notions but to ourselves in a sensible, rational, and reasonable way what it is that we actually think about and come to conclusions about in our reflection and contemplation.

Everything is now at the mercy of other things, lets itself now be used by other things, and exists for them. What is independent is only the original thought in its own purest sense. As everything is useful for man, man is likewise useful too; we pass knowledge to one another, thereby increasing each other's wisdom and usefulness to society. What essentially we do is to enlighten each other in a way that is most beneficial to the whole of humanity at large. Man must persist in the belief that the incomprehensible is in fact comprehensible, or else he would cease his quest for more and greater knowledge.

Another great achievement and fulfillment of the human spirit was, and is, the advancement in printing technology and in music through the use of electronics. When humanity found the ways and means to create electronic printing and music, the ethereal quality of transporting the mind became more than transcendental; it became a super-surrealistic actuality. The great wonder of it all is that we could succeed at such an accomplishment.

The world keeps changing, not only of itself, but by man's participation in its evolving nature. For better or worse there will be an answer to every problem and a question for every achievement.

The long history of metaphysics has continued through the eras of time, even to today. As we search out the truth of things and try to find simple explanations, we come to complications of not only meanings but of the qualities of those meanings. Some answers that we put forward to questions are beyond words, yet we give words to them as a satisfactory explanation to the expressions we conceive. The pure thoughts where questions and answers originate are, and have, a special significance to the evolution and development of a way of thinking that brings us closer to a philosophy and theology acceptable to our contemporary knowledge and wisdom. While we are attentive to the facts and discriminations of thoughts on the subject there is an ineluctable, not to be avoided or escaped from way of thought that provides us with acceptable and reasonable answers we quest for.

Even within our mind we can expect a world beyond time, a world of the future that proclaims itself in the presence of our thoughts. From any conception there must be a way and means to be expressed. Since language is the key source for our expression, its usage ought to be carefully woven into the fabric of our rhetoric, our language, precisely and effectively.

However the topic is considered the problem of language has never been a simple one. Grammar, syntactic structure, and semantic rules make language a study in itself, but we all seem to communicate rather well in a phonetic way.

And then there are some things that have no language to express them, like immediate feelings and emotions that just overwhelm us in the moment of an event. There is in the mind a sense that strives for release with no way to represent it except for tears or signs of intense joy by dance or meaningless voice patterns.

Historical contingencies that one may admire or regret are and were absolutely necessary for us to have come to where we are today. It's not what happens to us that is important; it's what we do with what we have that makes all the difference in the world.

Logic must look after itself. In a certain sense, we cannot make mistakes in logic. A legitimately constructed proposition must have sense about it. What makes logic so amusing is that there is an improbability of illogical thought. I think as well that just the thought of something illogical is highly entertaining. Some things that make no sense at all mostly lead the mind to creative intellectual imagination where sense becomes senseless and even inconsistent with any refined wisdom we have in the treasury of our sense-full mind.

Perhaps logic is full of primitive ideas that originate in nature itself, which is highly logical and as well has reasonable principles by which its laws stem from making logic the most sensible of all our innate qualities that the mind utilizes in judgment making and in decision forming notions of probabilities and possibilities. Once more we come to understand that the unknown must be logical.

The influences on us are numerous, variable, and unconditional. An idea in the mind produces the idea of the world, the universe, and the inner thought of oneself. The idea of world-origin must begin somewhere, so perhaps the best place to start is in your mind. From there you can go anywhere your imagination or memories take you. The world is transcendental and empirical all at once.

History and knowledge have always been associated with increasing challenges to procure wisdom. The development of practical methods of information retrieval and expression or presentation has been based on the use of a functional language system that clearly represents our thoughts and ideas. Without it the passing of knowledge to one another, or even communicating with oneself, would have no basis at all. So it seems that we use language in more than one way, deliberating thought, reflection, and expression. Even picture-thinking requires some kind of symbols.

Though not all people use the same language, our mental experiences have similarities common to all alike. Just as well we have similar feelings and emotions all coming from inside our mind.

In every case, the voice closest to the mind is our inner one; our conscience bears itself to the intellect and to the world. It translates the external world and gives meaning to our inner world. Since these concepts are indispensable to humanity we ought to have a cherishing for language, because it gives worth and value to our wisdom. It makes our genius come alive.

Reflecting on our passing knowledge to one another, a thought came to me from ancient times; I really don't know where or when — if all the seas were ink, and all the ponds were planted with reeds, and the earth and sky were parchments, and if all humans practiced the art of writing, they would exhaust neither reeds nor pens nor the ink to fill them expressing each and everyone's thoughts about themselves or the world. Not even writing about the universe or heaven could wear down the reeds or use up all the ink or fill the parchment with words from the heart and mind combined with all the knowledge either known or unknown throughout the ages.

There are people who think that thought is mundane, but those who labor in thought know the labor it takes to translate thought into word, by the use of their language skills, and write that thought and its explanation in a clear and precise way.

The wonder of it all is that the treatment of the metaphor and the determination of an absolute presence constituted as self-presence is an analogy to the realization of a thought in the mind. From the moment of realization this becomes just a simple understanding.

The same wonder leads us to consider the sudden appearance of words the ancients invented from their creative intelligence. The descriptive factor is one in which symbols and words take on their mystique. The introduction of words as a useable language was not only necessary, but inevitable. Our communication skills lead to the passing of knowledge to one another, which is the theme of this work.

Numbers take on the same significance as words, perhaps even more so; because they take us to science, physics, and geometry. In logic there can be no distinction between the general and specific. In our rational capabilities the solutions of problems of logic must be simple, since they set the standards for our simplicity of thought.

The general and specific coincide — the particular or specific is the general made manifest under a different set of conditions. The whole of existence is an eternal process of separation and union. It also follows that human beings, watching and considering this process, involve themselves continually in this separation and union on a regular basis of separating and uniting in more realms than just in thought. We alienate ourselves to unite with the spirit and unite ourselves to join in society's activities.

A faithful observer who reflects to some purpose is always more and more aware of his or her limitations, and then again is consumed with the idea of probabilities and possibilities given to their own potential once accepting the awareness of their own inner thoughts and the advancement of humanity, in general, as a whole community of thoughtful and logical, reasonable and rational beings.

The voice and writing are a matter of perspective. We ought to choose a vantage point that shows us the grandeur of the whole picture. Perhaps a view from outer space looking back at the earth will do, but the view from inside our mind will suffice for now. The greater view is only accessible from the International Space Station or from the Hubble telescope.

Though there is technique in the use of words in writing and in conversation, the words we use in our inner thought reflect how we think and not what we are. We are more than a thought; we are real with essence, spirit and body. It is the philosopher and theologian who close all books except for one; that one is the book of nature that we discover both inwardly and outwardly in both the realm of mind and in the real world. Beyond reality we can only think with words from reality about the divine and the unknown.

Self-evidence can become dispensable in logic, only because language itself prevents every illogical mistake. What makes logic knowable without experience is the impossibility of illogical thought. The all-embracing logic we adhere to makes things connected to one another in an infinitely fine network, a matrix of sorts, and becomes the great mirror of the mind and of the world.

We can describe the world completely by means of fully generalized propositions; yet the particulars require a different set of measures. The metaphysical must appeal to itself, because it is still part, and not apart from, the known, either from facts or experience.

In the conception and expression of ideas, though their origin may be in the mind, the logic we use is prior to all experience and when we go to express ourselves we first have to make our thoughts clearly logical for them to be expressed in a reasonable and logical way.

Confidence of Thought

In this world, in this day and age, we have to be confident and sure of ourselves in thought, because here we find our own stability.

Believe that the rational part of man in which his essence exists is of a self-motive nature, and that it subsists between the intellect and nature which both moves and is moved.

We need not restore confidence if it is already there; but to increase its sureness is an ongoing process. The loss of confidence is something begging assurance. Confidence is trust and faith in some sort of relationship that provides security for one's beliefs and convictions.

Life is not as simple as we make it seem to be. It is full of rigorous complications that from necessity need to be simplified. In the actual phenomenal world unity and harmony are replaced by strife and discord; the result is conflict. The employment of philosophy is to acquire knowledge to relieve ourselves from the complications life draws us to and to bring us back to a simplistic form of thought and thinking where our understanding can draw its confidence from.

We spend much time and labor on the problem of the Absolute and reach the only conclusion possible: that it is inexpressible in words. The mind falls back upon itself from it, unable to reach any conclusion, and must nevertheless create for itself some form of notion or idea about the concept itself.

In as much as intelligence is all we have to use to think, it is determined and limited to its own increase. Consequently the actual and real are sometimes misinterpreted, and illusion and fantasy find their way to dominate our thoughts. But the way around this complication is to evolve and develop a system of consistent thought patterns that bring reality back to its proper place. Perhaps it's all in the way we think and not in the how we think. From here we draw on our self-built confidence and become sure and certain with our own thoughts. Life is for the making; we cannot just live. Necessity finds its way into our own life and existence.

To know the truth is the impulse of every worthy mind. It is not enough to entertain plausible opinions. Apart from our shortcomings we seek the metaphysical knowledge that brings divinity to the human level. The pendulum of the mind swings back and forth between doctrine and speculation; our mind fathoms the most suitable answers to our questions and reaches a satisfactory conclusion that seems the most reasonable and logical within our own reach and capabilities.

There must be a division in the mind between the mind itself and the objects it is given to thought about. Even such a division can be made between what is thought and the thinking of that thought. It is incredible even that there is a separation between the spirit and the soul, though both are part of the unity of the mind.

The final point of descent into those philosophies which see the material order of things of the world and universe must not leave out that the same order, in all of its diversity, is but a reflection of the higher order of the mind, which can be seen as a united entitlement of all its parts, both the lower mental activities and the higher mental activities that allow us to explore and discover the peculiar subtleties of metaphysics and philosophy itself as a thought-provoking activity where we discern and question the answers our mind itself reveals.

We are strangers in a strange world, even to ourselves, but this intrigue can be resolved once the mind is put to good use through its own utility, abilities, and aptitude for learning what can be found and searching for what cannot be found from the deepest part of our intellect. It is our intelligence that separates us from the kingdom of wild beasts in such a way that we can develop and perpetuate ideas by the labor we give to thought and thinking.

So much is fascinating, whetting our appetites for more because it is there waiting to be discovered and applied. Applications demand creativity, and our intelligence can supply that, for it is nature's way in a curious manner what comes to our attention whether by learning or from revelation from an increase in our insight.

It is not what life is that assures our confidence of thoughts, but how we go about interpreting it from our wisdom. So with the increase in knowledge we build our wisdom, create our own genius, and succeed at having this sense of confidence of our thoughts.

There is a certain pre-comprehension that comes from instinct and from that voice within we call the will of conscience. Even the understanding we develop can be misguided from an artificial wisdom begotten from a deficient knowledge foundation; so we increase the basis of our elemental thoughts to secure that certainty we quest for.

Those who build castles in the sky have only the sky for a foundation. But those who build castles on sure ground start with confidence of thought and assured certainty in their thinking.

How we build this certainty is in the way we think and through a constant analysis of the procedures and methods we use in the way we go about thinking and imagining as we do. For sure it is the certain way of thought that brings us to the conclusions that we make.

It is our curiosity and questioning that leads to the increase in our knowledge foundation. It is not the answers that we find in life that makes us wise, but the type of questions we ask of ourselves and the formulation of those questions that give the wise their wisdom. It is the answers we find that increase our knowledge, but what we do with that knowledge is contained in our wisdom.

It is our creative intelligence, when put to good use through its utility, that increases the certainty of the knowledge we find in the world and within our own thoughts. All is not to be thought at once in the presence of the voice of the inner mind. We take apart and break into pieces the thoughts we have and put them back together in a way that has importance and significance to our individual character and disposition.

We think the way we do just because of the training we've had, and because of what we believe in and have faith in, determining the type of thoughts that surround us and draw our attention in our awareness, contemplation, and dreams in our waking moments of life. We think of the parts that make up the whole before we think of the grandeur of the whole picture in the vision of our mind. It is an amazing thing the mind can do when involved in the process of thought and thinking. Our imagination grows as we become aware of the actual process of thinking and the utility of thought the mind provides us.

Even when we take into account the grandeur of the big picture in the panorama of the horizon, in the mind's view, we see many of the various parts, think about them, then reassemble our thoughts, including in them some new knowledge found in our overview of the field of perception and our conception about what we have given thought to.

In a sense, we do not really need all of the exuberant growth of objects and desires, including religious interpretation, but we think we do; the mind allows thinking to make it so. The mind creates and selects, influenced by inner or outer forces to discriminate in favor of the best and brightest ideas we can conceive to move the will in the direction our destiny will take us by either action or by thought. As personalities, we share the distinction, arguably, of being intelligent judges of the world and of ourselves in a favorable way that is most significant and suitable to our own character.

Few dare risk such explorations. Certain delicate and dangerous questions are rarely asked of one's self; but those who labor in thought know the significance of asking and questing for answers. We can barely cope with the knowledge that we have, and adding more just makes one more thoughtful and contemplative.

A thought for consideration: zero has a designated meaning of nothing, except when it is found past the first numerical place as a digit, or symbol implying a greater meaning. One must remember that nothing has no meaning, like the great void between the planets and stars, except for something to give it meaning. In a sense then, the spirit created itself for that reason — to give meaning to the emptiness that is outside itself.

To be solid and substantial is immaterial. The appearance and impression that thought has on us as creative and intelligent beings is an illimitable apt conception of our patterns of thought and awareness to our own thinking. Though our creative imagination is seemingly full, there are gaps in it that are beyond explanation. It has been said in scripture that narrow is the gate and few are they who find a way in; but to recognize one's own awareness to knowledge and wisdom is a determining factor that puts us on the path to that gate. And though these words are hard to express, the gate remains within our own mind and thinking.

Ourselves, our mind, what could be possibly more interesting. Seemingly new at any point, the source is infinitely renewable, continuing the cycle of thought and interpretation, idea, and conception, the spiral of taking and giving of knowledge and wisdom. Thus this theme of We Passing Knowledge to One Another continues, even as the seasons change. This is my second beginning of summer passing my time on this spinning earth rounding the sun for yet another season until its completion, time allowing. It might just as well take a few more trips around the sun.

States of mind are all inter-related. The human consciousness is the magnifier of all our thoughts and notions that thinking brings to our awareness. The last great challenge to the mind is its own potential for creativity in thought, and it has no challengers except for itself. An invisible force is at work here; our intelligence could not have evolved as it has without some kind of divine intervention.

The ultimate is so immediate that it avoids detection. From its concealment we seek the revealing for the increase of our own genius. The least popular is the inner life of our mind, but at some point in time one must take on the challenge to explore and discover the potential and possibilities it holds in waiting for us. It is the infinitude within that remains the most eccentric discovery. We are not alone; we always have ourselves to consider in addition to the world that surrounds us.

Our confidence of thought reminds us that even consciousness implies limitations and qualifications. The cognizer and the cognized and the cognition remain in the mind, and all three are one within our actual intelligence. The evolutionary power of intelligence and mind create the link between the mind and its spirit, including the greater spirit of the world and universe the mind foresees as an inevitable force of nature we all partake of.

So inspired, consequently, the higher part of our intelligence can be a turbulent and reckless act of thinking, but our worldly reality, which occurs minute by minute, holds the innate idea of a center which can only be within our own mind and surfaces when we are given to its awareness on the surface of our thinking. There is no alternative except for our own alienation to ourselves, which is no acceptable alternative at all.

Rationality alone will not reveal, but may postulate, that there are experiences we encounter that will be sufficient in themselves to explain some of the mystical and curious phenomena we are exposed to in our lively existence, which is itself full of degrees of the possible and probable we all attempt to explain for.

Looking backward opposes progress, but at some time we all must; yet retreat and advance are in a precarious balance. We are constantly in a state of arriving and departing from our higher thinking with the winds of change provoking us to explore both directions, and still amidst despair there is always hope our questions will be answered in some way or another.

Chance alone cannot account for the way we have grown to be. In time small achievements account for natural selection and set apart those who labor in thought and those who just accept life for what it seems to be; and still there is a greater part of life that needs exploring and answering to. The universe is under no obligation to human advantage, for as many of those who think we are alone in the universe there are those who think of the possibility of other places like our own earth to exist without any doubt whatsoever.

In our thoughts we become enchanted with words because they form the symbols we use to describe our thoughts to others and to ourselves. We have an inherent aptitude for abstraction that leads us beyond the formal sense perception for which descriptions give us meaning, and in the realm of the surreal and mathematics it is our creative thought and thinking that yields numbers and geometry to our intelligence.

It is through our words and language that our intelligence expresses itself immediately and unconditionally of both realms our life exist in, the inner and outer, where the inner borders on the heavenly because it has metaphysical implications, and the physical world only has the natural laws and principles of nature to create its foundation for.

What should concern us is the weighing of our questions against the importance of discovery and the Adventure in Learning that our life consists of in our constant search for knowledge and wisdom to create what we call our own genius.

The spirit of the ancient wisdom lives on in our contemporary society and culture. Theosophical knowledge is about Man and the one we call God. In thinking about God we are led to believe in a Designer and Architect of nature. It is improbable our world, as well as the universe, could have come to be without such an entity. Our own spirit confirms this idea; yet still there is this constant debate as to the origin of both our world and ourselves.

In this sense we ought to be developing a sense of certainty about the sureness of our thoughts and thinking. Any certainty we come to must come from our own beliefs and faith in our own thinking.

Unintentionally we must let science be materialistic and leave thought and thinking to the metaphysical realm of philosophy and theology. For we have only two options: the truth can be scientifically proven or the truth can be reasoned in our creative intelligence. Our spirit cannot be denied, but our soul and God have similarities that cannot be denied neither.

Insight dawns that what is inward is not to be projected with imaginary detail. We must climb the central spiritual mountain and listen well and see far. Beyond such an unconvincing stand awaits the Absolute, which we all claim to quest for understanding of. This is actually true even if it is denied. Certain individuals want and desire more that the world can provide, so we are left alone with our mind and thoughts to consider and wonder.

With human strengths and weaknesses the Idealists manage to make all manner of mistakes, disagreeing among themselves. Some take the high road, and some take the low road; but all roads lead to the same destination. The end is just another beginning.

Humanity and the universe are worthwhile subjects to reflect upon. All else is just life, and we have the nature to take it as it is for no other reason that people, in general, have no need for looking into the past and can only speculate about the future.

Enlightenment seems, in consequence, to make something directly connected to the knowledge we gain from study and contemplation. Here then reality is to be found essentially connected with the state of the mind, and is neither foreign nor indirectly implied to what the individual believes or has faith in, recognizing itself to be at the center of its own world.

Pure insight is just that — insight into what we find in the reality of the inner world of mind and the outer world of the physical nature we exist in. One way of describing thought is a matter of knowing what sort of word is the object represented, from our insight into what words use, and by using a combination of representational words we can use describing the thought we intend to express either to ourselves or to others. The written word and the spoken word have a unique relationship. Spoken words are the symbols of a mental experience, and written words are the symbols of spoken words but are mentally exposed to our inner thoughts before they are used. We think before we speak. We have an idea of what we want to express and determine the appropriate words to express the idea behind the thought.

Language and writing are two distinct systems. With both we use our inner voice to set the words to thought, and for the expression of those words we use a logical pattern to symbolize that thought in a precise way. The certainty of our thoughts could only be described by the language we conceive and then perceive while exploring our mind and reconciling the world that surrounds us with this inner voice that circulates around in our mind seeking a means for expression. We come to trust that our expression is as clear as the thought that came to us as an idea or as a notion of some kind.

We ought to consider the concepts of stability, permanence, and duration as they affect the thinking we do in our lively existence. We all strive for a certain stability — we question the permanence of everything, just the same as we subject duration to everything as well. When we question stability, having confidence in thought, we must first consider that rules and laws exist from necessity.

A simple analogy comes to mind when considering a metaphysical approach to viewing life: if all games have rules, and life is nothing but a game of survival and learning, then rules that govern life must have permanence and unlimited duration to cover not only past generations but future ones as well.

Concerning rules and laws as principal factors in our life, we ought to perhaps give meaning to their necessity and question the frontiers that approach the horizon within the sphere of their own legitimacy. It is not their arbitrariness that comes to our attention, but the common factor of their determinateness, purpose, and final measure of worthiness to society and humanity at large.

Experience has always had a relationship with a presence, or a spirit, in the mind as well in nature, we can be certain of because the concept is a foundation for many a thought in our own thinking. Having an experience with this spirit is not only mysterious but thought-provoking, whereby we come to new knowledge and wisdom in the sureness and certainty of our thoughts.

Clearly we have some concept of elementary propositions quite apart from their logical forms. In our mind we create and invent by the utility of our intelligence the ways and means to communicate with each other so that we can pass knowledge to one another. We must be aware that our imagination has the use for words just as our mind does to represent our thoughts to ourselves as to others as well.

Just as our empirical reality has a use for words, and their certainty of meaning, so does our surreal reality have the same use for our mind to understand and comprehend itself. One must remember that the words and thoughts both originate in the mind and create a reality for themselves. Our words and thoughts follow in a perfectly logical order and find truth and its similarities to be at odds against themselves; so in our mind we configure the most logical truth and its significance to suit our own particular and individual nature.

We must not forget that the independent moments that make up the whole of our life have an individual worth and value of their own that accumulates and draws interest from itself. The growth and development of knowledge is proportional to the confidence we find in thought and contemplation of those thoughts.

The spark of the spirit, the trace of it, is in everything and in everyone, even though some know not of its presence. Much depends on our awareness of it and of our insight into its nature that affects us as humans living in the world of nature that has a consistency without doubt or compromise.

The trace of time, that permeates time as a significant whole, is that same spark which ignites the mind to wonder and brings the past to memory and dreams to our here-and-now concerning our future. It is a power within itself that regulates us according to nature's own rules and principle laws. You don't have to have experienced everything for yourself; some things we just have to trust in others' expression and interpretation of how they seem to be and how they actually are. Life goes on, and the minute hand of the clock passed the hour hand once again, only this time our genius knows better about reality.

If we are trained to calculate the effects of the movements of our mind as well as of our body, and to correct our mistakes before they clutch us in their hold, experience can make the difference, and it becomes clear that the more we do the wiser we will become. Knowledge is not beyond our years or experience; it comes with the proper training of the mind. We are blind half the time with this difference, and must learn to distinguish the truth of fact and the truth which is a similarity and learn to know the difference between reality and its artificial illusion that rebounds in the mind.. We ought to be taught to distinguish and differentiate the realities that affect us so much as to alter our reason and judgment.

The desire for self-preservation puts me on guard so that when I think I am safe the danger lurks around me and brings me to doubting, but with the certainty of our thoughts we can overcome dangers by the proper use of our training, insight, and revelation to what truth actually is and not just what it seems to be.

We find the door to the mind always open, but those who dare to cross the threshold and enter find a remarkable realm full of thought and wonder and curiosity which in turn brings out our wisdom, and we become all the more wise for entering this curious and strange place where imagination lurks freely and reason has to be summoned.

The metaphysical concept of time and spirit cannot adequately describe this element of trace or spark that is generated in the mind of the one who labors in thought. We only know intuitively that it is there when our intelligence is activated in such a way that causes us to give it to our thinking. The thought of it activates our mind into a state of comprehension and relative understanding of the subject whereby it becomes not only an object of thought but the subject of our present awareness and logical thinking processes, utilizing all of our abilities to rationalize the subject and object of our thoughts. As thinking creatures we know with certainty what we do and with sureness we know what we do not.

So I've come to an understanding that the confidence of thought is something inward and has no correlation with the outer world. Just like most things our world centers around the activity of the mind.

Let us consider just this one thing: if we had to wait for experience to teach us what we need to know, it might, perhaps, be too late. So in our education we must be taught the essentials and then wait for experience to teach us the rest of what we need to know, learning from our mistakes and learning from others and as well from our book learning. This will give us the sureness of thought we quest for.

And now we come to a major question one must answer for oneself. What is the cause of man's weakness? It is to be found in the disproportion between his strength of mind and his desires. It is our passions that make us weak because we give in to them, but the man of strength has developed a sense of control over his passions whether by reason and logic, or by knowledge and wisdom given to him from others or learning through study. To limit our desires strengthens our mind's ability to rationalize choice and employ discretion in those choices. It is a mark of our advancement in our intelligence.

Do we care what others think? I think not. All our cares are for the satisfaction of ourselves from the certainty of thought we have developed and the sureness of those thoughts from our knowledge; but our wisdom comes from learning control, which may be one of the hardest lessons to be learned in one's life.

What one thinks becomes problematic only because we have the proximity of understanding, and never really come to a proper understanding until an entire explanation has been learned, creating our own wisdom and genius. Our lives are compounded with a heritage of illusions and misunderstandings. The only correction possible is to re-learn what we have been taught from a different perspective, bringing an association of the truth closer to the real truth we all have the determination to seek for, while making our own understanding more pliable grounded in our beliefs and faith and reason.

The strength of mind is directly proportional to the life we live and the thoughts we bring upon ourselves, as well as the same thoughts that come to us from the outer world in which the mind gives thought to. The certainty of our faith and beliefs rests solely on what we understand to be truth and not just an appearance of the real truth. For this reason our curiosity and creativity in thought leads us on in our search and quest for knowledge and as well assists us in the passing of knowledge to one another.

To the extent that we recognize our thinking may have faults, as reason may imply, we ought to re-consider the knowledge we have accumulated and come to new terms with that knowledge, considering all the while what truth we seem to know and its similarities, which illusion allows to simulate the actual truth.

Our logical and theological prejudices ought to be countered with the increase in knowledge and wisdom we achieve, learning to uncover the foundations for what we seem to know and the basis of our thoughts and thinking, re-building from there a new structure of thought-provoking principles.

The order of nature is constant and well defined. If we would only consider what we have rather than what we don't, our world is a terrestrial paradise. Expecting too much can only change our opinion of the world we live in. The position in life that has come our way or that we have made for ourselves does not take away from the quality of life this world allows for us.

So in the course of human events and by the natural course of evolution, we endure patiently, attach the will to live to our being, and live as we can purely for our own survival and well being; but as for our aesthetic pleasure we procure and involve ourselves in a higher order than just surviving.

We ought to substitute calculating for reasoning, but that would surely take too much philosophizing, and most people are more prone to speculation than laboring in thought that philosophy requires. People are just satisfied with living and learning is only secondary.

A New Dawn for Philosophy

We mark time by the stages of our lives. We also gauge time by the passing of the sun — as the dawn becomes mid-day, and then twilight comes with the phases of the moon, all only to be replaced by another dawn.

The coming of age follows a circular motion, as do most things, as a constant of nature. Its duration is measurable and, as well, we can trace our life and the history of the world, and universe, by counting each new dawn through its stages and phases. Time and the space we live in are factors the mind must consider; it has no other choice for reasons nature holds to in its mysteries.

Meanwhile we must use what we know for finding what we lack, for inventing ways of redeeming the lacking, and especially for settling controversies in matters that depend on reasoning and logic.

Between rationalism and mysticism there is a certain complicity. The mind works in both ways; in rationalism it is logical, and in mysticism it is philosophical and theological in its interpretation and speculative understanding.

There is much food for thought in the matter of the price paid by the mind considering philosophy, theology, and metaphysics. It is only valuable and worth the labor-intensive thought due to it from one's own perspective and vantage point one takes on life. Classical philosophic reflection has left its mark on civilization and humanity in the contemporary point of view, but it does not stop there.

The future, which is just ahead of our present, holds a new dawn for our exploration and discovery of bold and creative concepts, which philosophy and the study of metaphysics hold concealed waiting for its revelation from our continuous study and reasoning.

Tradition is subject to change, just as everything else, by the increase in age and wisdom. The wealth and novelty of information is all around us and absolutely unavoidable if one were so inclined to seek it out. We live, today, in an age of abundant information, and the ways and means of obtaining it are ever increasing at amazing speed through our technological advancement as a civilization so set upon its ways for that acquisition of resources.

The pioneering of a new thought is no simple task, but our determination to understand and verify our thoughts has become an incredible part of our contemporary nature. Our own motivation and ambition have raised our culture to new and higher standards. This is all for the better, because if not for the increase in knowledge our own dreams would come to a standstill. We pass knowledge to one another by its very own necessity; without restrictions we come to terms with genius.

As for purposive enlightenment, it finds a point to feel free from the entanglement of previous thinking. The believing mind takes the absolute for a universal one, not only finding its own absolute reality as an object of something universal but for the individual consciousness too.

This sense of mind becomes its own reality and brings out our intelligent and creative genius. The creativity of the mind becomes absolute and infinite in its form in the utility of all its own resources rooted deeply within the inner mind, where each individual is taken into thought and provoked to wonder.

Enlightenment holds an irresistible sway over belief by just the fact that it finds its own consciousness the very moment in which enlightenment gives significance to its own validity.

Since our belief cannot be content to exist in some barren condition, it creates for itself its own reality that supersedes the real world. It stays within itself in the mind, discovering and exploring its own significant reality.

It is the liberation of memory and our creative intelligence that sets us free and apart from the other creatures on this good earth. It is our certain way of thinking that makes us individuals among the many that inhabit our civilization. It is our individuality that makes humanity what it really is: a collection of individuals that make up the whole. Together we capture the universal consciousness and revert into our own the general and specific contents of spirit and soul. Together we are the world and individually we are just ourselves as we really are.

What was written between the lines of volumes of works in this endeavor to realize philosophy at its height is the conceptualization and thought of the new dawn that is at the threshold of the era in which our lives are contained.

One should observe that the mind is the ultimate liberator of ideality and the notion of concepts we can only imagine. For ourselves, in a singular way it is the mind that determines the Ideal, and the means for achieving these ideals comes to the rescue from our reasoning and logical intelligence.

The production and management of our motivation and intent comes from the depths of our inner spirit and by ambition we derive from our own character. In the course of achieving new knowledge we have a sense of fulfilling this motivation to maximize the use of our own intelligence. The categorical determinants of our wisdom have their root in our achieved wisdom and the willingness to approach the New Dawn with a certainty of thought and open-mindedness towards the exploration and discovery of that knowledge we quest for.

The previous dawn that came to humanity brought one's voice to recognize itself and to understand itself. The new dawn brings recognition of that understanding to a new level of wisdom. We not only understand the inner voice as conscience and spirit; we recognize its value and worth and come to a determination of what we should keep and discard in our mind, while taking into account our newfound knowledge and wisdom and putting it to good use through its own utility.

Metaphysics and philosophy, along with theology, have constituted an exemplary system of defense for the mind to accommodate its own intellectual capacity.

There comes a time, about every generation or so, even considering generational overlaps, for a new voice to reply to previous generations and to address the contemporary thought we have grown to know and understand as a basis for our elemental thinking, while at the same time addressing the passage of knowledge to one another in a new era.

From the origin of thought to the present age of thinking, an abstract representation can be described as a system or method of thinking where one interweaves roots to an endless extreme, creating a matrix of thoughts patterned on a labyrinth of simple movements the mind can conceive, bending them to pass through the same points again, to redouble old adherences, and to circulate among their differences in infinite configurations.

There is no closure of knowledge; we are constantly adding to our treasury of thought with the evolution of that thought progressing with time, inspiring new thoughts and provocative revelations. The today part of time is our history in the making, which confronts the past and challenges the future.

The widest horizon of the questions we ask are in the answers we are searching for. Mythical reflection can reach unforeseen results on the intellectual plane. So too, is the case with reflection on the natural order, characterized by spontaneity of thought, when everything that is subject to a norm, or standard, is relative and particular when given thought to or contemplated upon.

We Pass Knowledge to One Another is a work of reflection and study. When one wants to study humanity one must consider those around oneself and the relationships that coincide with their interaction between a person's inner mind and the outer world. So to study humanity one must extend oneself and the range of one's vision with the utility of all the mind's resources.

One must observe differences in order to discover the properties that come to our senses and our contemplating mind. The original alliance man had with nature has all but dissolved and re-formed into a new alliance with different properties than at its origin. We know more now. We are a smarter people. Our advancement in technology has done wonders in our research and evolution as a civilization. We are a different people; but we are the same, only in a different time and with different constituent principles.

If it is true that nature has expelled man, and that society persists in oppressing him, man can at least reverse the dilemma to his own advantage and seek out the society of nature, a realm, of course, to which we belong, in order to meditate there upon his physical and emotional stability.

It is the constant duration of enduring until at last the achievement of enduring becomes more than survival when one can finally consider the fact of one's existence as aesthetic above mere necessity. Enlightenment illuminates that world of heaven with ideas drawn from nature itself. From the world of sense we project ourselves into the world of mind out of which this element of finitude is etched upon the mind and scored with the concept of infinitude, which only the mind can conceive.

Finitude and infinitude do not fall apart, because they belong together under the dominion of nature and the Almighty one we come to know in the fashion of spirit, which is indivisible from belief and the faith we come to know as the absolute truth.

Belief is never satisfied, and its illumination is everywhere without distinction and has a content of its own, which is more than a barren condition but finds its own satisfaction implicitly in the mind through which nature has given to us the ability to reason and understand the qualities of spirit we find in belief itself.

The spirit passes beyond consciousness into its own clearness of the mind and into itself regarding its own necessity, as a simple part of nature actualizes itself and finds its own place in pure thought, awakening its own enlightenment and illumination to itself.

This is the dawn of a new philosophy. The metaphysics involved are rational and simple. We can be overcome with thought, but still our mind passes from one realm to another without suspicion or a need for validity. Some things we just take as true and leave there without further concern because we believe and have justified our faith with sureness and certainty from our own wisdom and from our enlightenment.

Notes from the Pen of a Philosopher

The first principle is that of curiosity, a principle natural to the human mind, spirit, and heart, though its growth is proportional to the development of our feeling and aptitude for knowledge.

There are certain concepts that the world holds close to the mind, under the banner of metaphysics, phenomenology, and existentialism; consciousness and intuition keep their distance close by.

The human race has kinship to philosophy, because we are a curious kind, always seeking explanations and questioning everything, even the answers we find in our exploration and discovery of new knowledge.

The best-preserved bits of wisdom are those most accepted by society; and those bits may very well have partial truth. So we quest for certainty and learn what we can to verify our beliefs. This is part of our constant human nature and the activity of the mind. Its utility has bearing on the applications we use in our reasoning and logic. The human condition is not logical, yet we apply our own logic to it from our interior sentiment so that we can live in peace with our sensibility.

What should, ought to, concern us is the sorting-out of doctrine and ideology that has prevailed and come to our solitary and singular conclusions. One must always remember that opinion is infinitely debatable and theory must have proof, and to presume often leads to a lack of integrity in one's own thinking.

Any one hypothesis, a tentative explanation for an observation, needs further testing and investigation and can be presumed uncertain until our knowledge makes way for true wisdom.

Even to ourselves, in a colloquial sense, we are remarkably intelligent creatures and aware of our ingenious and enterprising means of coming to conclusions. One ought to distinguish between the implications of sociological factors and purely intellectual factors while considering all the while the emotion and feeling that come from both. The split between factual certainty and speculative theorizing has its own place in the mind. We ought to come to terms with both. Our primary concern is for our stability and well-being.

Considering the title of this chapter and the title of this work, knowledge is theoretically infinitely transmissible. That is perhaps our primary motivation for creating new works, not only in the arts but in literature as well.

Though brought up in the spirit of our maxims, accustomed to making our way through life the best we can, we ought not to be told something we do not understand. It should be brought to our attention and from there we go on our way exploring and discovering.

We always advance slowly from one sensible idea to another. It is nature's own simple way of setting the standard for progress. Our own place on this good planet earth is too small to conceive the great circles of the other planets revolving around us, the great unknown galaxies that revolve around our own, and our own place in the universe.

There are a series of abstract truths by means of which all the sciences are related to common principles and are developed each in its turn as we grow and evolve into the ideal in which we conceive that we, perhaps, could evolve into. This relationship is the method of the philosopher.

There is quite another method by which every concrete example suggests another and always points to the next in the series. This succession, which stimulates our natural curiosity, arouses our own attention required by every object, even in thought, in turn. My whole and entire work is to support education and the acquiring of knowledge to increase our own wisdom and genius.

We ought to learn to think for ourselves; it is something that cannot be taught, but must be acquired from experience and from the passing of knowledge to one another. What knowledge is within our reach we reach out to seize it; but that which is out of our reach we have to gain the advantage of creativity to attain it and only then try to comprehend and understand what we have sought to gain as our own. Well chosen questions will only bring well-enlightened answers which in turn will bring about more questioning.

Do you suppose that I'm better-off for the study that I do? I think so. Perhaps if more people would give themselves some time to read more and study some, the circuit of knowledge would be more complete and society would raise itself to a higher scale.

Pure reason may lead us to approve or censure, but it is feeling which leads us to thought and action. How shall we care about that which does not concern us; perhaps the answer lies in human nature and the necessity to have feelings of care in our disposition and character.

Could we discover a way in which all human need could be fulfilled, perhaps not simply because each of us has our own particular needs? We ought to be reminded that needs differ from wants except for those that ensure our survival. With the development of our knowledge base we can confirm the mutual dependence of mankind. This might be expected, but we are all for ourselves when it comes to survival; the exception is that knowledge has to be passed along to one another to ensure our increase in knowledge and come to value the aesthetic ideal.

How much must be known before we attain knowledge of man; this is the final study of the philosopher. Any limit must be denied as each succeeding generation overlaps the preceding one on through history from antiquity to the present contemporary day.

We have ranged the heavens and measured the earth, exploring the universe and earth to the extent that our abilities have allowed. We have sought out the laws of nature. Now we must explore ourselves to the quantum depths and discover just who we really are.

There is an abundant amount of quality knowledge in print, but experience teaches us the most valuable lessons. Whatever is left to learn, we ought to be searching ourselves for what we think is missing, because it may not be; it may be concealed in the recesses of our mind awaiting release from its concealment. There is more to the mind than we can know just as there is more to the unknown and unseen than one could actually realize. This thought keeps the philosopher busy actualizing, conceiving, and perceiving what there is to be realized from our awareness of the mind's utility.

Nostalgia is an effective use of our memory; for better or worse memory contains all the history we have been opened-up to during our life cycle. But considering the wonder of a dream, an active contemplation of a once reality can be exciting and emotional.

Our intellectual ability to think of possibilities, probable outcomes, and reason to conceptualize is one of our greatest assets. A transcendental regression is an important factor in our wisdom, but a transcendental projection has just as much worth and value to the human condition as it always has.

Our relations with one another have an original significance. Though they are occasionally a global base for experience, our relations with others concern recognition from necessity without emotional overtones. We are stronger together than we are alone, but alone we must go head on into the future with our own thoughts at the base of our experience.

We are no longer linked by oral tradition; writing and documentation have taken priority over this traditional way of passing knowledge to one another. First came the printing press, then we've grown up through the use of the telegraph, telephone, cell phone, and finally to the internet.

Languages are made to be spoken, even if we speak to ourselves as a supplement to speech. But the art of writing is nothing but a meditated representation of thought carried out through expression.

The contemplation of nature has always had a great attraction to the human mind as well as the mind itself. It is no wonder that we think about our external world, but the inner world of mind has just as much significant integrity.

When we are compelled to hear the call of nature we must answer; just the same we are compelled to hear the call of the spirit in our mind, the one we call conscience — our only link to the divine. We use our eyes to look at the world. We use our senses to realize the world in all its actuality; but there is one thing which has its importance verified and that is the abilities of our mind.

The mind works on both principles — a reluctant outward disposition and a self-contained inward hesitancy to search ourselves for the answers to all our questions. Life is fair. We have to have the knowledge to stay on top. Our options are limited. The choice has to be one from reason and a sureness, and certainty of the facts and that we cannot be challenged by fear; straight away we go into the world with our own wisdom and genius.

There is an intermediary between everything and nothing. There would be no nothing without something to give meaning to it. This something is our creative intelligence, the same intelligence that provoked the Holy Spirit to create itself from nothing but a thought to give meaning to the finite void of the material universe.

From this principle one can realize that heaven itself is beyond the bounds of the universe and still remains totally and absolutely in one's mind. It is our mind that thinks. We give thought even to our own thoughts. The miraculous and incredible thing is that there is something in nature that created a means and way for us to think.

This midpoint between contentment and complacency occupies the present, and its immediacy is a name for the total absence and the absolute plentitude in a state of consciousness about our condition. We live searching for this place without desire or want, believing that contentment and complacency is just another state of mind.

If one would consider a starting point, or origin of development of one's self — we must begin wherever we are, and the thought of the trace of the future that surrounds the present is a justifiable point of departure. For where else can we start except from where we are in the here and now.

Only the chosen few will hear the call and respond with the choice to awaken the power within and discover its potential. It is the way we look and think of things that determines the outcome of our thoughts and consequent actions from those thoughts. There is a certain amount of speculation that philosophy brings, but with our logic and reason we continue our journey through time.

The one who sees the whole picture with their senses sees with the mind as well, where each part should be. Like a jigsaw puzzle;

the pieces fit together in a systematic way, reasonable and logical.

The one who sees one part clearly and knows it thoroughly may be a learned one, but the former is a wise one, and you remember it is wisdom in addition to knowledge that we hope to acquire.

Self-preservation is nature's first law and principle. Everyone has their own specific needs and no two are alike. So from necessity we learn to exchange things and ideas. This one notion forms The Basis of Elemental Thoughts and continues in the theme of We Pass Knowledge to One Another.

We must exercise ourselves with courage and strength of mind. We must learn to accept ourselves and then quest for improvement. It is a useful occupation to use one's mind to the best of one's abilities to fulfill one's own potential. That is what we do; to seek out the ideal and strive for it. And then once more we learn that this new knowledge, acquired and applied to the knowledge we already have, assimilates, forming a newer form of wisdom and genius.

Clever ones are distinguished from others by their greater or lesser aptitude for the comparison of ideas and the discovery of relations between them. The way in which ideas are formed gives a certain character to the human mind and its own certain way of thought.

Everything matters to us, as we are dependent on everything, and our curiosity naturally increases with our desires and need. Nature does not deceive us, or God; we deceive ourselves with illusion and fantasy. In the end it all amounts to just a matter of thinking and a certain way of thought.

The picture of the world is what we make form and concepts of from our knowledge, determining our own wisdom from what we have searched out and brought to our own attention in thinking and in thought. How we observe determines the measurements that we make and the judgments we come to conclusions about. Our reasoning allows us this privilege separating us from other creatures.

The best way of learning to reason aright is that which tends to simplify our experiences or to enable us to dispense with them altogether without falling into error.

We must learn to confirm the experiences of each sense by itself, without recourse to any other. The mind does its share of interpreting what our senses become aware of; in fact, the mind has a sense of its own, depending upon itself for confirmation and verification. Then each of our sensations will become an idea in the mind and correspond to its original truth in meaning without verification, because we already know and understand without doubt about the idea's principles.

The art of judging and the art of reasoning are one and the same. Compelled to learn for ourselves we use our own reason, not that of others, to discern and discriminate the facts we come to terms with. When understanding lays hold of things before they are stored in the memory, what is drawn from that store is our wisdom and genius.

Humanity is not being displaced in the universe; we alienate ourselves by choice, chance, or from necessity. We are finding ourselves singularly intent within humanity so long as no one attempts to disrupt our disposition and natural composition we've made of our mind. Reality happens where our awareness and understanding come to terms with our intelligence.

Thought matters by what and how we think, and the reality of thought is not superficial, but substantial within the boundaries we create for ourselves, protecting our singularity and sanctuary of our own mental capacities which include our feelings and emotions.

We have to reach for information and knowledge which is outside the boundaries of social consciousness and define for ourselves a new reality within our own individual and singular mind, suitable enough to give us satisfaction and contentment in our inner-most thoughts and reasonable thinking. We need to consider as well our memory and our dreams of the past and of the future we create for ourselves and what we, as well, have created for ourselves in the world in which we live; in the reality of mind and universal natural reality.

It is in the character of being human that we are led astray by our passions. What then is required for the proper study of man? It is a great quest and a great impartiality of judgment to know what can be known of the qualities we possess.

Society must be studied in the individual and the individual in society. From necessity we have a mutual relationship with others, and for that reason We Pass Knowledge to One Another.

Thinking of ourselves we draw conclusions of our own reality but in the thought of our greater world; humanity becomes an immense abstract idea with people living at all stages of development and enduring survival, but those at the top of the pyramid live differently than all the others. Their aesthetic needs come before their survival because their survival is ensured, and therefore their time contemplating the higher levels of thought is consumed with their realization and fulfillment.

As we grow and learn, acquiring knowledge, we choose what ideas we shall attach to, and conform them into our own ... We learn to select and distinguish, calculating their importance and repressing others less significant.

The continuous now, that which is all except for the time of sleep, our surrounding here and now gives us the freedom in the moments of decision to make choices from remembering experiences of the past and considering our expectations and anticipation for a time in the future that comes to us as naturally as looking at the sky and breathing the air with no other concern than actualizing our experience of living to the extent of our abilities, all the while taking into account chance, opportunity and ambition —our prime motivation to excel in life and enjoy our own genius.

You don't have to have seen or experienced everything for yourself; but if you want to trust in another's objective notions remember that you are now dealing with the matter itself and another's interpretation. The whole of existence is an eternal process of separating and union of integrated thoughts in the matrix of facts and opinion.

Another Thought

The question is just how much do you want to discover about nature and your own nature? The obvious answer is as much as is possible, but that would require some effort on your account, and how many are inclined to put the work into these discoveries though the rewards may be invaluable to one's own disposition.

What is important here is our certain way of thinking and how we go about interpreting our thoughts, the thoughts passed to us from generations past, and contemporary thought. It is not our actual perception that matters, but the way in which we conceive these thoughts and bring them to the surface of our intellect.

There seem to be two separate systems of observation: one when we are observing something directly and the other when we are just giving thought to it. Both require an active mind and a certain amount of reason and logic, exploring probabilities and actual possibilities.

Your own mind has been creating multiple possibilities ahead of itself in anticipation of drawing reasonable conclusions and proper judgments about these conclusions.

Some things are just so amazing we cannot even conceive their possibility; yet we do and make up scenarios to explain them in some simple and understandable fashion.

We create our own reality, from the mind outward in the way we think and in what our thoughts provoke in response to the ideas and notions we conceive. We make thought just as real as reality itself.

There is learning in reflection, in contemplation, and in the self-intended meditation we do in thinking about our own thoughts. In the contemplation associated with thought, knowledge comes to us as inspiration and revelation. We ought to take this type of learning more seriously because it comes from deeper within our own mind than our everyday surface thoughts that arise with life-bearing situations. So we pass knowledge to one another realizing that wisdom is associated with each of our others' well-contained wisdom not often shared.

With greater knowledge and wisdom our dreams of the future grow proportionally. We call this enlightenment of possibility.

Everything factual is already theory — to understand this would be the greatest possible achievement. Common sense, which is said to be the genius of mankind, must first of all be considered in the ways it finds expression. If you can read, you should understand; if you can write, you have to know something; if you believe, you ought to comprehend; if we can recognize our real self, we ought to know of our own spirit; and if that is true we ought to know the spirit of the world.

Our fault is that we have doubt of what is certain; but the human mind is reasonable in spite of all the unreasonable things that happen in our cycle of living. We learn from what is not necessary, and from what is necessary we learn of its certainty.

The question comes to mind whether I can dictate the life I want to live and am going to experience. Perhaps the answer is yes, but one has to take into account chance, opportunity, and random encounters with motivated ambition and the intent to find some truth in what we have come to believe. Through our accumulation of knowledge we broaden the base and progress up the pyramid, always questing for a position nearer the top. Such a goal is most often common, and if not for the exceptional few who reach such heights the top would almost be out of sight. Yet we all can see there is a top and know those who reach such heights determine what happens to those below them, with the only exception for those who labor in thought and come to understand the basic principles of philosophy as a means to excel in thinking and understanding by comprehension and the aptitude for learning and the expression of that learning.

We have two choices: the first is to evolve in our way of thinking and associating our inner thinking with our surroundings. The second is to regress. Without knowledge we cannot evolve in a way that will assure our progress; but there is to be some gain from looking back for answers we may have overlooked or just passed by because of the lack of knowledge to look for what it is that we are seeking, which is a bolder and stronger wisdom.

So we explore the unknown with veracity and discover subtleties to the known and apply our newfound knowledge to our existing wisdom. It is all because of our natural and intellectual curiosity. We are constantly absorbing information and formulating it in our thought and memory while at the same time projecting it into the reality we think of as our future, thereby considering the future as just an extension of today because all of reality is connected in this way.

Ultimate reality depends on how we perceive it, always from the innermost parts of our mind. For thousands of years we have been exploring the significant understanding that we have, and all the while discovering new aspects of that reality which belongs to nature, including the part of nature which is above our knowing.

Reality ultimately comes down to how we experience it in its many and various forms and perspectives by which our senses perceive and by how our mind interprets those sensations. Above all it is the things, including thoughts, that are the objects of the minds own considerations.

What we are doing is trying to understand the human condition; with all its complexities we must, from necessity, find some kind of simplicity in our nature and in nature itself. We think of the universe as some kind of great clockwork mechanism that is above us and affects us in many various ways. But time is relative by the standards we keep and the moment of thought we are given to.

One must always remember that the past was once the here and now and that the here and now is absolutely true. It will be the same in some different time that the future holds so close to our attention.

I think what needs to be is a new realization of the actual power of the mind. If we would only turn it inwards as much as we do outwards, the conflict of human nature would come to a resolve. It is the quality of our intellect that sparks my intention to develop a bolder philosophy of our creative intelligence we ought to be putting to better use as a common one earns the quality of wisdom and genius laboring in thought of life itself.

We have to embrace knowledge that is unconventional. The new, and unfamiliar, knowledge we are discovering has more curiosity than we are accustomed to; but it sure is thought provoking and emotional inspiring. There's more to life than living; the thinking that we do increases our aesthetic pleasure, once past the stage of survival.

The Philosopher has two objectives. First, to understand the world as it seems to be. The second objective is to break it down into parts and discover what reality is made of; once past our inspiring mind we can explore the quantum depths of reality on both the macro and micro scale.

There are two principles that affect the philosopher's adventure in learning: the first is practical, and the second is the profound. The veil, the curtain, the threshold we come to needs revealing because what is concealed has its own significance and importance and has to be revealed for us to consider. One must remember that the unknown is greater than the known. So we quest for knowledge and arrive at a significant wisdom we can call our genius.

The reason philosophy is important is because it looks at knowledge and discovers the wisdom within that knowledge. Our own reasoning tells us so. We have to discover and employ the utility of our mind to the fullest of our own individual potentials. Collectively we are stronger than by ourselves.

We ought to be able to perceive measurable feedback in our life from the thoughts we introduce into the way we think. Conversation is the externalization of what we think internally and which we bring into the open clearing of society and civilization. We Pass Knowledge to One Another from necessity. We get tired of talking to ourselves and seek others for companionship and feedback on our own thoughts and emotions.

We give up our sheltered state for the freedom to face the elements and opinions of others concealed within themselves, yet revealed through interaction and dialogue. We do the same with nature, revealing ourselves to the elements and get satisfaction from our senses.

Conversation is the communication between two absolute individuals who recognize each other's limits and potentials and draw them to disclosure of those possibilities, and then bring them beyond their own capacities into a new reality of expression full of emotion and a new sense of reason and understanding within their own comprehension.

The reciprocal interaction brings out the best in each, both trying diligently to bring their point of view into focus. The veil of understanding is breached and unity is found in the common elements of the one spirit that holds humanity together: the spirit of knowledge and wisdom.

With the passing of knowledge to one another, whether by speech or writing, we come across superficial reflections which give way to more profound ones. This activity is part of the processes of the utility of our mind. We pass from one thought to another until we settle on one that occupies our attention.

These thoughts come from the great depth of our mind; no surface thought can be denied, neither the deeper ones our creative intelligence draws from its treasury of resources. These thoughts of ours are lured outward, through expression, in many and various modes of communication, including all the arts besides literature.

It is the inner working of the mind that surfaces through our objective perspective of the world. And for those realms beyond our own we conceive notions and imagine possibilities that are either probable or cannot even be conceived.

Our mind is formed through language so that we can recognize our own thoughts and express them to those who significantly draw our recognition and usefulness in conversation. There is one thing for sure: we talk to ourselves because we deem ourselves to be the most significant and responsive of all other creatures. We are so conceived that we think we can even talk to other creatures and unknown beings that we come to prayer expecting to be understood, and talk to animals as though they were other humans; but there are some animals that respond to our conversation with them, beyond a doubt.

A Philosophical Examination of the Nature of Knowledge

Every word may be spoken in hundreds of languages, and through its meaning, the word, thought and considered proper for the expression, is still an idea and has the form of its basis and foundation in the correct usage of it to complete the thought that expression fulfills.

The generation of a thought or the solving of a problem of necessity is leaped forward through the mind's power and directed towards the constitution of the intelligence within our capacities.

We can train ourselves to make better decisions and choices by increasing our knowledge and wisdom by adopting a language that even our conscience can recognize as well as the others that surround us.

In order to create a new future we have to leave the past behind. The feelings and emotions we've come to learn are a different task, but in order to bring a new future to our existence we have to create a new and novel network in the process of our thinking. We have to examine our thoughts and consider them, carefully sorting out what we should set aside and what we ought to bring forward.

The thought process itself changes and our certain way of thinking evolves even as we mature and grow in knowledge and wisdom. The neuro-net under new stimulus creates new avenues for thinking to become further improved in creativity and imagination as well as in a greater developed reason and logic. What we think now will affect our thinking later. Therefore now is always a good and proper time to improve upon our thinking and discriminating thoughts.

Life is but a page in an enormous book that takes us to the threshold of the unknown, where possibilities and probabilities surpass any reality we can be familiar with, using our present knowledge.

To create a new process in thinking and thought, we must be enriched with enlightenment and revelation of the possibilities of a greater reality than the one we already know. Perhaps just below the surface a greater reality exists, and it does — within our mind.

Adversity is the greatest teacher because it brings out the utility of our capabilities apparent within the composition and structure of the natural world we've come to understand and know.

Here we go again. Another day has come and it's full summer now in my second year of this project. Perhaps I'm just a quarter of the way through; but to excel one must have the intention, motivation, and ambition to succeed.

An unbelievable explosion, a powerful release of matter from some substance among the elements was in the beginning. Perhaps it was just a thought that emerged from the mind of God, like happens to us in the moment of revelation, and the universe was created, along with the heavenly realm. Even the homeless have to have sanctuary. So there is a home for God and all the angels, yet the mind of God, the Holy Spirit, has its home within God's mind, just like our mind is the home of our intelligence that holds our spirit and soul. Such a provocative thought requires a deeper level of thinking common to the metaphysician and philosopher.

Above all, technology has created the means for human achievement such as the invention of the printing press and this old typewriter. Thank goodness its electric and has a correct-a-ribbon.

I know we've come a long way, but as the children play the elders work to fulfill the kids' dreams. The origin is somewhere deep within our own mind concealed by life's everyday stuff, and emotions, and the unexpected. The primordial spirit of our being has absolute knowledge, but it is only revealed to those who labor in thought and philosophize of it. The metaphysical realm of intelligence and music make the connection, and the entrance to where creativity lives is opened to the infinite and to the possible.

We know with certainty that space exists above the clouds, and The Hubble Telescope confirms it exists for billions of miles; but should we grant this unknown matter a place outside the mind?

The answer ought to be yes, but the space within our mind is as much a difficult matter to explain. It exists because we do, and both are something rather than nothing. But the concepts of heaven, God, and hell and the devil are metaphysical questions that defy any possible answer or conclusion other than faith and belief, which are in the mind as are spirit, soul, and intelligence. As the evolution of humanity developed we created countries, states, cities, and the avenues of our communities for the purpose of separating and linking us all together. With the advent of the telegraph, telephone, cell phone, and internet we are now almost totally in touch with each other; yet our aloneness still remains.

It is imperative to learn of the existence of the elements of life. We learn through all sorts of media, including literature and music. It is music that brings reality to its heights in all forms.

It's not the lyrics that make the music; it is the music itself that forms life, and we revolve around our own thoughts as the music we listen to goes through our head into our mind creating fantastic images to wonder by and sounds to give thought to. It's in the mix.

Who would have believed we could have progressed this far? The future is real and we are living in it. It comes to us on a daily basis. There is no stopping it. Destiny comes to us; we do not go toward destiny, we only create it for ourselves from our thoughts and actions.

Something in nature propels us along the path of life towards our end, which is yet another beginning. We will know when we get there. Prepare yourself for a mind-expanding experience; just the thought provokes images and thoughts wondering with amusement and curiosity.

The mind, and its reality, develop in slow steps of growth, but after some time take on a new form: the quantum leap into the surreality of thinking.

We ought to have a self-consistent appeal to reason where tradition is embodied in philosophy. Mental things are alone real; what is called corporeal, no one knows where its place is except in one's own mind Through the spirit you behold it appears without substance, and only its essence is made known in your creative and intelligent imagination. Perhaps if one opened the door to the mind one would be opening it from the inside. And if one would open the windows of the mind one would be opening them from the inside as well.

We must understand that ideas, like passions, cannot otherwise exist than in creatures with intelligence and the ability for comprehension and expression.

We learn this premise from literature and music. To be a visionary is not to see a different world from others but to see the same world differently. Our experience is unique and individual. The more knowledge one has, the greater the experience seems to be. The living mind is free from restrictive limits of time and space. It is not subject to decay or death but lives on as an eternal intelligent spirit. Lost may be found in that realm.

We live in a world of ultimate possibilities that the mind can take in by the way of thought and thought projections in the media and throughout the world in the arts, architecture, humanly made things, and in nature. Reality is tapping our brain all the time. At the moment you interact with reality it becomes rock solid existence; until then, it is a vision or just a projection of our thoughts that we perceive and conceive the quality of realness determined by our knowledge and inspiration.

The passionate philosopher has two concerns: the deconstruction of the world, and the reconstruction that we do through our intelligent thinking and discriminative dreaming.

The deeper you go the more dynamic reality becomes. We begin to uncover rigorous distinctions separating things, and their entanglement with each other. Then we discover verification and the meanings things have on a deeper level than once previously known.

In passing knowledge to one another enlightenment becomes our newfound knowledge to those open-minded enough to receive it and to assimilate it to their own genius. Our maturity of thought brings new complexities to this paradigm and this enigmatic universe.

To the one who is given to thought there must be a consideration of the emotion prior to all kinds of reflection. It is our natural compassion for the accumulation of knowledge which is included in our curiosity to know and to understand.

There is an anomaly, a deviation from the common order, that takes place in the mind when it is active. It is the departure from the normal into the surreal. It is peculiar, irregular, and difficult to classify; but the mind takes into account itself and the annuity of knowledge towards our understanding, comprehension, and reason of the way things really are and not just how they seem to be.

The mind has an energy of its own and acts spontaneously in reaction and in creative contemplation. Imagination is the power that allows life to affect itself with its own representation. With the understanding that comes from wisdom we come to know what enlightenment actually is.

Imagination has the power to awaken and reveal what is concealed in the infinite possibilities. The mind's potential has the capabilities for reasoning and understanding through learning and the process of learning as we accumulate bold and revolutionary concepts that come to our attention spontaneously or by the way of experience.

Knowledge is not by deduction, but immediate by perception or sense at once. Knowledge also comes from wisdom of the ages in literature found throughout the world on dusty library shelves and in and used book stores, and also in new book stores, but there all the good books are either out of print and have to be ordered or the contemporary books on sale just say the same things as the older ones with different words.

The cosmic man knows spiritual reality exists as part of nature. The ordinary or common man perceives the world and only has notions of what underlies natural reality. To this effect he must learn the finer qualities of nature.

There is only one law or principle that works on all creatures and that is nature with all its properties, some of which are still, yet, unknown to us and remain in the realm of the metaphysical.

Living existence is immeasurable and infinitely various, and every creature follows the inner law of its own being. Life delights in life. On the wings of intuition our individual lives follow their own course of deconstruction or construction, or reconstruction, whatever may be.

Our sleeping potential rises to the occasion of enlightenment when awakened to the possibilities that surround our mind in idea, concepts, and notions of the universe we live in and partake through our existence.

We are asked to take nature not as given, but as a real presence that is indispensable to our outlook of nature itself, including our own human nature and nature as a property of the universe.

As our mind awakens to the infinite possibilities that remain concealed because of not knowing, the power which was held back transgresses its limits and reveals what lies beyond the concept of our limits and supersedes them through thought and reflection.

All that is in the mind is stored in reserve and can be called upon from the will, to access and remember at a moment's notice. As soon as the potential powers of the mind begin to function, the imagination, more powerful than all the rest, awakens and precedes all the rest of our actual intellectual abilities. It is imagination which enlarges the boundaries of possibility for us. The world of reality has its bounds; the world of imagination is boundless.

The imagination which excites other virtual faculties is nonetheless itself a virtual faculty — the most active of all. It belongs to nature's resources inherent in each of us awaiting awakening and enlightenment from the study of knowledge and wisdom of others as it is from the study of ourselves.

Along with our acceleration in learning comes a regression into the past as we consider the general impression knowledge gives to us. We consider and realize our projections into the future and their possibility, but we are bound to the past by a thread of remembrance; though this regression only adds to the flavor of our individual genius. We are not an island in the middle of the great ocean; we are a continent in the middle of that same ocean on a little planet somewhere in the east of our galaxy, in the middle of nowhere, but with significant meaning to the universe.

A Higher Realm of Thinking

When we consider the progress of philosophy and its qualities we must as well give consideration to the improved quality of our own reasoning from our increase and wealth of knowledge.

Our mind works in a circular fashion. It divides itself and comes back upon itself in concentric and eccentric circles, all the while moving from one overlapping center to another.

We cannot teach people how to live; they must learn on their own, but we can suggest to them what is right and proper. We can teach about concepts and principles, but as for morals and ethics we can only sway them into the views and attitudes of our culture. Our learning from experience is the most valuable, but let us not rule out the learning we do from books, for this learning cannot be learned from experience alone.

The natural progress of the mind is quickened, not reversed. Though age may creep up upon us and the mind seems to slow, it is only an appearance, because what is within is dwelling on some higher things other than the things of the world — it dwells on things that are kept in the mind, not in the world.

As we consider individual things and ideas we ought not to forget the big picture, the panorama of the horizon and its grandeur. Progress consists in gradual steps, always taking us closer to the infinity of possibility, surpassing our natural finitely conceived reality.

No one doubts that man is changed by his senses and state of mind within his intelligence. But instead of distinguishing the changes we confuse them with their causes. A value of virtuality or potentiality further introduces here an element of transition, and in our confusion we realize the need for hesitation in connection with the thoughts we give to our own considerations.

Lively questioning about cause brings up its own dialogue, but confusing cause and effect; reposing in a wrong theory does great harm and irreparable damage to the kind of thinking we are pursuing towards a higher realm of thinking and thought.

Living existence is immeasurable and infinitely various, and every creature follows the inner law of its own being. Life delights in life. Disengaging a concept of formal difference is the work of philosophy. A great deal of the burden of reasoning and of understanding is left to each of our own individual abilities of cognition and imagination.

Ingenious as it may appear, the analogies and conveniences of interpretation, natural as they may seem, present invention and discovery of new knowledge that may well have been accepted in the past and in the present here and now but that might be overthrown tomorrow by the increase in our own wisdom.

A regular succession in the process of thought requires revision and openness to new and bold ideas from our creative intelligence. We ought to keep in check the polarization of our thoughts. There ought to be a common ground where harmony of the chromatic scale of our thoughts is found. Our thoughts revolve in an elliptical or circular motion, and this rational axis must have a permanent center, just out of necessity to know our bearing and have a real sense of direction.

The joy and pain of each creature is the innate law of each living spirit, which survives by its own principles and personal genius. We live on the wings of intuition and realize the impact of our own principles and decisions in our reasonable choice making existence.

It is the mind that frames all varieties that abide in the visible world. To address the invisible and unknown is a natural response to our intelligent reasoning and rationality.

When one wants to study humanity, we must consider not only those around us but ourselves in a sincere and certain manner. We must also extend the range of our vision — not our actual eyesight but the inner sight of the mind.

One ought to first observe things' differences and similarities in order to discover their properties, elements, and essence; in effect, one must discover their actual substance that makes up their living Being.

The human race is so diverse in culture and social organization, the cultural agitation of its inhabitants brings us to the origin of the problem: we must first discover ourselves before we can discover other people.

As a matter of survival and subsistence we must consider the amount of work that goes into a task, and the intent, the motivation, and the ambition to get on with what we are set to accomplish. We ought to be industrious and contemplative to reach the heights of our destiny.

These two contradictory notions compliment each other. Difference only appears starting from a certain middle point and extending outward from the epic center.

The idleness that nurtures passion has been replaced by work, which represses it to a degree in that what spare time we have is already designated for rest from exhaustion. Before one becomes concerned with being happy, one has to be concerned with living.

The ever-present danger of perishing limits our ability to become contemplative, but those who labor in thought give contemplation its own time; and for reflection, memory and dreaming one has to as well allot some of their idle time for more eccentric activities.

The desire of man is infinite, his possession is infinite, and man himself infinite in mind and intelligent spirit. The whole of creation would appear infinite if it were not so corrupt and consumed with seeking after the material things that make our lives so comfortable.

A philosophical demonstration of this notion becomes a mystical affirmation once one applies their intelligent abilities to discover what actually is below and above the surface of reality.

The nature of the perceptible world captures our attention; but what is imperceptible, that which we know not of, seldom crosses our mind except for an occasional glance at random chance and what is called fate, or opportunity. The material world decays; the spirit does not, and remains spirit as a part of nature beyond our own comprehension and understanding.

We Pass Knowledge to One Another is a work that provokes thought and reflects upon thoughts from contemporary and past ages in time. It, as well, makes projections of thoughts into the future that may be relevant for observation and discussion.

As soon as one who labored in thought was recognized by another with thinking similar to themselves, the desire to communicate further thought and thinking that made one to seek the means to do so.

This is the theme and basis for this work: the desire and need to pass knowledge, to communicate with others, even as we communicate with ourselves with an internal voice, a recognition of thoughts and ideas through language and the use of words expressed through that language as a means to relate to each other notions and ideas.

When the ideas of people began to expand and multiply, and a closer communication took place in dialogue and literature, people strove to invent more numerous words to explain their thoughts. This is a chief result when we pass knowledge to one another: that we create a common ground for understanding in a more copious language form. "Copious" meaning yielding or containing plenty, affording an ample supply, in this case of words and meanings to explain and to describe what is thought in our thinking.

The windows by which light is let into a room is knowledge that is acquired and turned into wisdom and personal genius. There is one vital issue that requires further investigation and discussion: the mental nature of the phenomenal world and our living experience of the earth, and the heaven within that our spirit gives recognition to.

The world of the senses is closed by the gate of reality, but reality is extended into the world of mind and shut out by nothing except by the powers of the mind itself deciding to recognize or not anything it gives thought to or thinks about. With this point of view there seems to be, as is mentioned throughout history, four primary virtues: reason, feeling, intuition, and sensation. We bring into the arena of this world these factors and are struck with awe when thinking about them in our life.

If by ideas you mean immediate objects of understanding, or sensible things which cannot exist unperceived, or out of mind, then these things are ideas, real things, solid corporeal things the mind understands yet cannot either prove or disprove. This is reality at its height. The mind fathoms, but really does not know. It is the work of the philosopher to explain and describe these notions and ideas of the metaphysical realm of pure mind and intellect.

Before Creation all was solitude; the infinite and finite were not distinguishable. Eternity exists and all things in Eternity, independent of creation, exist just as well in the part of nature we still do not understand.

The heart sinks into the abyss of outer creation and beholds the deep of corporeal space known only to the mind. Infinity is observed, but not realized. We can only go so far on our own. We must seek the power of some higher entity — the great spirit that explains all. The mental nature of the phenomenal world is not a matter of correct thinking, but of our living experience on this great earth.

What is called the history of ideas is actually the passing of knowledge to one another. To ask the great questions is the movement of invention and the accessing of our intelligent powers. What is real I want to know. What is unknown I have to search for. Though the unknown may be, perhaps, real, it still has to be accounted for. The unending possibilities are fathomable through our mind alone.

You've got to wonder what this reality is that we live in. The truth is just a benign disguise of the concealed phenomenon we believe our existence is part of. The purity of truth can only be examined through contemplation and thoughtful consideration.

The differences of truth are in our own interpretation of it. Consider just what our thoughts do to us. They increase the imagination and diffuse our logic and rationality. In clear daylight we can see perfectly well; so does the mind when the clearness of daylight enters the mind. But when night comes we are filled with enlightenment from the day's illumination of our thoughts and ideas.

Curious as it may seem, conditioned as we are by materialistic assumptions, we can still arrive at and conceive from experience a state of consciousness in which the sensible world might seem part of our subjectivity. A self-evident or universally recognized truth is that though what we perceive is in the mind, reality actually exists both in the mind and outside the mind.

In the mind we conceive and interpret what is outside the mind. In nature God's countenance is everywhere known throughout the phenomenal world, just as it is known to the mind from the spirit within our intellect.

We are informed of nature by the living presence of a living spirit within our own mind. Even our conscience cannot deny this. Even the stars, the constellations, with all their forms are experience and not a mechanism of the movement of the mind. Just as they are part of nature, they rise in order and continue their immortal courses.

What our world is, is what we make of it. Revenue to the mind is knowledge and acquired wisdom. Its value is undeniable. This is why we pass knowledge to one another: to exchange revenue. Deception is an illusive reality that exists in the possibilities our mind creates and realizes as truth. When you look in a mirror you only see the reflection of yourself, but when you look into your mind you conceive and perceive the real you.

It was the Great Spirit that willed humanity to be social. The socialization of man has shifted the globe's axis of the universe. This slight change in the quality of mankind evoked the use of a common language and the written and spoken word so that society could function as a unit, instead of just as individuals grouped together for the common good. As our bonds in society increase, so does our feeling for consciousness and emotion for universal consciousness. United we stand strong, and together we circle the sun on this little planet called Earth, in the middle of nowhere in this great and grand universe. As life draws and lures us on, we create our own reality and live life as we make it as well as it comes to us eternally.

We live in a boundless invariable ocean of duration and expansion. We have a certain amount of aptitude for learning in our exploration and discovery of life, in all the possibilities and creative potential within us and in our surrounding environment.

All spaces and places are in reality created by the one universal imagination which in every individual being varies the ratio at will. Though what we believe may be in doubt, if the sun and moon were to doubt they would immediately go out. I've heard it said as well that the hours of pleasure and pain are measured by the clock, but of wisdom no clock can measure. Even a stopped clock shows the correct time twice a day.

Though time knows all things, all things do not know time. The succession of ideas in our mind follows each other, leading us to the one great spirit which knows time but gives it no mind.

This great spirit, creator of its own place in space and in time, lives on in our own mind. This realization can be nothing else but an original truth and principle of nature itself.

The question now is, how can there be thought and imagination? Think: who created thought with the capability of imagination? Thought and imagination are within nature, and yet nothing in nature can explain this awakening of the mind and its innate powers. This supplement to nature is its playful companion.

Through nature's play the seasons change and night becomes day; and the mind considers nature as a Great Spirit. Through this realization we come to recognize our own spirit and search for the end of the universe and for the beginning of heaven.

What is so great and so small that it cannot be found is why we are drawn to philosophy, science, theology, and metaphysics. There was a time when history was silent, before anything at all, at the dawn of time, when humanity evolved and developed the means for communication. Language was born and the written word took a quantum leap in recording events, thoughts, and emotional feeling. Once the written word became well defined people passed along their knowledge and wisdom in story, tale, and in literature.

In the beginning there was a great thought. This thought heard itself speak and conceived what it thought into a spark of perception. It created itself from that thought. It was the Holy Spirit. It thought of God and became the mind of God. Since it could only create itself because it was a thought, God created everything else. This notion, or idea, became a philosophy and a ground for theology.

Every so often you meet a person who seems different. Put the intellect aside and read into the emotion and feelings they exude. It is the spiritual power within that makes them so different. On a subtle level everyone is subliminally aware of this spirit within, and in the world. It's one of our natural abilities that nature itself has endowed us with — to recognize nature's own strength and power.

Even though truth is timeless, when understood by the mind and felt in the human heart, it makes all things new. The human spirit is lifted up to a new awareness of reality and of the spiritual possibilities in life.

Whether or not seeing or hearing was first does not matter; they both came before language as a well-defined means of communication. Likely before language we used some kind of communication with ourselves to relate to the mind what we were sensing and feeling. It was only when we crossed over to the world of language that we learned to communicate and give meaning to the words we use for expression.

But there is also another sense in which seeing and hearing come before words. It is seeing and hearing that establish our place in the surrounding world. We explain that world with words, but words can never undo the fact that we are surrounded by a phenomenal world.

The relation between what we believe and what we know is never settled. Our knowledge and the explanation of things never quite fit our certainty and understanding of them. Our curiosity never ceases even after a proper explanation is made known to us. It remains in the opacity within the system of rationality we create and can only be irreducible to logic primarily because the mind comprehends logic in its own origin.

When we use our words we ought not to forget their meaning and the thoughts that surround them in their use. It is because our thoughts are made up mostly of words and images, and the images bring to mind greater thoughts in the form of words. As knowledge is increased our language skills change character and become evermore so pronounced that we develop the need for more new and precise definitions to express the next generation of thoughts that comes with the passing of ages and the flowing of time in our existence.

The clouds bow to meet the Earth and Oceans. The starry skies extend themselves far beyond our own vision, yet we still imagine that great distance though we know nothing of it.

The progress of writing and thought is a natural process where the genius of the intellect transforms thoughts and images into words. The words themselves are just symbols representing those inspired to think and express themselves, whether to others or just to their own inner mind. The novel ideas we have approach our consciousness and become full with explanations and definitions materializing as a quantum leap in our mental capacities.

Our passion for clarity and precision goes along side-by-side with the definitions and explanations of the concepts in our newfound knowledge and wisdom.

The enlightened spirit finds itself in a world beyond expression and firmly established in emotion and passion. Only then does the enlightened one find words capable of expression of the passion and emotion felt through the mental and spiritual phenomenal event.

For a philosopher/theologian it is not uncommon to say something had an effect on them that was extraordinary and was reasonable to believe actually occurred. Then the measure of skill and talent for expression finds its own importance.

Our search into the origin and activity of the human element in nature is not metaphorical but an inherent quality of human nature and the mature disposition of nature itself seeking to be found out about and explained.

Living in the whirl of social life it is enough that a man should not let himself be carried away by the passions and prejudices of others. Let him see with his eyes and feel with his heart; let him own no sway but that of reason. The natural progress of the mind is quickened but not reversed. As learning is acquired knowledge brings itself forward with real wisdom.

Our attention is in a constant shift between meaning and verification. We subject ourselves to intense consideration of what we hold as true and certain. We calculate the degrees of our certainty and subject our present knowledge to verification.

It is the thinker, the philosopher, who breaks ideas and notions apart and then tries to re-assemble them in a more cohesive and coherent form so that thinking becomes a simple task. This is how we pass knowledge to one another. This work is presented and formed in a unified way. It is meant to be a work of art in the form of literature that is exciting and entertaining, as well as an informative and thought-provoking concept in writing.

Subject and Objectivity of Knowledge

What is sensible is not always intelligible, yet we create the means to comprehend and understand through our communications to ourselves and to others to make notions, concepts, and ideas known; then we do what we can to define and explain them.

Provisionally we understand metaphysics as a part of theology and philosophy, but there is more than meets the senses and our intelligence that we cannot understand, explain, and comprehend as well.

The experiences we have in our mind are just as real as the phenomenal physical world. The autonomous existence of things outside the mind is undeniable. Of all the known things created in this world and in the universe, invention speaks for itself. Invention is either naturally made or created by the ingenuity and cleverness of man, woman, child, or creature that habitats on this good earth.

One cannot overcome any alternative to expressing one's own thoughts without reinstating something unsaid. Pure representation is subject to metaphoric displacement and, as well, to the imagination subject to our knowledge of words and their usage, creating thoughts and meanings in their explanations and verification contributing to our sureness and certainty.

The question now is, in what space can one listen to oneself without the use of words in relation to one's own thoughts? This self-same idea created a worth and value for language and symbols. We ought to make and allow for ourselves time to think and to recognize the order of thought as we survey the horizon of our own intellectual and creative capacities.

We live in a theatrical culture. Everything is a drama as we live out our life, existing with reactions and actions from our continuous thinking challenging our own mind to use its potential abilities while interacting with others and ourselves. One event or thought leads to another full of emotion and passion, and hopefully with good, sound reason and logic. Just as we make the connection with others we connect to ourselves in our actual thinking.

In the time of contemplation and meditation we come to reflect on the nature of thought, on what it is for something to be, or be the content of, an idea concluding that we have concepts in our mind of what the real world seems to be.

Thoughts are merely images — that is, they are not essentially different from sense-contents and sensations but the progressive activity in our working intelligent mind.

We understand that the immediate objects of our awareness are subjective and have qualities inherent in them which are objects of our mental activity.

Perceiving is something we do, and the objects of perception are the things we are experiencing and given thought to. The psychological state is the act of thinking and the thoughts we come to be aware of in our thinking. The objects of thought come from either inside the mind or from outside it; either way the subject of our knowledge becomes and forms its own objectivity.

Our knowledge of the objects of thought, therefore, would have to be by some internal faculty, such as from reason or memory of some experience life has brought to us or that we have brought to life in the activity of our thinking.

The physical world becomes a cause for thought, and that thought becomes a cause for thinking. Nothing can be like an idea except for the notion of the idea itself. The idea is a concept the mind becomes aware of in the process of thinking; thus we are given to thought by our own will.

Those little bits of thoughts called ideas cannot float around the world on the air as the great spirit does; but inside the mind they do, and this concept cannot be denied. An idea is something that concerns the mind directly in the pursuit and quest for knowledge, and upon its revelation and discovery as a subject becomes an object for thought and contemplation. What we do is to put discovery to good use so that it leads to further discovery and fresh achievement, realizing along the way our true potential.

While we sort and discriminate the little things in our life and distinguish them from the bigger things, we ought to not forget the big picture and the marvelous grandeur we are part of.

Even when we are set apart in our aloneness and alienation, we still belong to the greater part of humanity. Together we live on this marvelous planet, but alone we must face the world and conquer not only it but ourselves as well. We will overcome the obstacles set beside the way and surmount the highest plateaus of our achievement. There is nothing we cannot achieve with the proper training and good will from chance and fateful opportunity. We must find our own road and travel it with discretion and thoughtful intention.

I find myself always coming back to consciousness — it is indeed as much awakening as it is re-awakening of this intelligent spirit that keeps me in thought, awe, and wonder of ourselves and the world we live in.

The pleasure which we all strive for is some stability in our personal life, where we learn the difference between want and need. At most times it is properly unimaginable to rationalize any real difference; sometimes the want of need overshadows pure want and desire for things we actually don't need. The exception is that our wants and desires bring with them passion and emotion.

From the various concerns in our personal lives we learn of want and need. All of what we want we do not need. The needs we satisfy for our survival. The wants we satisfy for our pleasure. The emotional factor plays an important role in our thinking. Sometimes wants and needs get confused when the emotional factor is considered into the equation. The common ground extends and divides our own realities. Here where reality meets fantasy the illusion grows truer — that just below the surface of our thoughts a truer reality exists where mind meets intellect and intellect meets with emotion. Where emotion meets with heart, metaphysical and spiritual matters become the only real reality the mind understands.

The imagination is open to impossibilities yet still entertains them as though they were achievable and sincerely possible. Our personal awakening and logical rationality divide us between the practical and impractical, between the possible and likely impossible; and still we strive for the impossible pretending that it is realizable and achievable.

Such is the paradox of the imagination and enigma of our conscious awareness of our present and enduring condition. Rousseau once said, "I shall set down in writing those delightful contemplations which may still come to me." So in the passing of knowledge to one another I do the same and relate thought and experience to you the reader for acquiring wisdom and knowledge to your benefit and entertainment.

Whether we turn to the annals of the world, or supplement with philosophical investigations the uncertain chronicles of history, we shall not find for human knowledge an origin answering to the idea we are pleased to entertain at present. "We Pass Knowledge to One Another" is a dramatic and affordable necessity of humanity.

One thought that has been pursued is that the reality of generality and universality exists only after that of specifics, and that absolutely everything real has to be wholly particular and singular. That's what gives us our individuality, which is so important, separating each of us into singular beings within the whole of humanity.

So each thing and creature has its own individuality, though known in a class of generalities of that specific class. When we do our utmost to conceive of something we have no knowledge of, we are all the while only contemplating our own ideas. This utility of our mind is one of our favorable qualities. After awhile you can work on points for style; until then you have to work with what you've got and continue in your own Adventure in Learning and discovery of the experience life offers to us either by chance or opportunity, or by acts of nature that compel us into action from reaction to those events. It's always a matter of choice on our part facing those little challenges just to see our reaction and to test our character.

If everything thinkable can be realized in an image or idea of it as a feature of it, then the concepts of the mind, interpreted as independent matter, could also be realized and actualized by the faculty of the mind's perception. This notion confirms the reality outside the mind and, as well, ideas of metaphysical proportion.

If we consider more than one theory about something, the most simple one ought to be taken in favor, explaining and giving meaning to the foremost thought on a particular subject. William Ockham seized upon this notion; to today this remains a matter of importance when applied to thought and thinking.

Once on the threshold of an idea or concept we ought to seek out the simplest explanation and proceed to understand it in that way, all the while considering newfound knowledge upon its discovery.

Whenever you write it is an experience in active thinking that surpasses time, because in the mind a generated thought or one that has been remembered is not confined by the time outside the mind that we all can relate to. It is our experiences that give us newfound knowledge and that knowledge we pass along to one another.

The opposition of dream to wakefulness is not that a representation of metaphysics can be thought but willed knowledge we know and can be certain of. The reality of a dream is just as real as true reality because the mind's interpretation justifies its taking place in the true time of the inner mind as an active thought and concept of our intelligent and creative imagination.

Imagism as a theory of what concepts are is hopeless, but an imagist approach to what we can conceive of — that is, to the concepts — is not open to the same objections and captures more directly the spirit of empiricism. It is empiricism freed from the concern to be nominalist. Imagism as a theory of the content of concepts, rather than the nature of concepts, consists only in the properties that we can conceive of as they are in themselves ones that can be presented in, or constructed from, features presented in the experiences we find in our actual living existence.

The Qualities of Thought

Question: What is reason? Answer: Reason is the spirit of the mind. Consider the idealist's developments in the current age. Not only are we aware of what is in our mind, but we are aware of what is outside it. These things give us reason to consider our own thoughts of them, and then with reasonable doubt. What is inside our mind only represents images and concepts of what is known by experience and our aptitude for learning.

If we see reality as it exists outside the mind, it ought to be the same within, but it isn't. They are two separate realities. Our imagination compounds reality, and with the blurring of mental vision and cloudiness that comes upon our mind we are open to misunderstanding and misinterpretation of what actually is before us.

This is the complex enigma and paradox the mind presents to itself for those who labor in thought and dream of possible impossibilities where concepts, ideas, and notions become actual reality in the mind of the beholder. There is a matrix in nature that changes dreams into reality and reality into dreams.

Not only is there a difference in the act and object of perception, but there is a difference which we are aware of in the thought of perception which brings images and thoughts to the mind and creates the reality of them which we can conceive within our deeper mind.

Such terms as ideas or notions of conceptions only add to the reality that takes place within the mind during thought, contemplation, and reflection. A proper discussion of this point only takes us further into the depths of philosophy.

One can only make sense of an unknown quality in relation to something known. If nothing of the matter is known, our imagination leads us to conceptualize the great and awesome wonder of the unknown. In the case of the one we call God we give human attributes to the word — name remaining unknown. There are others as well, such as spirit, reason, and logic; our understanding only goes as far as our ability that knowledge has brought to our wisdom. In the way of thought there are two roads, and they converge into one: idea and conception.

It is intuitively plausible to claim that the fundamental properties of the world must be like something in themselves. If we cannot experience certain properties directly, the defense of an idea as nothing but an idea is certainly sound reasoning.

At this point we must consider our own attitude toward spirit and its powers through nature, as nature created it formally. The perceiver exists just as well as what is perceived.

The objects of our awareness have different qualities and have principles with greater content than we could know. When I enter most intimately into what I call myself I can never observe anything but the perception. Here then the idea of a perception of myself is just an idea and can be nothing but an idea itself, again.

The difference between ideas floating into the mind and controlled thought is also difficult to explain considering such things as agency or will, which is a principle quality of the mind and is one of the essential qualities of being human.

The spirit that sullenly works and weaves its way through our intelligence passes without distinctions within itself away beyond consciousness and into a clearness of itself which only the mind can conceive and perceive. Pure insight with regard to its necessity and condition implicitly actualizes itself as one of the contents of our own thoughts and patterns of thinking.

Because this pure self-consciousness is a movement of the mind working in pure notions, pure self-consciousness collapses in fact into that unconscious working and weaving of spirit, which is part of its absolute reality that roams about the mind beside nature and part of nature itself.

Reality has a special significance because it is treated as an infinite consciousness within and beyond the mind itself. Reality arises into a pure and simple thing only compounded by the integrity the mind pursues in thought, imagination, and passionate emotion.

Inside you, you hear a calling; it's your own spirit, your conscience, and it always has something to say.

It is our understanding that makes our wisdom the more reasonable from the knowledge we gain, either through the adventure in learning or from experience alone in which our life exists in the phenomenal world. We are grounded in the basis of our own elemental thoughts; and it is this foundation that we have which determines the way we think and the certainty of our own thinking.

One can be sure that ideas do not exist outside the mind; reality is not an idea. It is a certain fact that it exists independent of the mind by nature's will. The words and notions, the conceptions we have are just an interpretation of reality as we come to know it.

The external world only provides ideas from the micro all the way to the macro; the universe is our world too. The mind therefore only comes to its interpretation from logic and reasoning. If one could take this conception a step further, it would consider the actual interpretation as a function of the mind by the certain way of thinking that we do and have opened ourselves up to.

The external world takes its share of causes and thereby explains itself as a phenomenal structure of elements totally uncountable. But the causes of ideas come from those same ideas which thought determines well enough to give its attention to occupy our time in contemplation and meditation of those same thoughts.

Although things exist in themselves, it is the mind that is the causal agent of discovery and exploration. Ideas are more than passive agents which extend themselves into the depths of the mind; they are the most provocative agents of the imagination and intellect combined.

The mind is contingently connected with every aspect of nature which can be named with one word: consciousness. And our very same consciousness is connected in every way to the unified theory of the whole, as one is made up of all its individual parts. Phenomenological judgments are difficult to evaluate, yet within the mind's ability we are capable of making such judgments with respect to our own individual, singular, and personal knowledge, and level of wisdom. Lively questioning is good for the mind, soul, and spirit.

It is plausible to say that you have feeling and emotion in thought, yet emotion and feeling are only supplemental to actual knowledge and understanding. They are two principles that come naturally but that for the most part are learned responses to events and supplement the content of our thoughts.

Berkeley was the one who said, "Nothing but an idea could be like an idea." Any representational realism an idea brings to mind is only an overwhelming continuation of that same idea in the faculty of the mind.

If people would only use the abilities and capabilities within their potential this would surely be a much better world to survive and live in. One ought to recognize as well that change takes time, though some changes take longer than others; it is the constant progression in change that takes place in time as one comes to know and understand.

Anything the mind concerns itself with directly becomes more than just an idea; it becomes a thought. Some are more complex than others, but thoughts are essentially what make us human.

Throughout the history of humanity, people have inherently thought about their own thinking. It is an absolute principle that philosophers have been trying to demystify our understanding of thinking. It is thought that gives meaning to spirit where all else fails in a proper explanation.

Upon discovering the will through thought there comes to be two distinct contents of inquiry. First is the intention, and second is their generality. This is what the purpose of this work is: exploring and discovering the properties of thought and the passing of knowledge to one another. Since you cannot form an idea of something unthought, thinking remains a mysterious quality of humanity.

No theory of thought can operate without a distinction between the thought considered as a psychological episode and what the thought is about. The objects of thought must be conceived as existing while the *unconceived* remain as ideas not yet brought to the mind's attention. Life goes on, and what we do is to think.

We need not be stuck in the present as we seem to be. Our thoughts bring us into both the future and the past through memory and dreaming imagination. Yet still the present is the only reality we know, because that's life.

There are mysteries which the heart of man, woman, and child can neither conceive nor believe. There are mysteries that you must at least realize are incomprehensible until the imagination catches hold of them. What is out of our reach we only strive the more to grasp and find some understanding in our reason and logic.

We have seen the road by which the cultivated mind approaches these mysteries of life. As they hasten the development of knowledge we come to a new and bolder understanding of life itself.

The way we relate ideas is by association and resemblance. Through each idea that comes to mind in thought I observe that there are particulars which have similarities and generalities, yet still have, and retain, their own individual qualities that separate one from the other.

The term knowledge has distinctions and divisions in itself. We have knowledge by acquaintance and knowledge by description. There is as well knowledge by hypothesis and theory. One can concede the title, unintelligible, to any field where no one has any knowledge of it at all. There is a fine line between vague awareness and where true knowledge begins. One ought to proceed from the generalities and universalities to the particulars, and from hypothesis and theory to a simple singular truth, beyond doubt, with a degree of certainty.

Propositions as well as ideas lead one on in thought to a sense of ambiguity that can only be reasoned through our intelligent logic as a function of the creative mind. People are inclined to think that there is a world of facts as opposed to a world of words which describe these facts. One is the inner mind and the other is the world in which we live. It is how we pass knowledge to one another through the world of words and the images those words and symbols create, bringing to mind those pure and simple thoughts.

Meaning in at least one important sense is a function of the word, image, and expression used to relate the impression of meaning. An idea has meaning when our interpretation has a reference to something that we have knowledge of. The truth or falsity then comes from its own verification in our Adventure in Learning, starting with the Basis of our Elemental Thoughts.

One must be given to consideration of the notions that words imply, the evidence and believed given truths of those words. Our thoughts circle around verification and possibility, all the while considering the probable and logical reasoning that we do in our thinking. We ought to be aware of the plausibility and proximity of the conclusions we come to relative to their truth and certainty.

What seems to be certain is the relation of a thought to the one thinking it. But through expression, whether written or spoken, the expressing factors are always in need of refinement of their distinguishing contradictions and precise meanings of the qualities of definitions we use and their verifiability.

It is possible — indeed possible even according to the old conception of logic — to give in advance a description of all true propositions. Their truth or falsity comes under the scrutiny of our own reasoning and logical deductions and judgments. So there can never, really, be any surprises in logic. In logic, processes and results are equivalent therefore surprises are sure to be non-existent.

We can construe our logic in such a way that every proposition is its own proof according to our reasoning and understanding within the capabilities of our own wisdom and genius. One thing is for sure: we cannot just get rid of the metaphysical unknown by its own logical probability. It is there as a part of nature, and though our will to know lures us on in the quest for knowledge it remains open to discussion and proper dialogue in a philosophical way.

The collection of ideas we accumulate and assimilate into a bold synthesis of the paradoxical enigma life presents to us to interpret is conditional on our aptitude for learning.

Hinged on the door of reality is an entrance to another realm. It is important to consider which way you open that door, from the inside out or from the outside in; both realms are part of nature.

Once at the threshold of an open door one can look back and see where one came from and see just to where one is going. The world is just so sublime and surreal it is beyond our conception, and still our awareness is enlightenment from our own imagination and genius.

It is the descriptive meaning in the words we use that express the nature of our thoughts. Through images which words produce our explanations become realistic and conceivable. Through the faculty of our mind the images we interpret become the thought once conceived; but now perceived we can see into our own mind and into the mind's of others through the use of language — the provoker of thought and wisdom we use to pass knowledge to one another.

It is our certain amount of common sense and devotion to truth that brings us to where we are today. Philosophy only adds to its mystique. Being endowed with reason we have a motive to listen to that same voice of reason our mind creates for itself. Conscience persists in following the order of nature in spite of the laws of man.

Doubt with regard to what we ought to know is a condition too violent for the human mind; it rebels in the quest for certainty, and it cannot be long endured. In spite of itself the mind decides one way or another, and it prefers to be deceived rather than to believe in nothing.

Some of the mysteries that surround us and penetrate into our own mind are impenetrable and are beyond reason, so we fall back on our imagination and creative intellect. Through this imagined world each of us forces a way for themselves which we hold to be right, but none can tell where it will lead. Still we long to know and understand but realize that there is a limit to the knowable. We prefer to trust in chance and theory rather than see what really is, because for the most part of life the metaphysical and spiritual has no definite proof and cannot be realistically defined other than in a casual way.

If I must accept general laws whose essential relation to matter is unperceived to me, how much further I have to go to realize creation is much greater than I once thought. It is no more possible to conceive how my will moves me and my thoughts than to conceive how my sensations affect my mind and emotions. For my own part the only possible assumption is that the chances are infinity to one that the world is as it is, and I am what I am. And who I am just another human working out my own existence, taking in all that I can to increase my potential abilities and come to a reasonable conclusion about the world and myself.

I was resolved to admit as self-evident all that I could not honestly refuse to believe, and to admit as true all that seemed to follow from this. All the rest I determined to leave undecided, neither accepting not rejecting it, but yet not troubling myself to clear up difficulties which did not lead to practical ends.

I am now convinced of the existence of the universe as of my own. It is I who moves myself. My will alone causes this movement; once started, the mind energizes itself into action from the thought of that action. The world, on the other hand, is not some huge animal or creature that moves itself of its own accord. Its movements are therefore due to some external cause, a cause which I cannot perceive, but the inner voice makes this cause so apparent to me that I cannot watch the course of the sun without imagining a force which drives it; and when the earth moves, which I cannot perceive either, I think of the hand that sets it in motion.

These words, I think, are philosophy at its best — considering all that there is to think about and find suitable explanations for. What we have to do while translating thought and word, familiar as it may seem with all its similarities, is to challenge our thoughts to become words as symbols of images with clear and definite meaning. This then happens from the conception of an idea: realizing it and then giving an explanation of it through the proper use of words and symbols. From this series of events we do pass knowledge to one another.

Anything recalled to the mind is like a souvenir, a token of remembrance, or treasure to be cherished; and when implied in a new context becomes an elaboration of a past interpretation, and explanation reminds us of what was even while it is changing and becoming something new.

In the non-verbal context our mind works with words and images that have no quality of sound, only a relationship between symbol and the object of thought. The notion of conceptual thought is our consciousness at work with the will in the sense that the will and spirit are in communication with each other at all times. Our thinking and thoughts are eternal companions. The more examples I take, the more causes I have to explain, without ever finding a common agent or element that controls them with the exception of the Great Spirit that oversees us, the universe, and all that there is within.

I can understand that the mechanism of the universe may not be intelligible to the human mind, but when a man sets to work to explain it he must say what men can understand; beyond that this intelligence works with nature and quite possibly may even be nature itself.

I judge the order of the world, although I know nothing of its purpose, for to judge this order it is enough for me to compare the parts one with the other, to study their relationships, and to observe their united action. I know not why anything at all exists, but continually see how it is changed; even with the thought of it I find the only constant is change itself.

Our Expanding Horizon

There are times when we express an idea in its propositional form that can be factored into two notions of form. The first is what is meant by the proposition, and the second is that the same proposition is a reference to something pointed at in the present or remembered in the memory of some distant reflection. And, still further, a proposition can be thought of in the future tense of the mind. All three notions make a reference to where the idea will lead the mind.

This work, this book of mine, has been designed to present a spectrum of points of view and carefully considered thoughts regarding the use and accumulation of knowledge that we call our own wisdom, from the intelligence within our mind. Through its vital understanding we come to expression by our logic and reasoning of the factors our thoughts and thinking lead us to believe.

The relative orientation of our "spirit" and "being" determines our point of view of the world, including our certain way of thinking; how we interpret that point of view depends on our experience and the extent of just how much knowledge has been passed along to us or that we have found out along the course of our Adventure in Learning. From this stand we can then proceed to pass knowledge along to one another and consider our own thoughts and patterns of thinking.

Of course there are two ends to this spectrum: there is a shift in the balance of ideas, and secondly there is the weight of the shift being that some know more than others and the others just have more to learn, though they may choose to neglect their incomplete knowledge foundation.

In our expanding horizon there are progressive stages of certainty that come to mind. Our awareness of what we know has an effect on our determining the horizon of our awareness, which is our own world. The inner and outer interplay of reality itself has a profound coincidence of relationships in the faculty of our thinking.

The whole picture is made up of all its parts; consequently in order to completely understand the whole picture we have to have a significant knowledge of the parts that make up the panorama of the horizon.

Through contemplation we take possession of the heavens and stars. Through our industry we take possession of all that can be known. There is no other creature on earth who can make fire and hold an admiration for the sun. Are we much better than the beasts that roam free in the world? They have no chaos in their order, and we create our own chaos from the order that we have.

When I meditated upon man's nature, I seemed to discover two distinct principles in it. One of them raised him to the study of the eternal truths which the wise delight to contemplate. The other led him downwards into himself, which made him slave to his passions.

Man is not one — at once he is a slave and a free man. This is no coincidence; nature made it so. We have free will and choice. We are decision-making creatures, just like the beasts, but we have an intelligent reasoning mind which is creative and imaginative as well.

We are one step above the creatures because we can believe and express ourselves about matters that come to our attention, as well as notions, conceptions, and ideas about a higher power we call God. The one we call Jesus must have had a reason for being born as a man, and the one we call His mother Mary must have been so pure and innocent that God would have given her the right to birth that same Jesus. It really gets interesting when you think about the whole situation. The voice of reason is not a passive one; moreover the inborn heart is not silent either.

Human understanding is both directed from our senses and from the faculties of our intelligence. One must soberly and diligently consider the way by which we are accustomed to proceed in the investigation and discovery of things as much as ideas and the notions of conceptions we have of those things and ideas.

When man addresses himself to discover something, he first seeks out and sets before him all that has been said by others and then begins to meditate for himself upon those ideas, evoking his own spirit of intelligence to consider the worth and value of his findings and coming to a realization of the parameters of those discoveries.

The scholars, the readers of literature, should be impartial and examine themselves as they examine the knowledge and wisdom in writing. It is not only the experience we derive from life that is important but how we value the worth of that experience and our interpretation of random chance, opportunity, and deliberate motivated intent.

One ought to suspend one's judgment on the conclusions one reaches until that time when one comes to a sure and certain reasoning. To be sure without doubt comes from modest contemplation and reflection on the beliefs and convictions we come to with our accrued understanding and genius.

We ought to be moving towards our horizon as it intrigues us with its own extension into the distant future, beyond our sense of sight but within our own intelligent imagination.

My will is independent of my senses. I know very well in myself when I have yielded to my passions or acted with reasoning. I have power in my will, but not always the strength to move it. The voice of my soul is the conscience itself; conscience moves the will and empowers it. Intelligence is no better known to me than my own spirit. My freedom consists in this very thing — that I can will what is for my own good. Our judgment is the motive power of all action. Providence only oversees our freedom and opens the way to decision and choice.

Supreme happiness consists in self-content; that we may gain this self-content we are placed upon this good earth and endowed with freedom, tempted by our passions and restrained by our conscience. If we are content to be ourselves, we ought not to complain of our lot.

When our fleeting needs are over, and our mad desires are at rest, there should also be an end of our passions and our crimes. God is intelligent, but how? Man is intelligent when he reasons, but the Supreme Intelligence does not need reason; there is neither premise nor conclusion, nor even a proposition. The Supreme Intelligence is wholly intuitive; it sees what is and what shall be; all truths are one for it, as all places are, but one point and all time are but one moment. In this way Man and God are the same.

We may be men without being scholars, for there is another way: now that we've found our conscience, the spirit of our being will be our guide through this vast labyrinth of human thought. But it is not enough to be aware that there is such a guide; we must know her and follow her, and give heed to the inner voice that calls to us.

Philosophy being nothing else but the study of wisdom and truth, it may with reason be expected that those who have spent most times in search of greater knowledge should enjoy a greater calm and serenity of mind, and greater clearness and evidence of wisdom in their own knowing of the universe and themselves as part of it.

The doubt and difficulty we have within our own understanding comes only from the capacity to view our world from different points of view. It is the masses of humanity who walk the road of plain common sense who have no more of an idea of the grandeur of this world and universe than a grain of sugar or salt.

It is a hard thing to suppose that right deductions from true principles should ever end in consequences which cannot be maintained or made consistent with our own convictions. The knowledge is out there within our reach if we would only set our will to explore and discover it, from not only old dusty library shelves but in our natural reality and in the infinite metaphysical reality of nature.

I cannot bear to conceive that we raise our own dust and then complain that we cannot see; but human as we are, we do. One must walk softly on unsure ground and open one's mind to the infinite possibilities held within nature in our finite but expandable creative intelligence.

It should be to our own encouragement that those who had come before us have explored the great designs of thought that we now have come to terms with. The mind can frame itself to any notion or idea of abstraction by reference to association or similarity in its own utility. Our confrontation with contradiction and enigmatic perplexity can be unraveled though entangled in the labyrinth of nature through a sincere contemplation and reflection of our thoughts.

I exercise myself in lofty contemplation. I consider the order of the universe, not to explain it, but to revere it without ceasing. I have done all I can to attain to truth, but its source is beyond my reach; and if I can go no further it is for truth to draw me near. The grandest ideas of divine nature come to us from reason only. Behold the spectacle of nature; listen to the inner voice that plays in your mind.

In our awareness of the quantum factor of an ever-expanding universe we are conscious in mind of both the grandeur and minuteness of both our inner and surrounding worlds. Those who are not perfect strangers to the writing and disputes of the philosophers acknowledge that there is no small part of them that do not concern themselves with the working creative intelligent mind.

Logic and metaphysics are no more complicated than life. We create our own difficulties and are well acquainted with them, but the actual simplicity of natural reality and the sublime and ethereal part of nature is not so hard to comprehend and understand if we could only see it in its actual simplicity.

We are told that the mind is able to consider things with abstract qualities. As the mind frames itself to more abstract ideas there comes the difference between those of excellent faculties and those for whom common sense is their ground. We are not all tied within narrow bands of reason; those who consider philosophy as part of their nature and labor in thought know the mind is boundless because of the achievement of wisdom, accumulation of knowledge, and their aptitude for learning.

The mind in its imperfect state has a need for abstraction for the enlargement of knowledge to which it is naturally inclined. It is the great toil and labor of the mind to emancipate its thoughts into the realm of the unknown without verifiability. It cannot be denied that words are of excellent use in that by their means all stock of knowledge accumulated by those inquisitive to put themselves to study are aroused from the will to know and find some understanding of life.

Whosoever is designated to read these sheets of words and the ideas they bring to mind, I entreat them to consider the thinking about them and the process of thought as a gift from the Creator.

Let us therefore seek honestly after truth and yield to its presence before us. As we submit to reason the truth will be known. The witness of man is nothing more than the witness of my own reason, and it adds nothing to the natural means which God has given me for the knowledge of truth. I wonder what the day before the first was like.

It is one thing to acquire knowledge and have it; and it is another thing to use it, and know how to use it, acquiring the skill of applying applications.

It is evident to anyone who takes a survey of the thoughts that envelop human knowledge that they are ideas that are either imprinted on the senses or conceived by our creative intelligent mind and that are formed with the help of memory or from our imagination.

One can conclude that neither our thoughts, nor our passions, nor ideas formed by imagination exist without the utility of our intelligence. The common factor is just the ability of the mind to think and to conceive without the use of perception, except that of the mind's own power over itself.

We are thinking creatures that react and act either spontaneously or through meditation and contemplation of consequence. This one factor depends on our thinking and how we have developed that pattern of the way we go about thought. This separates us from the beasts that roam the earth without an emotional thought of their behavior.

When someone shares knowledge with you, you incorporate it into your own. When you hear or read something you do the same. This is the primary principle of We Pass Knowledge to One Another. It happens that way every day and has been like that throughout the ages for eons upon eons; even the creatures of the world and unknown creatures, and nature itself, participate in this train of thought.

If we restrict our studies to what is useful we evolve and develop ourselves in a way where what we learn can result in the use of its affections and applications. The way is open; we do not have to be set in our ways. Change is inevitable and a primary part of life. This voluntary course is apparent in our daily life routine and throughout our very existence, extending way beyond ourselves.

The inner world of the mind is a spiritual realm in a sense, but what is that? Only after a long course of questioning do we come to matters of this type. What is spirit? What is God other than a spirit? When we reflect upon this difficult questioning, how can we be able to understand it except for our own reasoning? To learn what God is, you must first understand nature and then reach into the abstract field of metaphysics. Let us think what pleases us, and to go further in thought we ought to consider what we have been taught and what has come to our own experience.

It is therefore important to cultivate the faculty which serves as judge between our guides; conscience and society; which does not allow the conscience to go astray and corrects the errors of prejudice, and that faculty is our reason.

In this age of philosophy one must be able to distinguish virtue and resist temptation to stray from what seems right and the truth of that right and proper action of thought. Love is an illusion, I grant you, but its reality consists in the feelings it awakes. The only real virtue we ought to adore is that love for knowledge, wisdom, and truth.

One must be careful with one's wit. The power of knowledge has its own consequences. Our reason and judgment are heightened and our common sense becomes highly uncommon, so that only the chosen few may know its treasure. The most dangerous snare, the only snare which reason cannot avoid, is that of the senses; if you ever have the misfortune to fall into its way you will be filled with nothing but fancies and illusions, consumed with fascination and troubled judgment you would not be able to escape nor willing to believe its truth.

There is no one in this world with a heart without feeling or a mind without discernment. Intent merely on the objects of our pursuits, we behold the space between the thought of those objects and the objects themselves. Wrapped in thought, I cast my heart upon the sea of tranquility and found the dark side of the moon full of the light of enlightenment. An ode to the distant memories of fairer times, my reflections became the lines of inspired verse. We do not merely consider the beginning and the end but all that is in the midst of the two opposites and all that is contained within them.

The journey itself is a delight, and its exploration a wonder of amusement and entertainment. We pass the time with various pleasures, but the most pleasing is our time given to thought itself. It is knowledge that makes us curious enough to want to know more. As with life itself, one thing leads to another, and we make our way forward while all the time caught in the grasp of memories and clinging to our dreams.

When someone shares their knowledge with you, you incorporate it into your own. It happens to people like that all the time. It happens to most of us by the means of our life experience. With age comes knowledge and wisdom. Our conceiving and imagining power does not extend beyond the possibility of real existence or perception in our discernment; but along the way of life we miss things, and when brought to our attention we quest for clues to the unknown.

Some truths are so near and obvious to the mind that one need only open one's eyes and mind to see their reality; but once our thinking is open to these new suggestions the infinite mind penetrates to the core of our being and we raise ourselves to a new level of thought.

Of all the Creator's creations only man, woman, and child are illuminated with the gift of thought and the process of imaginative thinking. Our lessons are timely; we live to learn. It is our evolution that makes us what we are. Our becoming is a continual process and an essential part of our life experience. So I prepare myself for each new dawn and all that comes with it, then in the evening before I retire give thought to the history that has been made and dream of the future.

– III –

Part Three

A Deeper Thought

There are many ways of knowing things. First by sense, second by reason, and third, but not final, is what we know from the creative intelligence we have been endowed with. Even if you do not know what something is, or its qualities, you may have an awareness of a relation this thing or idea may have with something else. In some way our intelligence gives us a relative idea, and no other idea is like the one we ponder on in the moment of revelation and enlightenment.

Through sense we have perception, through reason we have logic, and through imagination we come to the notions of discernment and wisdom. We perceive a continual succession of ideas that combine into new and bolder ideas and conceptions in our thoughts and thinking. Though there may be no apparent cause for the evolution of ideas, we do know that some attract and others repel in confrontation and contradiction.

The nature of Spirit and consciousness act this way, not being perceivable, yet known and observed in our thoughts. Whatever power I have over my own thoughts, I find that the ideas actually perceived through my will to recognize them are not dependent on my will but by our natural curiosity and the inherent faculty of the mind's own utility.

The question comes to mind: How can we know the world and ourselves when our senses are imperfect and our knowledge limited? When our mind is ready the truth becomes known by its own natural attraction and by the power of suggestion. Enlightenment comes as a gift of revelation through study and contemplation of the ideas that come to our awareness and draw our attention.

Amid the uncertainty of human life we ought not to give heed to false prudence, which seeks to sacrifice the present to the future; what is, is too often sacrificed to what will never be. If there is a time to enjoy life it will always be in the here and now, but let us not lay up regret or misery for the future by false thinking today. We should be subject to the laws of wisdom over the tyranny of popular beliefs and find out for ourselves what the real truth holds firmly to.

Within our mind we become understanding of life's illusions and see through them into the truth. From this truth we create our destiny by acting and reacting within our own reason and understanding. Into the unknown we traverse universes in our mind and become even more aware of the different planes life holds to in natural reality, in the surreal reality of metaphysics, and in the inner working of our intellectual capacities.

Just as shadows are born of light and die in darkness, we raise our consciousness to the illuminated enlightenment of insight and of acquired revelation through study and contemplation of our knowledge. A single thought can be broken with an idea, but that same idea can bring back together all that has been broken.

It's a paradox, the enigma; life is a curious wonder. Our thoughts our knowledge; the wisdom only adds to life's own flavor. In the beginning there was a perfect darkness. The light wanted to live, so it created itself to give meaning to the infinite void. Once the light became a vivid response to the darkness it illuminated the universe with its own wisdom and genius. It became a beacon that all of nature would be attracted to. Its radiance became a principal necessity that all of creation would recognize and explore. Its will would manifest itself. And then there was a Spirit born of the same Original Thought.

The illusion of separation and alienation can be further broken with our consciousness and intelligence. The tyranny of the unknown has fallen with our increase in knowledge. This is the true purpose of passing knowledge to one another.

We give meaning to the symbols we have known. Our interpretation may be misleading; the truth exists only in our own belief. The moment of clarity comes in the realization of purpose. Our learning is that purpose — it is the increase of our own wisdom. What lies behind is only history filled with memories. What lies before us is only an imaginable future with all possibility conceivable only through the ultimate faculty of our mind.

It is the restless shifting changes the mind goes through that occupy our attention. Finding contentment in thought is subject to our acquiring new knowledge to shore up the wisdom we already have. The moment within itself is doubtlessly just a phase of our insight and revelation into the knowledge we find at hand, which finds its usefulness in our processes of thinking. Since conflict and confrontation appear in thought at the same moment of contentment, our quest to find stability in that contentment of thought becomes a primary objective and a source for inspiration and discovery. The world out of which we find ourselves thinking about our own thoughts becomes the motivation for further investigation and study.

Insight becomes an actual concrete consciousness within itself. Insight, as well, finds itself as true knowledge in the matter of our thinking; and in the way we go about reckoning our own thoughts. When I enter most intimately into what I call myself, I always have some reason to stumble upon some particular perception or another. I never catch myself without some type of perception and never can observe anything but that perception. The seasons will come and go; we are open only to change. The difference between ideas floating into the mind and controlled thought is a difficult one to explain.

However difficult this attempt of mine may seem, when I consider how many have come before me in the same design, I am not without hope that I may bring to the light of day some new perspective those before me just might have passed by. The spirit of knowledge leads us to our final destination: the sureness and certainty of what we have already come to know and understand.

The path to our knowingness is the Adventure in Learning. That learning is The Basis of our Elemental Thoughts. From these two considerations We Pass Knowledge to One Another with our awareness to the truth, and with that certainty and sureness we come to a new and bolder grip on reality which is both internal and within the real world, and universe, in which we live. The grains of sand pass through my hand, but their memory remains.

There is no quick apprehension of anything except for the feelings and emotions that come from the heart. They require no thought at all but are spontaneous and reactionary.

From experience we are not passive in our relationship with life. Our active role creates a succession of ideas and thoughts in our mind. What appears to me is that we are placed by nature in the midst of events and circumstances, and by being given to thought about them are aroused by discovery of our real being and of nature itself on the grandest scale. Langston Hughes once said: "When you turn the corner And you run into yourself Then you know that you have turned All the corners that are left."

It is important to relax our mind to use it in our concentration, exploring our own knowledge and conceiving ways of utilizing that wisdom to the best of our abilities.

It is the curious eye and mind of the philosopher, and artist, musician, or poet who brings out the subtleties of nature that are in plain sight yet cannot be seen by the ordinary person of the street. It is the things of the world that give us thought, and from those things of the world our thought expands according to the ability and faculty of each of our individual minds.

Because the Creator was so ingenious creating reality, could it not be so that this same ingenious Creator would give us the mind to conceive not only the Creator, but all of creation? It is our abilities that allow us this privilege within reason through language, be it written or through voice with wise contrivance.

The abundance of information conveyed to us is our wealth and treasure of knowledge. So this is why it is passed from one to another for the general good of all of humanity, for each of us to use as we will. What excites ideas in us is the spirit of wonder and curiosity. What brings uniform existence to our ideas is our reason and logic. What invigorates this reason and logic in us is our own spirit and will to know and understand what we conceive and perceive as the essential reality of our inner self and the greater surrounding world.

The question is now: How can man claim to be the master of his subject when he is taught that nothing is unnecessary? Nothing is one of the most important factors, because it gives definition to something which is its own opposite.

The question comes again: How can we claim to know so much when we know so little about anything at all? And when we claim to know ourselves we really know so little.

Goethe once said, "A man who thinks indulges a curious habit of replacing an unsolved problem with a fantasy he can't get rid of even after the problem has been solved and truth made evident."

It takes a special turn of mind to grasp formless reality in its essential nature and to distinguish it from the figments of the imagination which thrust themselves urgently on our attention with a certain semblance of reality.

It is worthwhile to reflect a little on the qualities of our ideas and not the quantity of them. Though the parts make up the whole, it is the parts we think about, while keeping the whole at a distance.

The question is: how can one even make a tolerable sense or meaning of existence? The answer is that it is just part of our nature to do so. It is worthwhile to reflect a little on the motives which induce us to have presuppositions about life; but in the end we withdraw the assent that launched us into the ground above them.

You think that we are screened off from the providence of the one we call God and are left to ourselves by our own wit; but this fable is not true. You say you are granted moments of thoughtlessness for your own relief; but thoughtlessness is only a reaction to the stress that survival projects into your mind.

We cannot act without thinking; we cannot live without thought. We are thinking creatures and believe in fantasy as much as we do in reality. The face of reality has many colors; fantasy must be perceived as illusion. The truth will prevail.

With our new found wisdom and the influx of provocative ideas our sympathies must be aligned with knowledge and understanding.

The Philosopher

With all the ideas we are acquainted with at present whatsoever seems possible may just as well be so. One more year has come and gone. The seasons are changing again; winter is coming. The world is changing too, just like ourselves. Freedom has its price, but freedom of thought is priceless. Nature tells us part of what we need to know, and the rest is the instruction of reason.

It is most worthwhile to reflect on the tremendous power of infinity, which we must understand is such as to make it possible that all things share in this affinity. It must be a very difficult task to be the one we call God, with so much responsibility. The burden is no less than the weight of the position. Like us, God positions its own essential being with some serious preoccupations. If God is the world itself, and the universe, what can be less restful than to be revolving around the heaven's axis at amazing speed, without a moment's rest, keeping its course aligned to nature's own specifications.

A philosopher, whose thoughts take in a larger-than-life compass of nature, having observed certain similarities and differences in the confrontation of truth and illusion of that truth, creates an anomaly in thinking, explaining the world as a grand attraction of opposites and then considers their agreements that thought brings about. What we create in our own mind has its roots, not from only within, but from the curious world itself.

It is the will of our spirit that helps us claim the happiness we seek in the contentment of the mind, free from disturbances of the thoughts that seem to overcome us in the moments of triumph where actual peace is achieved; but as always it's something that draws us away from that peace and contentment. So our quest is to strive for its return to our consciousness and equilibrium.

For a moment, then, consider the unlimited magnitude of the universe and the space within your own mind. The something is greater than the nothing but its influence is no less than the thought we give to it.

We know our being because we know ourselves; but our will is something different, just as is our spirit. It is the will of our spirit that moves us to action and reaction. It is our will that allows such movement. It is the will that has a cause and searches out for a proper and reasonable effect. It is the will that affects our spirit as our spirit affects our intelligence.

It is just as in nature as it is in the mind — that ideas become real, and there is a wisdom in nature as is in our intelligence. It is the will of nature that has similarities with the human will.

The largeness of our comprehension has its factors in the knowledge we have gained through study and experience. What is most agreeable to us, and sought after by the mind, is the probable conjectures about the past and about the future. Our here and now has the most certainty because of its proximity to our own personal reality.

Logic is not a body of doctrine but a mirror image of the world. Logic is transcendental. It surpasses all other forms of reason because it is a principle of nature and is infinite as the universe itself. The question of whether intuition is needed for the solution of any problem is, in the case of language itself, provides the necessary basis for that same intuition of the desired answer.

The possibility of describing the world by means of Newtonian mechanics tells us nothing about the world. But what does tell us something about it is the precise way in which it is possible to describe it by these means. We are also told something about the world by the fact that it can be observed and described more simply with one system of mechanics than with another.

If there were a law of causality, as it seems to be so, it might be put in the following way: There are Laws of Nature which cannot be denied. But of course those Laws are made manifest in our present reality, forsaking all ideas and notions of fantasy and their illusion which appears in our present concepts of reality, including the very notions contained in metaphysics and spiritual reality which only can be fathomed by our individual human creative intelligence.

Time is one thing, thought is another; though thought is timeless and memory is a gift from the Creator. The present we already know because of the thought and attention we give to it. Reminiscing is one thing, dreaming is another; but fantasy grows with illusion and has no truth for it to abide by except for the utility of the mind's creative power. Still we must assure ourselves of the grounds we have for our own reality.

We should proceed warily in our course through the present, because we are apt to lay to great a stress on analogies, metaphors, and the prejudice of truth — that the eagerness of the mind is carried to extend knowledge into the general and universal from specific and particular cases.

Could it be the will of a governing spirit that sees it convenient to hide some things from us and reveal others? The answer may be yes, because each of our individual abilities to comprehend and to understand has the range and breadth and depth of assorted variations in realizing and actualizing the utility of our mind.

We ought to propose to ourselves nobler views, and exalt the mind to enlarge our notions of the grandeur, wisdom, and beneficence of the Creator — being unperceivable to sense, remains in itself similar and immovable relative to each of our centers of consciousness.

We are obliged to make sensible judgments and conclusions of unknown things and of the metaphysical aspects of nature and of our own nature in repose with our convictions and beliefs.

Mechanics determines one form of description of the world by saying that all propositions used in the description of the world must be obtained in a given way from a given set of propositions: the axioms of mechanics. From there, any development of notions and ideas, whatever it may be, must somehow be constructed with these building blocks of knowledge and personal wisdom.

We are also told something about the world by the fact that it can be described more simply with one system of mechanics than with another.

As a philosopher, whichever issue you touch upon may have in its own right a weak spot where our understanding is compromised. We can claim that the appearance of God is only in thought and not from our senses. It is within the powers of our mind to think so. Any visual image is only discernible by similarities to our own reflection; and that is why our mind, when directed at these things, believes that their nature is blessed and eternal.

We take refuge in the equal distribution of our thoughts and say that, since there exists a mortal nature, there must also exist an immortal nature which gives reason to the expression that the spirit and soul in our mind has these same immortal qualities.

There is a difference between the rational conclusions of an argument and simply pointing something out; for the former reveals certain hidden and, as it were, arcane facts, while the latter indicates things which are evident and out in the open. Moreover, since there is nothing left if you deprive man of sense-perception, it is necessary that nature herself judge what is natural and what is supernatural.

The Philosopher must conclude that there are transcendental maxims, which have influence on everything and every creature that we do not understand just yet, though conceivably we realize must exist.

A great many inexplicable difficulties arise in trying to explain the unexplainable and unimaginable possibilities that exist in nature; but we do that, indeed, by our irresistible concern for explanation.

Though the mind has the potential for comprehension and understanding, it is the explanations that defy words.

No idea can be rejected for its uselessness; all thought leads to further development and to its own evolution as a natural part of the continuation of evolution and to its unique development. This is the work of a philosopher who spends considerable time laboring in thought through the considerations of theology and unique qualities of the metaphysical nature through speculation and imagination.

Upon the principles of philosophy we can be assured there is more to the mind than can be revealed. We spend our life doubting due to defective reason and false logic. You divert the busy mind from vain research; it seems necessary to inquire into the source of the perplexities that amuse our attention and, if possible, discover common principles and the solutions of them.

It is important to relax our mind as it is to concentrate it in thought and reflection. Here again we ought to find an equal distribution between the work the mind does and its repose.

The doors and windows that we open and close each day and night determine the quality of life we will live; for it is our perspective and observation, our reasoning and logic, our comprehension and understanding that form the grounds for our thinking and thoughts.

Either you reach a higher ground today from newfound knowledge and acquired wisdom, or you exercise your strength in order to be able to climb to the summit of learning tomorrow. I seem to always come back and remember this one thought. Learn today all you can. It is the learning that we do that enables us to comprehend and understand what it is that we seem to know. It is that same exploration and discovery that brings about our wisdom and genius.

Comprehension is one thing and understanding is another; the two surround our life with everything that there is, was, and will be. Few begin with anything like a clear view of what they ask for from life; any answer they look for depends upon how the question was asked. The closer one gets to their own center, to their own essential being, the clearer their destination and questioning becomes.

The rhythms of nature need not be disregarded, because we have our own that follows nature closely. Our essential rhythm with nature takes on a more bold and colorful flavor when our thinking coincides with the properties nature holds close to fact and truth. Notice that your inward peace not only upsets your world but the immediate world that surrounds you. The whole world that you view and experience has its own center: and that is in your own mind.

What is this peculiar activity that occupies the mind? It is the struggle after ideas and notions not only conceived and created by the mind itself but implanted by the world with impressions of reality and life itself. We go from place to place in search of experience questing all the while for truth but find similarities everywhere and the real truth hidden in concealed places, which we seek to reveal from our expanding horizon of experience.

The treasure is real wisdom that highlights the truth in its own natural light. Any enlightenment that comes from its finding only adds to our own knowledge and genius. We should allow ourselves to step out boldly into the reality of the world and universe and find out for ourselves what this knowledge has in store for us. We Pass Knowledge to One Another because many candles are lit from just one.

The first sight of a lighthouse from sea gives us bearing and warns us of danger. Just the same is the wisdom we acquire; it gives us bearing and warns us of illusion and false truths.

Life comes at us pretty fast. Robert Frost once said there were three words that summed it up: "It goes on." John Milton once said, "The mind is its own place, and in itself can make hell of heaven, or heaven of hell." Sensible words are everywhere spoken, but we have to listen to hear them.

Thinking makes progress from one thought to another. One only has to remember where they started so that they do not end at the beginning. One should remember to use what talents one has and leave the rest to those others with more adapt skills. In the spirit of adventure we learn to boldly go where we have no real expectations. The only anticipation is for some new learning and profound knowledge. If there is some responsibility for our mortality, then there is a greater responsibility for our immortality. The mind holds in it what we call spirit and soul; these immortal qualities have a cherishing to the mind's own intelligence, for without them we are just like the beasts and other creatures of this Earth who live for living and imagine nothing past life itself.

When new enchantment grows in the mind, and the seasons

change, earth's breezes bring the clouds across the sky, and our imagination soars to the heavens and beyond. Oh what a joy it is for mankind; not far away is kind-hearted laughter of the sureness of our knowing.

When I come to walk the streets and avenues of life I am alone, just the same with myself and my own thoughts. What our inner life consists of is dissolution until proven otherwise by the reason we are endowed with in the sanctuary of our own thoughts and thinking.

A single footbridge crosses the abyss of the unknown, and we cross it with our own hesitancy and curiosity. Nature's own mind was made so simple; yet ours creates its own complexities. The dark mind and heart are lightened from thought and art. Literature has its own mellowing tendencies. Poetry goes to the heart and philosophy to the mind; and theology conquers both.

When the weather is fine and mild, a deity escorts us across the different meadows; but when the weather turns the other way we face life on our own with only the wits and skills we've learned from the knowledge we've learned and wisdom we've acquired.

A glass roof lets in the skies grandeur, and an open mind brings forth genius of all sorts. Nightfall brings out the stars and daybreak brings out the wonderful blue hue that surrounds our world with a passing cloud that shadows our thoughts with sincere and hesitant doubt. So we cross the threshold of our intelligence and find comfort in the celestial rays that pass by our way.

When joy comes from the labor of our striving the inquisitive keep asking how, and when, and where, and why; but those who labor in thought know better than to ask these questions and just wonder.

Men's gravity, great perils, and conquering zest — these come from education and awareness that there's a goal: the high worth, the best that's shown by what exists, and relics of past discoveries.

But those who are the elect know what the real truth is and not just what seems to be. Life comes from its daring, bold and lofty aim, and what we find is all there is contained in our own mind.

There is just so much in this world that we do not understand, even ourselves. But there is a reason for that notion, and even that reason we do not understand. We cannot see past our own understanding, and the choices that we make depend on the level of our reason and proper use of the understanding which we have achieved. Considering the choices we have to make we ought to be able to bear in mind the consequences of those choices; but the immediate plays more of a role in our life than the future.

There is no escaping reason; it is the prime motivator of the will, and our intent is solely based on the power of our reasonable will. Our discretion and ambivalence leads us to uncertainty and indecisiveness as to which course to follow. So our individual and singular life goes where it wills, closer to pleasure than pain, in spite of consequence or the immediate reactions from our close associates.

There is only one place where pleasure and pain coexist, and that is where love finds its way from our mind to our heart. Not in any day will we find happiness; once happy we redefine happiness so as to be happier. Those who wish to live in happiness must find good reason to live as they do, among those who they will live, and by the grace of providence to protect us from harms way. Our indecisive behavior amounts to the knowledge we've accumulated and to the use we put it to.

What I must do is all that concerns me; others may express an opinion, but the final choice is mine alone. We are all the same. The height of wisdom is to take things as they are and endure what we cannot escape. Just as with life itself; its finality is but a dream, and along the way we live in reality and dream of better times.

The legends of spirits live within our mind. From time to time they return, not to haunt us, but to guide us towards our destiny. In a short time see how much has passed away and how much new has come our way. The sphere of our Earth is adorned with so much and we realize just how little we know. So life goes on and the minute hand of the clock passes the hour hand once again.

No one was meant to go through life alone, but those who do can set their own pace; with another they must wait for each others' readiness. Life is full of give and take and compromise; we must yield not only to ourselves but to our significant others as well. We must yield to nature also. Freedom is just a state of mind. We are all bound to something or someone inevitably.

We must hold to our ideals and maintain our enthusiasm from the heart of our will to succeed in capturing our dreams before they fly away out of our reach. The real voyage of discovery consists not in seeking new horizons but in our evolving perception of reality. Perhaps what makes life so worth living is the Adventure in Learning and the curiosity life brings forth from its own accord.

It is the philosopher's position to entertain suspicions concerning the most important truths and bring them into questioning to discover what makes them so valuable and hold to their worth.

My own understanding has become strangely enlightened to comprehend some of life's greatest mysteries. These riddles of life have the most common of answers, if only one would take the time to ponder upon them. To exist is one thing, to be perceived is another; but the original conception remains part of the mind's utility, a faculty worth mentioning and entertaining in thought and reflection. If you try with all your will of thought to conceive an idea, in some time a perception will evolve, and its reality, though in your mind, will find some reality in the absolute world beyond thought in nature itself.

It is not those who examine the widest and most obvious notions who make their mark on society, but those who labor in thought over inquiry of the philosophical paradox of the nature and truth of reality as it seems to be from not only our senses, but from our own actual thoughts and the sensations of the mind. There is more to visibility than just plain sight; it is insight that takes the mind on its journey through discovery and comprehension that brings out the most reluctant principles behind what can be plainly seen.

On Meditations of Ideas

As our mind passes from one thought to another, one thought significantly captures our attention as the other is let go by the wayside. Here the mind is forced to admit its own diversity, and temporarily cling to one idea over another because of its own preference or attraction. The mind knows its own objective reality and knows the causes of its own preferences. We take reality in the sense of nature; but its other establishment is in the working of the human mind.

Though we are moved by chance and caprice one must not eliminate sensibility and the results of logic and reason. Though our passion is moved by pleasure and the avoidance of pain, our sensibility takes control over any reason we have to call our own.

Seeing with the mind is one of our natural abilities that has to be honed like the blade of a sword to cut through the veil of appearances. The real truth of something is not always apparent and has to be found in reality — not of the kind we create for ourselves.

What I once supposed to be real I found to not be; but a different reality paralleled the most obvious. As for the rational deducing of causes from effects, those ideas are beside inquiry; it is the perception of ideas, and their creation, that finds quality in our thoughts and thinking.

By one means we have images and representations. By another we have immediately perceived recognition of something that has its own validity. It is our meditation of ideas that utilizes the ability and capacity of the qualities of the mind. Though at times we may seem to be alone, we are not; we are with ourselves and the angels of providence who see to our safety and protection, while looking after the thoughts we think and ideas that come to our attention.

From experience we ground our senses to form recognition of qualities, but from the mind alone, through our creative imagination, we conceive what cannot be perceived. These are the ideas that we meditate upon in inquiry and through exploration and discovery of the knowledge we find by study and that knowledge which is passed along to us from literature and from our significant others.

I find it is impossible for us to conceive or understand how anything but an idea can be like an idea. It is most evident that no idea can exist without the utility of the mind.

The idea of comprehensible is broad and is defined by our understanding of the idea at hand. The whole system of nature in the world, or the system of the universe, is comprehensible but at the same time immeasurable. We, ourselves, act in the same way; we are comprehensible but immeasurable based on our own understanding of who we are and what we are becoming.

The Author of nature actuates the universe, and all that is within it, including ourselves; but as for our free will and our creative intelligence we are apt to be on our own with our own reasonable intelligence and sense of understanding within our own ability to comprehend what it is that we think we know or have a familiarity with.

You must call your imagination to your aid, because reason is not enough to explain nature — the nature of the universe and even our own nature. Everything has its own simplicity in the midst of its own complexity; this is the eternal enigma and paradox of life.

Can there be anything truer than to put an issue before the public and leave it to them to conceive, even give thought to and consider, to hold to be true, or to debate the issue and still be so divided as to a reasonable conclusion? Yes, an open dialogue is the most sincere work of the philosopher in each of us. There are so many ideas in this world open to discussion and still have no verifiability. Creation, God, Jesus, Moses, and all that have come between. So much constant debate and more every day. What is this world coming to? That's the big question. And everyone has an opinion. That's just as true as change is a constant.

Though we agree or disagree, the outcome of an open dialogue is the passing of knowledge to one another. It's just what the world needs to evolve and mature. Perhaps just how far we can go is really up to us, each one and all.

An infinite mind could be necessarily inferred from the bare essentials of our existence that necessity of sensibility in an irrational world brings amusing ideas to the mind. The infiniteness comes from our expanding intellectual horizon and from our creative intelligence. So we get to wonder how the mind works when it plays out the events that occur in our surrounding world, including our singular and personal inner world.

Moral consciousness brings out our actions into reality. Self-consciousness brings out our rational sensibility and inner thought into our personal and worldly greater reality; it is the instrument used by the former for the realization of itself. The two ought not to be suppressed but brought into conformity with our inherent natural reason, part of our rational logic and reason that occur in the faculty of our mind's utility and functional abilities.

Our impulses are the springs of life and give us our nature and character by the way of thought and our tendency to think the way we do. Sensibility is a kind of nature, which contains within itself its own laws and principles and springs of action brought along with our ambition and motivations. The harmony between sensibility and reason is implicit within their own establishment in the faculties of our mind. The connection between the two is undeniable and its consequence affects our entire being; it is always incomplete and constantly compounded by the new knowledge and experience we acquire along the course life has in store for us. The key here is learning and experience in applying that bold new learning.

When we, our mind, are caught up in contradiction and confrontation of new and bold ideas it is essential and necessary for us to bring into the open clearing we coordinate for the mind's use, to bring these new and bold notions and ideas to a successful comprehension in our understanding, which of course brings satisfaction to our permeated central intellect within the actual limits of our own sensible understanding. To know is actually to have an understanding and a comprehension with our aptitude for learning.

In the attempt to understand an Idea, it is at one time to have validity simply and solely as the unrealized thought-element, and at another is a product of pure abstraction realized as a function of the mind's ability to rationalize thought.

Since the distinction on which the Idea rests is its conception of something tangible or not must be thought, passes into one which does not any longer exist even in words but in thought alone totally as pure conception and nothing else.

Pure consciousness is nothing more than the realization of an idea that has been actualized from a condensed thought to an expanded thought, all inclusive of its own subject and its qualities that surround the perception of the conception of the idea itself. The idea is an action of the mind that perhaps may be termed abstract phenomenalism because it rests within our intelligence and only appears outside the mind when it takes form constructed from its various parts that become realization and actualization of the thought itself.

The question is: how do ideas come to the mind? The answer is that they come to the mind from our natural curiosity and imagination, and from our reasonable insight into something that attracts our attention and occupies our thoughts in the moment when our mind is at rest from its other duties. Any liberal philosopher would call this moment of relaxed thought constructive idle time.

We see ideas produced in our mind after an orderly and constant manner; it is natural to think they have some regular fixed occasion, but at the time they are excited in the mind their appearance takes hold of our attention and we devote further concentration on the occasion of their appearance. The world does not go around ideas; in fact ideas go around the world in each of our mind elements and draw us to them from our own inquisitive nature.

One of the only things we can be sure of is that knowledge builds up within our intellect and brings about creative ideas that emerge as notions and concepts we devote time and consideration to while exploring the resources we call wisdom and personal genius. In some way or manner the interplay becomes our knowledge foundation.

In the beginning all we could do is wonder. Then we began to think. Though our comprehension and understanding were limited, our perception was keen, and our senses were, as they still are, well tuned to experience, even as we attempt at conceiving things greater than our understanding allows.

Knowledge, all you know, is that you have a certain idea or appearance in your mind of the recognition of similarities of signs and symbols we give determination to about our conceptions of ideas or from the perceptions our senses give to our mind.

The nature of knowledge is just a relation of perception and conception of notions and ideas we hold to truth and certainty in our mind from our creative intelligence. One could even go so far as to say that our imagination has some basis on our knowledge and accumulated wisdom that comes with the graying of life.

Once firmly established in our convictions we can only be open to greater wisdom from the passing of knowledge to one another having as a base the distinguishing qualities of our conceptions and ideas, and some relative understanding of their nature.

The world imposes itself on us, and still we maintain that we create our own world from deep within our mind and from the experience we gain from life becomes our greater world, a unity of a sort between what's inside us and what's outside in the larger world which we live in, including all the unknowns in the universe above our clouds.

We are no greater than our thoughts and no less than the considerations we give to them. The perfection of human knowledge is only just an ideal we seek after, which is a better understanding of what we just think we know. But actually we know so little compared to all the knowledge that's out there to be found, and there's so much explaining to be done for what is already known. Our limits become the bounds of our determination to find answers to our questions; but in the questions we form the answers we seek after, so the phrasing becomes the important idea and the notion of the question becomes the key to finding the answer we're looking for.

Philosophy is only a deeper level of thinking than one is accustomed to, considering our ordinary and daily thought patterns. Though we are not accustomed to think deeply, those who labor in thought know that serious thinking results in enlightenment and furthers our imagination. I have an immediate knowledge of my own mind and my own ideas because I can be sure of what I know and of what I do not. I have a sense of my own being and well being and I know when I am not well. I am more sure of myself than I am of the world.

As for everything else I only have an awareness of these things and a comprehension only as far as my own understanding. Many things exist though I have no notion or Idea of them or of their qualities. This I cannot deny; but those things must be possible either by probable deduction and logic or by necessary consequence of the causes distributed by providence throughout nature including the universe.

Although we believe things to exist that are not verifiable or provable, those things which we do not actually perceive we can conceive and represent through images created in our intelligent imagination. Their possibility is only as great as the probability we assign to them from our own reason and logical deduction.

We communicate by the means of words, and all have their own connotations. Words are not to be used without an attachment of meaning to them, because without meaning they are just utterances or prehistoric mumblings or grunts of excitement or passion with feeling. There is more to reading than just the words; it is the thoughts they bring about that make us think and use our intelligence. The thoughts that the words bring to mind are greater than the words themselves.

If not for the words we use in our own thoughts we could not communicate with either ourselves or others. The significance of thought has a dependency on words and their appropriate meanings and connotations. For this reason among others we pass knowledge to one another and gain insight and enlightenment into our deeper self. I am therefore one individual principle nested amidst the background of greater principles.

Being conscious of ourselves and the world that surrounds us, reality breaks up into the plurality of circumstances indefinitely in all directions: backwards into its condition, sideways in associations, and forward into consequences. Life holds to the rhythm of time, continuously without interruption except that it is surrounded by our sleep.

When knowledge is considered in those relationships we are conscious of the moments that make up our life and bring consciousness of these moments into our reality. Most of the time our mind interacts with itself, and other times it interacts with the significant others that share the living existence we endure and survive through. Even as I sit here by my window side I know that reality is on both sides of the pane of glass that separates us; and still we wonder.

Sometimes my own head even puts aside the facts and fills itself full with emotion and passion that come with desire of need and want.

Conscience is part of the circle of life. It knows itself, and is not empty because it is the keeper of our spirit, and gives us our sensibility, along with our mind that gives us our reason with the natural intelligence we are endowed with. Our consciousness of conscience co-exist for one another and give us this self-certainty of its own proper truth and as an essential principle that recognizes our soul, not in some abstract reality but in the pure reality of our existence and in the things, beings, and creatures that surround us in the course of our livelihood.

By observing how ideas become general we may better judge how words are made general as well. It is the words that give meaning to the ideas in our thoughts and to the things and creatures of the world. Thinking deeper I know that there are moments between thoughts when ideas hold firmly to our attention. It is the words that give meaning to the ideas we have and are conscious of. And it is the ideas we have that give meaning to our conscience in our thoughts, actions, and behavior that combines both qualities within our intelligence and creative aptitude for reasonable and sensible thinking.

There is some proof that the mind is in an imperfect state. It has the need for notions and general ideas, whether they be real or abstract. Whenever there is need, there implies the lack of something, and that something has to be filled for perfection to be achieved. We, as humans, will always have this need from our own curiosity and desire for more knowledge and wisdom that fulfills the promise of our own genius.

The mind makes haste to call for these ideas and notions with our endowed intelligence for our convenience of communication, and for the enlargement of knowledge — to both of which it is naturally inclined.

What can be easier than for one to look into their own thoughts and recognize what they know and what they are sure they know nothing of. Much is here said of the difficulty that abstract ideas carry with them and the great toil and labor of the mind to raise their thoughts to such sublime speculations of the metaphysical and of the supernatural that clings to reality in a nature beyond our own comprehension.

When one considers the great pains that for so many ages have led to the cultivation and advancement of knowledge, it was not without the thought of abstract ideas that we retain clearly in the darkness of our own uncertainty and curiosity. The ideas formed by the imagination are faint and indistinct; they have besides an entire dependence on the intelligence within our own mind. We can imagine only as far as we can conceive. But the ideas perceived by sense are more vivid and clear.

If only one could raise their senses through an increase in intelligence unknown and unperceived, things which start as conceptions would then be perceived by the increase awareness of them and their natural qualities. To know everything that is knowable is unrealistic, but to endure our own imperfection is a natural emotion, and still our desire to know more cannot be resisted. The nature of divinity is a natural attraction to the human kind, and its distinctions create a labyrinth of paradox in our enigma of life.

The making known of anything which was unknown before is an innovation in knowledge and comes by the means of laboring in thought. These are the novelties; these are the uncommon notions which shock the genuine uncorrupted judgment of mankind. The more we can know how things and ideas are connected, the more we can know of their qualities and nature. This phase of study is what best suits the philosopher — to discover identities and the meaning of their curious natures.

Our knowledge is no further real than our ideas are true representations of those originals, which come far and in between original thought and its associations to those originals. There is a light in the darkness of our own ignorance; it is study and the laboring in thought those inquisitive minds go through in the stillness of their reflection and meditation upon novel ideas and notions that attract their attention and lure them to a closer investigation.

Though we can be certain most people have a sense of recognition in similar ways, the ideas in each are varied and not similarly affected though presented with a common idea. This one notion gives each of us our individuality and character and reveals our certain way of thinking and as well how we are given to thought.

By annexing a collection of thoughts to my own knowledge I can conceive that matter exists outside the mind and is perceived by it, while still believing that conceiving and the conception of thought remains part of the activity of the mind alone. As well through the annexation of the same collection of thoughts I can conceive there is a spirit; though I do not know it I can realize its presence.

The distinction is quite small that since both have a certain sensible and intelligible existence in the mind, they can be known by the thought of them through reflection and meditation upon them. The mind is a fascinating and peculiar thing which is more than just an idea; its actuality makes our living experience all the more pleasurable when not consumed by the consistent anxiety and stress the world brings to our reality from outside and from within.

On Sentiment and Recognition of Knowledge

My endeavors tend only to unite and place in a clearer light what comes to me as thoughts of truths without compromising history or my own beliefs. That which before me was shared by others now becomes shared with me for the purpose of Passing Knowledge to One Another. Here these propositions and conclusions find their place on the printed page for contemporary and future generations.

Though we immediately perceive real things, and real is a genuine expression of our interpretation of real, it is the thoughts and ideas we possess which have their own reality in our mind and find their expression through the use of words we define the qualities of our reality and realism through their definite use and related meanings and the understanding of them.

I need not turn my whole world around; just my thoughts and think of them with different and various points of view, and with a variety of perspectives.

The truth can be known only our interpretation of it may be different or change — it matters because of our certain way of thinking we interpret the world we live in, and ourselves; life goes on and we think of it all the same with questions and curiosity. As an idea becomes a conception in the mind, one in particular surfaces; the soul always thinks.

Descartes believed that the soul thinks because as it is somehow connected to the conscience it is the holder of the spirit, and the spirit is intelligent. Once conceived that consciousness, i.e. thought, is the essence of the mind, so it can never lack; it draws upon itself. But essence as substance has desire and our will to fulfill desire constantly requires the elimination of lacking for its own fulfillment. The notion of conscience, spirit, and soul are abstracted from our own thinking via our intelligent creativity of thought and the intellectual process of thinking.

There were many new things to conceive with this newfound

wisdom that enlightened my mind and brought insight into the same wisdom that I called my own genius.

The ordinary became everywhere a miracle. I had realized the splendor life actually held. Everywhere there was something new to explore and discover. Inside me there was as well; in my mind I had revealed from the concealed the newness of exploration and discovery about my own thoughts and certain way of thinking.

Even the most clear and cogent demonstrations of our wisdom contain in them paradoxes which are irreconcilable to the understanding of humans, and even a small portion supply any real benefit to human kind. Otherwise they provide an innocent diversion and amusement to our thoughts and process of thinking.

There are years that touch us and moments of time that evoke feeling and emotion differently, like the passing seasons of the good Earth. Our awakening is timely, so we have to prepare ourselves for the future that wakes with each rising of the sun from the horizon.

By night there is much to think about, but how many do? All day long we experience the day, live through it, but how many really give it any thought? I find myself up late, even past midnight, thinking and reflecting, on the events, actions, and reactions that the day brought with it; and by night, after the thought, seek the comfort of rest in my comfortable resting place. We must be acutely conscious that fiction has disrupted the order of reality.

The aesthetic wonder comes to our attention only after our lower needs for survival have been met. The aesthetics of life have requirements, such as a full belly and comfortable living conditions. Only those nearer the top of the pyramid know the worth and value of aesthetics. The real wonder of them is that they are naturally occurring coincidences the mind goes through when given to thought about the beauty and splendor of life itself and the things and moments in life that we treasure.

When we stand back and ponder the answers to our questions we ask, the endless range of meaning finds its way into the essence of our being. We become what we think and still find avenues around what we choose not to think about.

There is nothing more nor less than a recognition of the difference between words and the echoes they create in the mind. The artifice of the philosopher is the only means to Pass Knowledge to One Another from history to the contemporary. It takes cleverness and skill, not to mention wit, but I will to embellish all the promises philosophy and metaphysics hold within their grounds of composite reality. You articulate some things and with others are content with general knowledge. Our wisdom becomes our own genius.

There is nowhere to turn to except to our mutual powers of illumination. It is one of the greatest things to add enlightenment and insight to another's life. Intelligence embraces annihilation, making the reality principle a sublime potion for our life to pass on to one another, concealed in the mystery of life itself previously unknown ideas and subjective principles.

The more we increase our knowledge our wisdom leads only in one direction. Our spirit is alive in our mind and knows its own soul, and with this departing body we reach the philosopher's dream: eternal thought and its enchantment.

The transcendental and extraordinary become part of nature's reality we never really knew until we passed into it and lived a life beyond our own knowledge. It is an extraordinary experience we can only conceive, but not perceive, and still our speculation bears its weight on our own thoughts and thinking.

We think, and read, and listen to music to repair our solitude, which is lost in our everyday world where business takes its toll on our casual existence. We lose ourselves taking care of necessity, and the real me is secluded in some safe sanctuary in the recesses of my mind, put off for my own protection. The deepest motive for reading is the pleasure in the quest for knowledge and wisdom, besides getting lost in the characters and theme of what we read. Worldly wisdom is rarely wise, but philosophy and metaphysical wisdom serve to enlighten our patterns of thinking and open to us new windows and doors to insight into ourselves and to the world.

Life is a grand dramatic irony. To be aware of our conscience is not merely a determination of existence, but a determinate constant of our spiritual essence. What ought to exist has here essentially only by its being known to be pure individuality gives itself the expression of who we really are. The self enters existence as pure self and is conscious of its own nature.

The self we find in ourselves is real. We know it is spirit which, having returned to itself, is certain of itself, certain in itself of its truth, of its own act of recognition knows, in truth, who we really are. Conscious of itself as a being with essence it knows its own reality full with emotion and passion.

This world was so created that the utterance, or self-thought language of the inner self, knows its own voice as an echo which always returns to itself and has no need for verification because of its certainty of itself within our own intelligence.

The silent fusion of the pithless unsubstantial elements of evaporated life has still to be taken in another sense of the reality of conscience; the objective moment of realization appears in the mind as part of actual reality as we know it from the outer world to deep within our own mind.

If one can break away from the obligations the world imposes upon us, an awakening of freedom exhibits its sanity on us that we are not really bound to survival. The paradox is that survival need not be all work and that our sanity necessarily requires a certain amount of personal luxury in quiet contemplation.

When we call upon the freedom of thought, and of the will, the suggestion that wisdom plays a dependent role is not far off the mark. To have control over our will we need a mind-set not only from free choice, from contemplated thought, but from a relative commitment and conviction to secure the knowledge that leads us to our own security in the right direction without having to choose to do so. It is an obscure thought that becomes clearer the wiser we become; without regret for lacking that potential with our aptitude for learning.

It is evident to anyone who takes a survey of the knowledge of ages since long gone, or of our contemporary intelligence, that there are ideas and word associations in language that bring to mind the objects of our senses or notions that circulate within our own mind.

With the help of memory and imagination we can search ourselves for the significant thoughts we consider as prevalent ideas. The farther we go into thinking of our own thoughts, or the thoughts of others the deeper we are entangled in difficulty and intrigue of interpretation, all the while coming to conclusions that are unfounded and border our imagination.

Our judgment is divided among the facts and our own speculation along with the notions of others who have passed by the way which we are traveling. We find these others in our real life and in the literature we read of people and their ideas which we incorporate into our own.

No knowledge is too excellent that it is beyond our reach, but still there is some that causes us to ponder and wonder because it has fascinating and purely amusing qualities that surpass the realm of reality as we know it.

There is but one means for an idea to exist, and that is that it has been conceived and perceived by our own intelligence where lives our mind within our own spirit, soul, and being.

Some truths are so near and obvious to the mind that one need only open one's eyes to see them; others require one to labor in thought over them and come to one's own reasonable conclusions.

To be convinced of this, the reader need only reflect and try to separate in their own mind the being of a sensible thing from its being conceived and thereby able to be perceived and realized. If we look but ever so little into our own mind and thoughts, we shall find it impossible to conceive a likeness except only between our own notions and ideas that surround our thoughts and progressively distinguish the real from the sembalance of what seems real.

I know its been some time now since I've given it some thought, but time goes on sometimes without notice. Now past the middle of my life journey I can vividly recall the immediacy that newfound knowledge startles me with freshness, increasing my own sense of wonder. Beyond wisdom secular transcendence has a spiritual root which embraces our own spirit and being, essentially expanding our consciousness of the knowledge we hold to be our own.

Being concerned for the affection I have for knowledge that comes from the printed page, I've found it worthwhile to consult back to ages long since passed and review the enlightenment of the ancient sages mused with thought of life itself and of the universe our world exists in and even deeper into our own mind. From this point of view I can realize my own insight and enlightenment, which has increased my own understanding of the development of the human intellect.

From my own emancipation from ignorance by the freedom of thought and sincere thinking I can never be completely detached from the world, yet I can move from the reality of the inner mind to the reality of nature, and beyond to the higher level of nature that includes the spiritual realm of metaphysical notions and ideas.

It is through an exceptional awareness that enlightenment and insight come from the awareness that we have accumulated from study and contemplation. Humans are the only creatures we know who have this ability, with the exception of animals that stalk their prey considering each move to achieve the capture of their next meal, only to satisfy their need that hunger drives them to use these inner resources within their own intelligence.

There are a lot of people who can see in what I've learned whether I have known how to choose what would enhance my theme, and others have said what I cannot say so well; but our interpretation increases the worth of our understanding and capability of rational logic. In the reasoning and invention I plant in this theme my only weakness is hidden and concealed under what has already been said, so by engaging thought the already rich soil of wisdom produces our individual genius.

Some who turn the pages in works already written find curious words and bring them into their own. We become part of what we think and read. Our involvement becomes part of our reality.

Philosophy writes the same in all languages, but in our mind we borrow and add to our own thoughts the thoughts of those who thought before us. Once I have read what I have written I am given to increase my own thoughts on this theme of Passing Knowledge to One Another. Even as we think of our own thoughts the expanding horizon of our thinking becomes an ever-amazing Adventure in Learning. As The Basis of our Elemental Thoughts takes on new ground our real genius becomes even more apparent, and our wisdom grows even as our life journey continues.

The Adventure is just beginning. With knowledge at hand we traverse the heights of pure thought, realizing the unknown and conceiving what was once imaginary to be just the secret part of reality we can now perceive with our insight and intelligence.

It is language that mystifies us, and words are a means of enchantment. It is the language of conversation transferred in the form of a written work that brings us to the conversations we have with our own being and increases the scope of our thoughts.

It is our own knowledge and wisdom that rises to passion. What we are is in search for a deeper learning experience, but that comes with life so we have to search ourselves on a deeper level. All for the love of wisdom that becomes our own genius. The high-noon experience comes from our morning experience, anticipating all that memory can hold until the evening comes and we can reflect upon the day, bringing revelation of what our expectations have brought to fulfillment.

One must have the ability of mind that can conceive ideas and the sensibility to make the life equation reasonable and logical, but often enough life just has too many variables and abstracts. So we have to make due, endure, and learn all along the way the best that we can, knowing there will be surprises and unexpected arrivals of events that require most thoughtful consideration.

The voice of reason never rests. It follows us even into our sleep. It is loud enough to hear and remains in our mind and begs to be considered. It will not rest until it is heard and is the perpetual disciple — a voice just as strong as the will, perhaps even stronger, because the voice of reason leads the will to action.

I find I can excite ideas in my mind at pleasure and vary and shift the scene as often as I think fit. It is no more than willing this making and unmaking of ideas that dominate the active mind.

Whatever power I find I have over the contents of my own thoughts it is still in my power to choose to continue them or dissolve them at a moment's notice. All that we learn by experience is imprinted in the treasury of the mind, and to that we only add distinguishing factors and compound them with our continual thoughts of their original notion and the ideas produced by them.

Even in the most philosophic reasoning we pretend difficulties and inconsistencies that the most apt reader will collect a sense from the words we use to describe things and the ideas they represent. Even the most far away things as the stars in the sky, we think them to be so close because we can see their brightness, and for those ideas so far from our sense we bring them closer with the activity of our intelligent mind.

With a clear-sighted aim in view, this work's purpose is to furnish us with ideas and precepts that serve to explain all there is, including the unexplainable, to the best of our abilities, giving our reasoning a clearer insight ordinarily thought impossible without a pertinent philosophical point of view. So we are persuaded to take a course of action, in our thinking, to make even the most abstract principles clearer in our own thinking.

Life goes beyond our own brave exploits, and we give meaning to the simplest things that are measurable with words; but those things we experience that are beyond words are the specific ones that need addressing and a closer examination, even those things we think about that are concealed deep within our own mind.

To set this matter of ideas in a clearer light, I observe that there are different amounts of reality due to them. Ideas are not at random produced; there is a certain order and connection between them, like unto cause and effect. There are also several combinations of them made in a very regular and artificial manner discernible to the curious thinking of a philosopher.

It is worthwhile to reflect a little on the notions and ideas we have of the unperceived and how they are excited in our mind by some force we deem it necessary to reckon with. Is it not so that ideas beyond our knowing have such an attraction and luring that they draw our thoughts close to them in our quest for truth and certainty? We can scarce part with them they are so riveted in our mind, clearly beyond our own reasoning, yet we ceaselessly try.

It is a very curious thing that the mind retains so great a fondness, against all evidence of reason, for ideas that have no real proof or grounds for validity; yet we find in our own ways to conceive a proof by our own wisdom and knowledge to endeavor to support an opinion of the bare possibility of these thoughts' existence.

Worldly wisdom is one thing and does no other good than further our understanding of the world, but divine wisdom is larger than we can absorb. A wealth that already is ours is activated through the spirit that is a unique strength and is the beginning of true wisdom.

Those who bring human wisdom back down from heaven through the laborious and useful business of philosophy pass knowledge without excitement but assuredly have the most lofty and natural motives: to increase the capacity of our knowing and understanding.

It's one of those things, being human, to recognize our own strengths and virtues, and of course our weaknesses. Through considering the wisdom of the ages we do ourselves a great favor, roused with courage and fortified with patience to endure and overcome the human vice of prejudice against knowing — that we are capable and have the ability to raise ourselves above the common and ordinary into a realm of understanding the extensions of nature that reach our soul.

Once the circumference of our mind has been taken to its outstanding threshold and crossed its integrated radius a new dimension combines the universal element together with nature and finds within us perpetual sympathy with *unfound* wisdom.

Our words, by which we are inventors, unveil the permanent analogy of things by images and ideas that participate in the life of truth as we know and understand it; and still the unknown lures our curiosity in search for unmistakable sureness and validity. Our unmitigated quest for learning cannot be denied nor tarnished.

Knowledge is power, but what we do with that power is entirely up to us. One must remember that the increase in knowledge brings us to a newfound wisdom and personal genius; any further explanation comes from the passing of knowledge to one another by way of prose, poetry, essay or philosophy, all of which contain in themselves the echoes of universal and eternal principles that account for nature in its physical and metaphysical forms.

In the advancement of learning the saturation of a new age will restore the wisdom of the ancients. This new age is just a moment in time that we see in the contemporary just after the turn of the century and is the accumulation of all that is in the here and now we recognize as our present condition in life.

Wisdom is esoteric though essentially original and in no way mystical. Our wisdom comes from the foundation of knowledge we build for ourselves. What we learn and how we apply our learning becomes our own genius. Whatever wisdom we do gain from learned knowledge we must keep under our sense of reason and sound logic.

Our wide-ranging curiosity about the world and universe and its inhabitants only brings us closer to knowing ourselves, which is the truest wisdom one can achieve. A teacher can only teach what is known, but a philosopher can give new light to the mind and open new scenes of previous times to prospect and probability, just as a sage addresses not only things but the thoughts of things and ideas, and multiplies his words and expressions about the notions of them.

Whenever I attempt to frame a simple idea of time, abstracted from the succession of ideas in my mind, I find myself entangled in extricable difficulties. From the standpoint of earth the sun knows no other time than its own; the moon and stars abide by the same, and our mind only knows time by the succession of ideas it gives thought to. Whoever shall go about to divide their own thoughts or abstract the existence of a spirit from its cognition will, I believe, find it no easy task.

The knowledge of nature is only half the task. The philosopher is required to estimate the happiness and misery of every condition, observe the power of passions in their combinations, and trace the changes of the human mind as they are modified by institutions and accidental influences, conditions, and events in one's life.

I perceive no other condition for life than the living for the interaction we have with others and the things that occupy our time in thought and recovered memories.

Even as our thoughts move about inside our mind, philosophers who have a greater extent of thought, and more just notions of the systems of things, discover that even the earth itself moves about the sky above, circling the sun, even moving in accord with the motion of the galaxy in the universe among the heavens, which is so grand it is even beyond our own comprehension.

Nothing can be plainer than to consider my own thoughts, but to consider the thoughts of others is well worth the time required to think of them. If every grain of sand on a beach beside the great oceans of the world were individual thoughts then one would know the whole story of life itself.

There are two thoughts here of fine importance; the first is greater and the second smaller. If one could believe in the ten or hundred thousandth of an inch than equally possible would be the same in the greater sense — ten or one hundred thousand times larger. Is this how our mind works? Yes, I think so. There is the smallest part of the atom and the greatest part of the sky we still think is unknown.

Knowledge of Heart and Mind

There is no one whose imagination does not sometimes predominate over their reason, nor who can regulate their attention wholly by their will. Our ideas come and go with no command.

What happens to us even as we face reality is the grand human experience. There are those who indulge the power of fiction and send their imagination out upon a wing with fanciful disguises, and there are those who face reality straight on.

Through all conditions of life we endure and concentrate our hope for better days, all the while searching for our own security and happiness. Faith and belief cannot get us through alone; it is wit and skill that rescue us from life's traumas and dramas.

Though it seems the general opinion of the world and within the design of nature and providence that the end of speculation be the improvement and regulation of our lives and actions, we consider the pains we take, no less than that of others, to perplex even the simplest things. We spend our time doubting those things which others seem to know and search for ourselves the real basis for the real truth. In time some particular train of thought overtakes us with ideas and notions we expect to lead somewhere, but what happens is that we end up just chasing our own fanciful speculation.

Then fiction separates itself from reality, and one must distinguish among our conceptions the appearance of truth from the real truth. We are curiously faced with comic realism that makes light of situation and condition. This safety net for our emotions is real. It is our natural response to the fear and anxiety inherent in our lives.

In the beginning the pure self starts life empty and is filled by the surrounding environment. As a child grows it explores this environment and comes to conclusions about it. Everywhere we are filled with knowledge that brings us to our individuality and personalized thinking, but not without influences from others. At some point we stop thinking for them and begin to think for ourselves.

At this point in our decision making, learning and accumulating wisdom makes all the difference in our life.

The highest degree of culture is to know the spirit of Nature within ourselves. The wisdom literature passed down to us through the ages has brought contemplation to its philosophical heights. There is no clear sky to view into nature's true reality; but we can, in time, tear down the wall and raise the veil of illusion to see through the darkness into the light of enlightenment and pure insight.

We have an inner enlightenment and insight that occurs between the heart and mind which is an acknowledgement that what matters most is the open mystery and mystical amusement of the majesty of providence. It can be suggested upon, but never stated clearly, because of the labyrinth of complications inherent in the paradoxes and enigmas that dominate the mind's relationship with itself and the world.

The question is, what is our purpose? The answer is that everyone has a certain mission to accomplish, things to learn, and relationships to develop with significant others. If we find fulfillment, then we are no longer compelled to call earth our home and are called to the other side of reality, heaven if we may choose, or are given another mission to fulfill. Providence has its own reasons for everything.

It is with our perspective that we survey the world, and our observations with an extensive view remark upon the busy scenes of crowded life. Sometimes we can find ourselves truly alone, or alone in the midst of the masses that surround our lives. The snares that cloud our human fate is found in reason that guides the stubborn choices we must make. We pierce each scene with a philosophic eye and logical mind that toys with reason and possibilities. From age to age we pass knowledge to one another, but what we do with it is our choice, to respect it or discard it to the heap of accumulated wisdom that seems no use to us. Our wit must sort this out.

We have an increasing debt to those who came before us, but only those who labor in thought and contemplate what they have learned have this novel revelation. New powers of the mind we gain received from history's sway bring us to this one conclusion. The multitude of days protract our struggle with strength and still we endure.

Any building you want to build must have a sure and certain foundation, so we still search for new knowledge with our aptitude for learning and seek out wisdom that will be the most helpful in this process of building up our mind, and its abilities.

When the mind reckons up its resources, our imagination and intelligence gain a novel source of freedom; our abilities are more than we know and long to be revealed from their concealment.

The whispers of fancy and caprice consume our attention, yet the phantoms of hope replace our deficiencies and we are lured to the study and contemplation of the facts that reveal themselves from the truth and from the similarities of that same truth.

Surrounded on every side by insurmountable summits we are destined to a journey through a labyrinth of trials, each with its own reason and consequence. The philosopher's chief amusement is to picture himself in a world he has never seen except for his rampant imagination and intelligent thinking patterns. We extend our mind unchecked, without restraint — frequently, wildly, and menacingly.

Freedom comes with a price. Knowledge is all around us, but the importance of study and contemplation cannot be denied. The question is: How much do you really want to know? The answer may not be what you expect or want to hear, but the real truth will be known. The question is: How much do you want to know about your true nature, and the true nature of the universe? The answer is yet to be found out by science and the depths of spirituality.

Why does quantum mechanics really matter? It doesn't, but the world and the explanation of it depend on our perspective and the understanding we have achieved up to this particular point in time. We are faced with an acute observance of the facts reality shows us, but there is more to reality than can be known by the human mind. Let us remember that the unknown is greater than the known. Time isn't what it seems to be; there is more to know than our intelligence can perceive, or conceive, or that reality reveals to our senses. There are so many things that are so amazing we cannot even understand their complexity. The regular simplicity of things is compounded by the complexity we make of them. Only twelve men walked on the moon. All the rest of human kind can only imagine what it must have been like for those special twelve.

There is a story and a drama in every event and circumstance we live through. The real story is what our mind goes through besides the facts that present themselves to us by our observation and perspective on the human level.

We must have an analytical mind to even make some sense of what we are and what the world, the universe, really is. There is just so much more to know than we can realize or even imagine, so we study and equip ourselves with knowledge and wisdom creating our own individual genius.

The stream of plenty has many tributaries scattered throughout the world constantly flowing, just waiting for discovery. We live in a world where many parts are never seen, entangled in the imaginary thoughts we create for our own amusement, which as well includes the metaphysical world. We can only have ideas and notions about them in our singular conceptions.

The effort to reconcile our notions about the complexities of nature may take a lifetime, but the immediate conclusions we reach seem to be sufficient to get us through the labyrinth of our own thoughts. If we put the mystery aside we engage the mind with notions of genius tried by adversity. We busy ourselves with so much that we forget our solitude and imagine ourselves inside our own mind looking out into the utter chaos with fearful anxiety.

Though disaster dogs us, it is our responsibility to endure and move on with our individual lives. Even the wisest are unparalleled with scholarship and criticism. The immediacy that promotes pensive reflection becomes the solstice of higher thinking that leads us to concentrate on the metaphysical and philosophical matters that affect our inner being the most.

Conscious of our own play and thoughts, we reconcile ourselves to ourselves. We consider others' opinions and speculations and reach for the stars in our own way. I have seen the sunrise and sunset now for fifty-two years and still have questions and few answers. My original curiosity has not been abated, though my inquiry and endeavors have supplied me with a source of inexhaustible material for the passing of knowledge to one another. Many of those who labor in thought are unrecognized. In Thomas Gray's "Elegy" one insight can be observed and confirmed: "Full many a flower is born to blush unseen, And waste its sweetness on the desert air." The range of persuasive skill runs from embarrassing and painful failures. What makes the difference is our attitude towards the world and ourselves and the characteristics of the persons in their audience. The skills, techniques, and things to watch are within the grasp of anyone who wants to achieve them. Ideas are indeed quite fragile and need more care in unwrapping them than articles of commerce. But few realize this, and for this reason we are given to pass knowledge to one another with wit and skill.

Ideas may very well be alive within our own intelligence; but for them to truly come to life they need to be shared and transferred to others to gain any substantial worth. Though old ways linger on, once past the generational overlap in society a new age is at its dawn, and today is only the beginning of tomorrow.

We can distinguish between an interest in understanding the world and an interest in our understanding the world. The same applies to ourselves. In this case the perception takes on a deeper significance. There are logical relations among these ideas. There is a difference we must distinguish between what is known and what we think we know; similarly, we may look for the characteristics and qualities, the qualifications, that make an idea relevant or irrelevant to any concept that we question.

A huge range of the human experience is understood in terms of various concepts. Our explanations have many and various certain variables. At first an explanation does not attempt to dispute or add to any facts, it is only an examination. This part of philosophy is our main concern: the examination of the facts with sincere speculation.

Whoever reflects on what passes in their own mind cannot miss the notions and ideas of that reflection. Quite apart from its intrinsic worth, however, an attempt to understand the concept of mind and other mental concepts is useful for those who are interested in understanding the mind itself and its usefulness given to thought.

When we seek out knowledge we need to find wisdom that promotes its immediacy in the mind. One does not dig far beneath the surface to be enchanted by this newfound knowledge which becomes your own personal wisdom; but further underneath the surface you will find treasures like silver, gold, and diamonds.

We need not find any over-emphasis on sentimentality and superficial aspects of the facts, but when real truth presents itself we find our own genius. Though there is a variation in the parts of the whole one must not forget to remember everything is interconnected in some way or fashion by the principles of nature.

We need to distinguish between the light and shade of our knowledge and its black brightness that of course is its own conflict and contradictions. We need to reason our own context of thought, the degree of sensation it brings out, and the intensity of our sensibility. We must be able to recognize the structural changes in society; as well we must be able to recognize the immediate index to a changing perception. We must be able to provide specific operational wisdom for all the contingencies of life, and that comes from our actual accumulation of knowledge and wisdom.

The young student today grows up in an electronically configured world. It is not of wheels but of circuits, not of fragments but of integral patterns.

Old ways linger on, but change is slow and constant. Each human being is a more complex structure than any social system to which they belong. In our quest for truth we come to respect certitude. Certitude is the belief that we are absolutely right. Certainty is the external, unattainable truth which has not the least possible chance of being proven wrong at any time, though we still strive to attain its essential concept.

Albert Einstein once said: "No amount of experimentation will ever prove me completely right, but one new fact can prove me completely wrong."

In the science of passing knowledge to one another, exposure of ideas and proposals to other minds allows many other facets to be seen from different points of view. Naturally since the dawn of philosophical thought the mind has been a favorite field for speculation; there is probably no major philosopher who has not advanced some views on this topic.

To examine the experimental basis of a scientific theory is a matter for scientists; to examine its conceptual foundations, however, is to philosophize, which is full of analogy, metaphor, and speculation of things that have no actual proof, like the study of theology and metaphysics.

Your imagination prevails over your skill, but all the while you get better at applying what you've learned. The life devoted to knowledge silently passes away, except for what was passed along to another remains in their memory, which may be a constant thought.

Once I found the delight of knowledge and felt the pleasure of intelligence, invention came to me like at no other time in my life. It was and still is the invention of thought that leads me on. At first, being in possession of our faculties, we find strength in our invention and imagination, and then elegance and refinement of expression comes with the wind of thought and contemplation. This brought me new purpose and the spread of my attention has widened; no kind of knowledge would be overlooked.

The activity in my life has made me acquainted with diversity of opinions and abstract speculations about metaphysical notions. From these I add to my own treasures and resources and bring myself to a new and bold interpretation and understanding of human life and the human mind.

Today, more than at any in the past, people of all conditions, and abilities, are eager for ideas and greater wisdom. They are more willing than ever to listen to those who offer the slightest chance of satisfying their need for inspiration. Our innate need to find explanation and understand our changing environment demands that we form attitudes towards this overwhelming flood of information.

Everyone still seems to feel that they have an obligation to improve themselves, their family, and the condition of their life. It is undoubtedly an innate trait for even those who have little ambition or motivation to find within themselves that self-improvement stands its ground under all circumstances and conditions. Our primitive urge leads us on in this direction, even with unemployment, as our basic needs must still be met. Our lifestyles may change but our optimism cannot be shaken.

The commingling of problems and opportunities is characteristic of those periods in history called Golden Ages; but the gold seems to have turned to lead, and our inherent optimism seems to be wavering in its firmness. We live in a time of great contemplation of the facts and are in desperate need for answers.

Great works are performed not by strength, but by perseverance, enduring hardship for the sake of the great reward of leisure and time for contemplative thought.

In the pursuit of newfound knowledge and the discovery of things and ideas yet to be known hiding in the crags of the mountains of ancient works, the mind finds fulfillment and pleasure in learning. The satisfying act of just knowing that something can be known, experienced,

and achieved is a great and noble accomplishment. This one aspect of life makes it all the worthwhile for living.

The real voyage of discovery consists not in seeking new notions but in having a new perspective to view the old ones. Our belief at the beginning of a possible endeavor is the one thing that insures the successful outcome of our perseverance of the venture. Our thoughts, actions, and reactions take their hue from the heart, as landscapes have their variety from the light that illuminates them. Enlightenment acts the same on the spirit radiating its luminescence.

The fortress of our intellect rebels when our lower needs have not been met. Once our survival is secured we can then procure through our liberty our higher cultural needs through our leisure.

Has wisdom the strength to arm the heart against calamity? Consider that eternal things are naturally variable, but truth and reason are always the same. Recommendations come from both sides of the street where rich and poor gather in the market place of life.

What can hinder the satisfaction or intercept the expectations of him whose abilities are adequate to reason the logic of consequences, who sees with his own eyes the whole circuit of influence, and who chooses by his own knowledge the tempered way of real happiness in the comfort of his own wisdom?From the mind we discover the heart and from the heart we discover true joy and find a deeper satisfaction. The more we inquire the less we can resolve, because as one question is answered the factors that surround it are as well-inquired into and just beg more questioning. Through deliberation and delay, prudence prescribes to irrevocable choice. Once one has made a choice and decision we must bear the consequences and have no regret from our affirmation of that choice. Whether by emotion or opportunity we can be certain that we create our own destiny through what experiment and experience teaches as we apply reason to our logic.

The comprehensiveness of knowledge comes from our adventure in learning, from the basis of our elemental thoughts, and from the passing of knowledge to one another. When our opinions are fixed and our habits established, only our wisdom can save us.

Long customs are not easily broken; those that attempt to change the course of their own life often come upon chances and opportunities that require deliberate contemplation, deliberation, and reflection.

How can we do for others what we cannot do for ourselves? It is through the passing of knowledge to one another that we affect another's being. Stubborn as some can be, there are still those who can change and accept change as a part of life. There are thousands of disputes reason can never decide. The choice upon an answer must be our own thoughtful consideration.

Minds susceptible of new impressions are most likely to make use of experience and wisdom collected in our adventure in learning. Nature sets her gifts at the right hand and left; only one can be taken. There is always our choice that makes the difference in our decisions, which all have their own consequences.

To know anything we must know the effects they may bring to our attention and not just the cause of those effects. All affect us in some way. We can note that at many intervals in time the world made great steps in changing. The variable factors are too numerous to even count, but can be conceived. The year One A.D. changed the world in a miraculous and fantastic way, for example. We cannot change the history of the past nor re-write what had happened. The only thing we can positively do is to alter our perspective on those events, conditions, and situations.

From that one day forward humanity had to look at life itself and consider a new age of thought. The metaphysical had come to terms with nature and became a realized part of nature still being discovered.

The present state of things is not the consequence of the former but the certain way of thinking we bring to ourselves. When the mind or imagination is struck with any uncommon event the next transition of an active mind is to the means by which we use contemplation to enlarge our comprehension of new ideas surrounding the event. Perhaps to recover some lost memory or to envision a new dream to strive for. Very little is actually injured by time because time heals everything.

The hunger of imagination which preys incessantly upon our mind must always be appeased by some enjoyment our intellect brings to the imagination by its own empowerment.

Wealth is nothing but as it is bestowed, and knowledge is nothing but as it is communicated and understood with all its applications and accessories. So we have found the true reason for passing knowledge to one another: to communicate wisdom for each one of humanity to consider its value and worth to their own position in life and aptitude for learning and applying that learning.

The state of mind oppressed with a sudden calamity is like that of the fabulous inheritance of the newly created earth who upon the first night had thought that day would never come again; but with the new dawn and day break were delighted with a knowledge not beyond surprise or expectation. With a delightful anticipation the light illuminated the earth with revelation and enlightenment.

The continual flux of change brings just the same to the mind except we gain experience and knowledge with each passing moment.

Distance has the same effect on the mind, as on the eye, and we glide along the stream of time approaching the horizon only to find it renewed along the way, adding to our perspective and continued thought of the distance we create from our ability to conceive what we perceive.

One must always be sure to recognize the differences between conceiving and perceiving; the difference may result in obscure conclusions and only bring to mind further questions with the anticipation of greater answers.

At times we can turn our mind from remembrance yet we resolve to never forget because of the importance of memory within our own intelligence. To the philosopher integrity without knowledge is weak and useless, and knowledge without integrity is dangerous.

I thought myself honored among thinkers who have ideas the likes of mind and in thought as a virtue, all the while conceiving new notions about the principles of thought and thinking.

Recollections of a Philosopher

Only the eternal can divert us from our mortality. In recollection of the faculties of the mind and the ability to utilize it one must find pleasure in their own thoughts and must conceive for themselves the possibilities of all their ideas. So in effect, they must labor in thought and actualize their creative intellect.

The mind dances from scene to scene and unites all pleasure in all varieties of combinations to its own satisfaction. In time some particular train of thought and ideas fixes the attention and recurs constantly to the favorite conception and feasts upon reality as well as dreams, continued in thoughts of reality and the existence of the metaphysical within that same reality.

Everything supplies us with reason for contemplation and for stimulating reflection of our inward conditions and outward views of the world as it really is. My retrospective of life recalls to my attention significant discoveries about myself and my worthiness. Though there are many times of neglect, much time squandered upon trifles, and much time lost spent in idleness — though idle time is good for thought — my mind is burdened with no heavy crime or regret, and therefore I compose myself to tranquility and endeavor to keep my heart serene.

Therefore I am resolved to happiness beyond compare and am content to live as I do, in spite of circumstances unforeseen, in search of knowledge to add to my own wisdom and to pass along to others as I see fit, at least to those whom I deem able to respond. As for myself I will continue to labor in thought and come up with some reasonable conclusions and answers to my own questions.

At times one must open their heart to the influences of the light which, from time to time, breaks in upon you. This enlightenment encourages and brings serenity to a heart filled with passion, but let us not forget there will be good times and bad that come with our passions and secluded emotions we share only with ourselves. The one we call Creator is good about grace and mercy, but still we have the responsibility to make things happen on our own.

At times one must think about opening up their heart, with emotion and passion, controlled with the intellect, to the influences of the light which, from time to time, breaks in upon you. This enlightenment and added insight into the way things really are encourages and brings serenity to a heart filled with the passion and emotion that sometimes overwhelm us, disregarding all the influence our intellect provides. We ought to keep our intelligence reigning over our emotions, all the while storing up our wisdom and subduing the passion and emotion that get us in trouble. In this state of life we bring upon ourselves consequences that have no reason because we let emotion guide us. If we let our wisdom guide us in the anticipation of change, the change is nothing more than a convenience of nature, even though we make of it more than it actually is. The world is nowhere near exhausted, and tomorrow always brings a certain newness in the adventure in learning we see on a regular and daily basis in our elemental thoughts. Several factors have produced the hunger for intellectual stimulus. Perhaps the greatest of all is the rapid communications of the internet and cell phones, as well as transportation. Intellectual activity is a universal phenomenon. As knowledge increases all we can do is to keep up with its various factors. Perhaps it's like the automatic updates on my laptop. We have to constantly tune-up our mind, perspective, and thinking to keep up to date with the latest information, and our awareness has to be keen and sharp with our inner thoughts and outer view of the world. This is what we can call laboring in thought — the prime mover of the activity of a philosopher.

We are living in the age of Anxiety and Fear because of the unknown factors of economic conditions beyond our control. It affects our mind and is causing widespread calamity and affliction. Our innate need to understand is beyond our comprehension; all we know is survival, endurance, and meeting the challenge.

Our changing environment demands that we form attitudes towards this overwhelming flood of information. We cannot deny its being there because reality demands its acknowledgment. The burdens of present uncertainties and the drastic scope of alternatives that have become apparent in our time oppress the minds of many and have a subduing effect on those great thinkers we depend on for solutions to the answers of our questions.

Explorers some centuries from now will survey and look back on our time as a golden age, like others, with distress and fulfillment contradicting one another, causing civil unrest and the personal fear and anxiety the minority of us are going through because of the economic upheaval affecting the majority of unemployed middle class Americans.

Though we feel that some kind of optimism is possible the times when it is not present gets to be the most depressing and creates a feeling of despondency that is hard to rid ourselves from.

How to achieve this optimism seems to be the relevant question, but the variables abound. Accepting rejection only makes the job search more challenging. Failure is not an option, and I will meet the challenge straight on as most of us will have to do. "Deal with it," they say; but it's easier said than done.

The ideas themselves existing in the thoughts of the mind make the simplicity a complex matter of decisions and choices. I think it's all just a matter of considering consequences and actions from a concentrated effort in contemplation. Risk is one thing and chance is another; together both rely on logical deduction and reason.

Our only refuge is the solitary confinement of the sanctuary of our home or favorite place of rest where the monochrome contemplation of the mind takes on its hue and color. We cannot underestimate our opponent, the world, and we must survive and endure, compromising all along the way to the best of our abilities to secure the unrelenting pleasure we at least can find and eliminating as much pain as is possible, assuring our rest and contentment and peace of mind.

Clear objectives focus our energy and give each part of the mind its duties and responsibilities. Sometimes we must even focus on our conscience to connect with our inner self and the spiritual side of nature's pure reality. Imaginative and unexpected deployment of reason unbalances the opposition and contingencies absorb counterattacks as afterthoughts. In the process of our thinking it is important sometimes to remember that when man's desire gets the best of him, the rational element of the mind is reduced to a simple standby while desire and passion reign fully with their own power.

Since a man may not only find himself drawn one way by desire and another by reason he may be also a prey to conflicting alternatives and remain undecided because of his own knowledge and wisdom. The final stand is met by his determination and resistance due to the choices and decisions based on the resulting consequences considered in the spirit of conscience and intelligent logic of a reasoning mind.

Our traditional values have changed; we live in a new world. Nothing is secure anymore, and our moral and ethical values have changed along with our social and political values. The age of a new reality is here upon us, and to cope and endure has become standard protocol and policy. Our addictions have overtaken us and become the norm and status quo. There is no turning back; all we can do is to look back, learn our lessons, and apply our knowledge to our present conditions and situations.

In this critique of the mind and its thoughts and processes of thinking we assemble and examine ideas that make the mind a cabinet or chamber full of psychical entities that are interrelated in certain ways and function as a complete, united, faculty.

The actions of the mind can be compared to the blowing of soap bubbles: growing, floating off into the distance, carried by the wind and then popping, disappearing into nothingness. But we remember.

Within this theme of passing knowledge to one another, the greatest part of mankind owes its knowledge to the information of others, which we assemble into our own wisdom.

Wonder is a pause of reason which lasts only while the understanding is fixed on some single idea; but when it divides itself it becomes entangled with reality. Only then is progress made equal to the labor of enquiry and invigorated with confidence and astonishment of the heights to be reached with our creative intelligence.

Consciousness is not able to escape its limitations, but in recognizing that fact it is able to transcend them. The widest excursions of the mind are short flights frequently repeated until the final achievement is some sort of definite comprehension and understanding. The proper ambition of the philosopher is to enlarge the boundaries of knowledge and pass it along for others to evaluate and stimulate further introspection of the reality they create for themselves inside the greater reality nature provides.

After thousands of years of explosion in our civilization we've reached the stage of implosion. We've extended ourselves about as far as we could, and now the world is collapsing in upon itself. I've experienced this for myself from the present economic conditions now alarming our great country, as well as the effects it has been having on a worldwide scale. When the money is gone, it's gone. What has become of us? Perhaps we just got to big too fast? The effects of this implosion have come down to the personal level of our citizens. The government has been helping the rich while the middle class and poor are getting the crunch of this economic and political manipulation.

Sometimes in the pursuit of knowledge we have to go down a path already trampled and beaten down to find some relic yet undiscovered. At other times we must travel the road less used and discover along the way some new found treasures. Either way we must follow others' examples and come to new conclusions or blaze out on our own in search of an idea still concealed from thought and bring it to realization for further examination.

Let us not forget to continue to follow our heart and dreams. We can meet the challenges ahead of us straight on with our wit, skill, and elementary reason. Though we challenge our own logic, the insight we gain from learning and experience can become beneficial.

Experience is our primary teacher. As we live we learn, and the longer we live the more knowledge we add to our own wisdom.

You can bring a teacher to a student, but the student must be willing to devote their attention to the principles of learning and discovery.

Wit, like other things, is subject to a changing environment. Even as our environment changes we have to create for ourselves a new and bold certain way of thinking to solve our most relevant problems at hand, mainly protecting our survival and finding new ways to cope with the changes that affect us most personally.

Either something new has to be learned or something already learned has to be retrieved by recollection or inquiry. This is the work of the philosopher who labors in thought, one who examines life, and all that it consists of, and then re-examines it over and over again in search for some absolute truth.

Great labor directed by great ability is never wholly lost; there is always an unexpected truth to be found in contemplation.

The pleasures of the mind imply something sudden and unexpected; that which elevates must always bring the surprise of enlightenment. What is perceived by slow degrees is truth that always remains truth, and reason by the same degree remains reason.

They have an intrinsic and unalterable value and constitute that intellectual gold which defies distinction. But gold may be so concealed only a chemist can recover it, and sense may be so hidden in unrefinement that only the words of a philosopher can reveal it from its concealment. Even the alchemist finds the inner gold of the spirit like physical gold; and human mortality finds bits of deity in the simplest and common human being.

Excellence is an exceptional skill acquired with diligence, patience, and endurance and comes from our innermost ambition and personal motivation to excel at all we attempt to achieve.

It is something we all are inclined towards, but few ever reach the goal without persistence, an aptitude for learning, and applying those skills they acquire.

Presentation of an idea is similar in many ways to fighting a battle. There are of course rules of strategy and tactics that fill shelves of books, but mere knowledge of rules does not win wars.

Training teachers the rules only provides guidelines; experience teaches the exceptions. Gaining experience takes time, and with our developing skills we gain proficiency at the task while the increase in knowledge brings our intellectual development to its heights. This same result comes from the passing of knowledge to one another.

Man is not only a rational animal but an emotional one as well. Our purpose in what we endeavor has roots in our own feelings and emotions about any idea that crosses our mind. Our intellect addresses the logic of our emotions at every cornerstone in our life experience.

The final measure is up to us and our will, to know when the time comes to address a situation and its conditions with all three factors: Emotion, Reason, and Common Sense.

We are not so far removed from our ancestors that we have completely abandoned their ways. Sometimes we reason forward, understanding consequences, and sometimes we reason backward from the effect to the causes. It is in our inherent nature to think about our own thinking and processes of thought.

Common Sense is the conservative force in human existence. It is validated on a regular basis throughout our lives. As our intelligence grows with our wit and skills we increase its value and worth. The training we get reinforces the structure of our patterns of thinking that our intelligence depends upon. This notion raises the foundation of our thinking and provides the necessary structure for the faculty of the mind to be successful at every endeavor we strive for.

We can move mountains and cross great plains with the increase in our knowledge; and this forces us to depend on others even as we depend on ourselves. Common Sense is more valuable to those who labor in thought, considering alternatives and perspectives, than to those who just think and react from events and causes.

Where imagination is called to the aid of reason, thoughts which are occasionally called forth could only be produced by the creativity held within the faculties of our mind, to the highest degree. Our unlimited curiosity sparks reason to find its own validity and sport the wide regions of possibility.

Reality is just too narrow a subject for genius because its own intrigue surpasses where imagination soars within the heights of our intelligence. When knowledge is accumulated and impregnated in the mind, fermented by study and contemplation, and exalted by imagination, wisdom becomes our genius, an excellence without exception.

As for opportunities they may vary with external events, invention, new knowledge, and discoveries that alter our view of what we could previously plan for before opportunity rises to the occasion.

So I take this opportunity to relate a story once told to me by a philosopher/theologian who by chance became a good friend some ages ago. It is a story of mystical and mysterious quality one ought to have a chance to consider in the passing of knowledge to one another.

The primary concept of the story is that something rather than nothing exists solely in the mind. It concerns a time before anything at all, when the only thing that existed was a thought in the midst of nothing, where our imagination soars freely with our creative intelligence.

Long ago, so very long ago there was a time when something was and nothing was not. Nothing existed except that something. It was this great spirit that made light shine out of darkness. The nothing resisted but was overpowered because of the significance it brought to thought. From that same thought it created itself, the only thing that could do that. It then thought of the Author of Nature who would create everything else, and rested itself in the mind of this Author whom we would call the Maker and Creator of everything but itself. It became the conscience of the Creator just as we, ourselves, have a conscience that we believe is our spirit.

It is reasonable to say that God does have a conscience. God's own morals and ethics are the most fair and just. These qualities can only come from the mind and conscience. From our conscience comes the soul and spirit as we know them. Since we were created in the image of God, God must have these same qualities.

Nothing is a great emptiness; something is the fulfillment of that nothing. So the mind is full of something, thoughts and memories which in the realm of mind are significant somethings and not nothing because of their quality of substance and essence. The power of thought cannot be denied. An idea cannot exist without its counterpart, the mind, and a mind cannot exist without a shelter for its existence.

This one principle becomes a permanent Basis for our Elemental Thoughts. The slightest thought gives the mind its motion and empowers it to the process of thinking. Just the same is the motion of the thoughts of the one we call God where the Holy Spirit acts as the mind of this same one we call Author of Nature and Creator of everything besides man's own inventions. Just the same, our being rests in our mind as does God's own rest in the Great Spirit.

I was reading some of John Keats' work one day and subtle parts of the poem "I stood tip-toe upon a little hill" came to my attention: "I stood tip-toe upon a little hill, the air was cooling, and so very still . . . And many pleasures to my vision started. . . His mighty voice came upon the gale . . . So that we feel uplifted from the world . . . On the smooth wind to the realms of wonderment. " These lines of verse ring true in my own mind, and I give thought to them often in my amazement of this glorious universe in spite of all the conditions that bear down upon us.

To such an end it is that I aspire. The deeper we delve into the mystery of life, the more knowledge we gain to fulfill our own satisfaction of understanding; and still so much remains a great mystery. Perhaps some day, or night, revelation will come and bring with it insight and enlightenment.

By the means of constant re-evaluation of our thoughts we bring simplicity to the complexity of our thoughts. As a matter of belief we set aside our convictions and bring to the open clearing of our mind some well-defined compromises in our reflections.

We are always testing the bounds of reality with our fantasy and succumbing to illusion, bearing in our mind as something to be challenged and overcome, knowing that we are alive in a living dream waiting for the storyline to shatter the illusion and bring us back to face hurting reality with some kind of sympathy without apathy for finding happiness, still within our present conditions.

Isn't it ironic, don't you think, how people derive joy from pain, all the time questioning without finding acceptable answers? We look for answers to our questions where none can be found; yet we just seem to believe in some unquestionable truth that has no real explanation.

Though the idea that form follows function has its own relativity, one must find some comfort with the inner essence and the essence of the surrounding environment. We are necessarily adept at keeping our inner mind secure while finding security and certainty in our place in the world within the universe.

Purpose is the greatest influence on form; inventiveness and taste come next. Experience and insight know no boundaries. Here we find the real foundation for the passing of knowledge to one another: to expand our creativity with the knowledge we gain along life's great journey.

It is one thing to write because there is something which the mind wishes to express, and another to solicit the imagination because the mind requires something to be written of passion and emotion. So as I continue in this endeavor closer to the end than the beginning my passion and emotion for understanding challenges the theme "passing knowledge to one another." Consider the shifting sands of governance and our autonomy, and the conclusion comes to mind that providence always makes a way.

What we have to do here is to tether the intellect to a human scale, and others will accompany you on the ascent to new mental heights once thought possible, but not probable. But with a little help from my friends and history it is an achievable goal.

Let our minds measure and realize what they can of the infinite and mysterious and bring it into the finiteness of our present thoughts. The two worlds, one of worldly knowledge and the other of spiritual wisdom, make our genius what it is: pure contemplation of our thoughts and the patterns of our own thinking reaching into the depths of insight and revelation from the proper use of our intelligent wisdom.

The probable is a curious thing and the possible captures our attention entertaining the differences in the explanations we come across as well as our perpetual configuring of our own. The Creator does not appear partial in the distribution of wisdom; only those who labor in thought realize their potential from the motivation and ambition to learn and communicate that learning for the benefit of civilization and humanity as a whole made up of its specific parts.

Wisdom always tends to some end; but with regard to man, a frequent reflection has an effect of revelation in the midst of facts and fantasy. Think how often we are carried away with a continual thought until its final release comes in some specific way.

There is more to life than it seems. Not only are there lessons to be learned but the details of life have more to them than we already know. It is our constant probing that brings the micro and macro inspection to the heights of realization. Just the same, there is more to ourselves than we actually want to admit. Our constant inspection brings the details of life into the open. From there we are brought to new conclusions and a more definite understanding of life as we are of our own being.

A Philosophy of Man

William Cowper (1731-1800) summarized a thought about our intelligence that goes far when considered: "Knowledge is proud that he has learned so much, Wisdom is humble that he knows no more."

The universe is a system whose very essence consists in subordination — a scale of beings descending by degrees, from infinite perfection to absolute nothing.

This nothing, on the quantum level, has more to it than we all could imagine. It is a fantastic something. Just the same is our finite universe that expands so far we only think it is infinite.

We can consider ourselves closer to the infinite than one could believe because of our intelligence to know the difference between our mortal finite end and the infinite substance of our spirit and soul, which only our intelligence knows.

There is of course the opinion of an infinite property our being has: in principle, our spiritual inner nature. Our existence is not without this sustaining empowerment. Our understanding is less than perfect certainty but accrues to the heights of the universe where no finite end can even be found. But some day we all will find some kind of truth that we can be absolutely sure of.

Our life experience is just the passing of time and the passing of knowledge to one another. Each of us has our own lessons to be learned, and we have to compromise the conclusions we arrive at.

Every reason which can be brought to prove that there are beings of every possible sort, including Angels, will prove there is the greatest possible probability to acknowledge their existence.

Our relative imperfectability falls into this category, some better or worse than others; we just cannot deny anything. Whether due to misfortune or greater skill we rise and fall by chance or coincidence, not due totally to our own powers; providence has its own role in our singular and personal lives. The means of character, ambition, and motivation bring us to challenge the most common events of our days. Our natural state in this world has some cause and we only experience the effects of those greater causes.

This system seems to be a concession of reason to the variety of people we've found in social and cultural humanity throughout the civilizations across the world.

Though we all try to find our center, just who could tell where that may be? Even the highest being, mortal as we can be, has often been observed to be at an infinite distance just below the realm of infinity; though heaven is at our doorstep we still know not where the threshold may be. Just as well, the lowest being must be at the infiniteness where nothing at all can be found.

To these meditations humanity has been made unequal; those who labor in thought know the difference. No created wisdom can give an adequate answer to the condition of humanity except what we create for ourselves. All we can do is to suffer the consequences for our actions and endure making way for change that comes so slowly it can hardly be realized. We grow old and everything else just gets old. A paradigm example can only be between a rock and the human mind. So often we challenge ourselves to know more or choose to not know at all.

Notice that intelligence can never eliminate all doubt, but it attempts to minimize the total uncertainty by any and every means. It uses the most reliable data available and checks it with rumors, observations of others, or anything that can help fill the vacant areas of knowledge. Its final conclusion is always a judgment, never the clinical certainty of a formula or sound reasoning of just one other source of information.

An analogy can be made by referencing the score of a symphony; though the score presents a wonderful piece of music it is up to the musicians to play and interpret the score to make a charming and aesthetic musical presentation. We must always consider the human factor. Machines fail but humans always make mistakes.

Though we may conceive the possibility of our self-sureness, one ought not to eliminate doubt while the possibility of the probable presents itself at times the sureness of our convictions must have a standard beyond reproach.

In earlier and simpler days, one brilliant man could do all the calculations in his head, but in our present times we need the assistance of technology. Our concept of simplicity has gone astray. The complexity of our present condition has compounded all of our calculations. The clear and present danger that faces us is that we might have gotten too big for our own good.

The road we travel these days is more perilous than at any other time in history. We are sacredly pulled along in history with all kinds of dependencies. Not a one of us can be declared independent. Though we act in the name of autonomy providence will eventually have its way.

As we progress along with the rites of passage there will ultimately be unexpected events that change our course and plans. Contingencies must be made; alternative methods facing change only add color to our lives. The one fortunate thing about unexpected change is that we accommodate it with our ingenuity, creativeness, and intelligent innovation.

Even the longest journey begins with just a single step. The common man wants simplicity of ideas to match his thoughts. He rightly resists when being steamrolled by insolent high priests who insist on change that is fashioned in a way that brings relief to a few and leaves the many to fend for themselves.

Every human being has some creative potential. Everyone does this in their own unique ways in order to survive. Some retain this ability to seek and encounter new knowledge with the wonder and delight of a young child. Others resist and fall by the way side. The first are high-voltage idea generators. The second are merely stimulated from action-response to avoid boredom. The term "serendipity" entered our language as a description of this phenomenon. We are indebted to the English writer Horace Walpole for this very expressive use of language to pass knowledge to one another.

I've said it before: life passes us very fast and if we don't stop once in a while it will just pass us by. In our passage through time we often think of the reality of our thoughts and come upon misconceptions or alternative understandings from our perspective of the land, in our mind, that approaches the horizon because as we near it, it moves from us, always changing.

Like seeing a rainbow, you turn and it has moved, or you stare and it changes form. So it is really our perspective and understanding that varies our interpretation of not only life but of ourselves.

You may have overlooked the brief periods in which you are conscious without thought that are naturally occurring and are a spontaneously curiosity in your life. Your perceptions become crystal clear as if insight and enlightenment have come to you.

To the mind, all is not significant. What we dwell on arises in our span of attention. We ought to become at ease with this sense of not knowing, because providence will always have its way and allow these shallow interrupted times to come about for our rediscovery of what we make important to us.

When you become at ease with not knowing you surpass the mind and live in constructive awe and imagination. A deeper knowing is the non-conceptual ideas that arise out of that state.

Poverty comes to us in all kinds. The worst of all is the poverty of the mind due to the actual lack of interest in knowing. There are so many just content with not knowing and are satisfied with the mediocrity of life without excelling from their own ambition and curiosity.

The want for riches of material things has less importance than the want for riches of the mind. The want for genius is a hard road and those less likely to pursue knowledge fall by the wayside.

There is an unlimited level of want and desire within us. We have to deal with it regularly. It's always better to have the intellect over the emotion, because if emotion gets above the intellect curious problems develop and emerge as conflicts of interest. Who knows one's self better than that person? There comes a time when we have to let go and other times we just have to hold on.

We involve ourselves in the busy pursuits of a scrambling world. The want of knowledge is the only opiate capable of bringing our insensibility to certain sensibility. We find logic in the most illogical. We make sense where none can be found. We are truly a creative intelligent race of beings in a civilization full of uncertainty, anxiety, and stress for our own survival and peace of mind. Repose doesn't come easily. Nobody said it would. We have this certain need to find out for ourselves just what we come to conclusions about by the rites of passage in the course of our life.

Divine knowledge is instinctive and different than knowledge acquired through study and education. It comes to us by insight and comes as quick as lightning flashes. We hear its roaring thunder echoing in our mind and throughout our being.

Life is more than a realization in the mind. We sense life within our own intelligence from sincere reflection and contemplation and make of it what we will. As for our will, we empower it from the being of our spirit and realize it through our awareness of our consciousness of it.

A little learning goes a long way. With our achievement in learning comes the responsibility of applying that accumulated and accrued wisdom. The more we add to it the greater our genius becomes. Of course some instruction is always a good thing, but we have to have an aptitude for learning and do the work required of us on our own by motivated ambition and the will to succeed.

In our everyday thinking we use a certain set of concepts that in different ways involves the notion of attention. Our attention is what keeps us focused on a specific idea or task at hand. We cannot take an interest in, enjoy, or think of anything without at least momentary attention. Consider for just a moment a drop of water falling into a still pool. That single drop creates a ripple effect, and the concentric circles expand, like a thought in the mind, finally reaching the shore and the pool becomes still once again, opening the way for more ideas to stimulate the mind.

Don't search for opportunity in the distance but recognize it right where you are, here in the moment of your own tranquility. Awareness, consciousness, and noticing are all closely related to this one notion. We cannot adequately describe the process of paying attention without referring to the object of our attention.

This characteristic is the most common to the human element. We notice what captures our attention and are conscious of what holds us to it. So when we pay attention to something it holds our interest; when we do not, we become careless and reckless, allowing our emotions to overpower our intellect. This is one common factor of all creatures.

We ought to consider the conceptual suppositions that shape our thoughts and patterns of thinking. The reformulations of basic principles conform to quite a different picture of reality as it is commonly known. We sometimes make an extensive approximation to actual reality, but become along the way overwhelmed with passion and emotion making reality into an illusion of the mind foregoing reality as it actually is. Here the simplicity of it all, life, becomes more complex considering naturally occurring anomalies and variations in the natural order of things in our overall perspective.

When we sincerely repose ourselves we can bring to the surface of our consciousness what has been latent and dormant in our unconscious. Easily recallable knowledge and memories are the first to surface. Secondly, the stable thoughts stored in a pre-conscious state in the mind are unveiled or retrieved from concealment. The storehouse of our knowledge and wisdom can be found within our intelligent spirit. When demanded to arise these thoughts rise to the surface of our attention for contemplation. A hallmark of mental activity is its purposiveness — its goal-seeking character of thinking, dreaming, and remembering.

As one considers thought we should not forget the mind's abilities of recognition, conception, judgment, and attention. Though what we think comes from either inner or outer stimulus, it is the quality of thought that becomes our genius.

The magnificence of a house is always a conception of the one dwelling in it, who calls it their sanctuary and home. The same conception of the magnificence of the universe adds to the ideal of a Supreme Being, or Creator, who we believe is the Author and constructor of the magnificence the universe holds with our own sanctuary or home planet Earth.

Within our mind is that spark of the Creator which gives us a sense of magnificence with our intelligent and creative imagination, and our logical reasoning powers to make conclusions about our judgments.

In all this, there is nothing that can silence enquiry of curiosity or calm our doubt and uncertainty.

In deep space nothing is either high or low. If the event horizon of a black hole does exist then whatever crosses the threshold has no way of escaping and is ultimately drawn into its center, forever. This one idea is not only a brilliant observation but an absorbing notion that draws its respect from the power of a star collapsing in upon itself. Just like the supernova of an exploding star the implosion may very well have the same power held within its nature.

The question still remains: what is on the other side? And so the same question arises when we think of the spiritual side of nature. The consistency of thought approaches the same relevance.

Any observation is relative to the distance and size of the observer to that which is seen or noticed from our attention we give to that observation. The comprehensive universe, described as a whole, is compared to a single person in the mass of humanity.

We are a little more enlightened by a philosopher telling us where we are in the universe than a theologian reminding us who we are, how we came to be, and where we have yet to go. While having knowledge is one thing and having consciousness of that knowledge is another, we become enlightened to both from the endowment of a sense of wisdom from our Creator. We are more than an animal; we are the human race of spiritual beings.

Though the road we travel may be long and seem arduous along the way, the distance we travel brings to our attention many details that are curiosities and that lead to our destination with momentary stopping, lapse of reasoning, and a sentimentality to the joy and pain we experience in our rites of passage through time.

Philosophy gives one no special competence to understand the behavior of things and creatures beyond any competence one may possess as a parent, teacher, lawmaker, psychologist, or sociologist. Its task in this field is not to explain the behavior characteristics but to explain the different kinds of explanations that we offer to our amateur or professional capacities.

It is language and concepts in our ways of thinking that furnish the philosopher's material. We are provided by everyday language and thinking not only with the means for referring to particular factors in our explanations, but also with a number of words, ideas, and concepts whose job it is to classify different kinds of explanations and kinds of things that may on occasion occur as factors in those notions of our realizations upon our conceiving explanations.

The one who thinks indulges a curious habit of replacing an unsolved problem with a fantasy they can't get rid of, even after the problem has been solved and truth made evident. Sometimes I just have to put down my pen and think.

Shakespeare states his awareness that true social and political navigation depend upon anticipating the consequences of innovation: "The providence that's in a watchful state finds bottom in the uncomprehensive deeps, keeps pace with thought, and almost like gods does thoughts unveil in our human mind."

When I was enraptured in the description of explaining yet another thought, I have now decided in my own mind that there is relevance in the studying of dirt that covers only one third of our planet; the rest is covered with water and is still seemingly yet another realm for enquiry of both the water and the dirt it covers over. So I'm left in despair to explore only what can be humanly touched.

So I sit here at my desk with my typewriter and look out the window at the blue sky and white fluffy clouds moving north with a southern wind at their backs; my CD player on with my favorite music; a fresh cup of coffee; on the seventh day, in the third year of this work; not actually thinking, but living in a sense of wonder and amusement of the magnificence of providence.

The wind has picked up a bit; along with the fresh blooms being tossed around are my own thoughts. More than occasionally I just have to pick up my pen and write, or load a fresh paper into my typewriter and just key thoughts directly onto its surface. Sometimes it has to be by the means of my tape recorder or my laptop computer. Technology has made all the difference in the communications arts and media presentations.

Labor surely is our saving grace; it keeps us from rest and leisure. But there is more than one type of labor. The labor in thought is restful and leisurely. The labor of expression has the same quality. Actual labor in time is beneficial to not only our wallet but to our physical and emotional stability.

Labor is at the same time elevating and resourceful. It gives us worth and value. From my own experience unemployment is the most devastating factor in our society today. From my own experience my compassion goes out to those affected by this condition who are forced to the streets and the local ESC Centers across this great nation and around the world.

If God could have excused us from labor surely that same God could have exempted us from poverty; but the way of humanity is based on work and labor, on self-improvement and the quest for knowledge and securing new wisdom. Still the mind of humanity is conscious of laboring in thought and working for our own survival. Surely the poverty of mind is as bad as actual poverty, but perhaps our own ignorance can be avoided while actual poverty is just circumstance.

It takes a special turn of mind to grasp formless reality in its essential nature and to distinguish it from figments of the imagination.

Who could have imagined the way we are, and the conditions that we live in, in our present age, in the continual process of creation. What we are is an evolutionary, reactionary creature living in a revolutionary and constantly, consistently changing environment.

Life is but a succession of events, thoughts, and emotions of improving states towards the ideal; sometimes we have to go back to go forward and make mistakes, learn our lessons, to reach that ideal. But who could imagine what that ideal could be?

Our paths still go further. Human lives are born and lost along with bright clouds up there even in the night shadowing the stars and moon even when it is in the dark phase; so we have to keep ourselves in the light of revelation and enlightenment.

Her fair eyes looked through her auburn locks, wisdom did, over which the mind did often consider. Coming into the blue with all her natural light she came upon man and gave him insight to the great mysteries of nature and the mind.

She had an upcast eye, tender, pondering what would become of man without his creative intellect. We smile upon the storyteller and think what made the sage, the muse, the poet tell his own interpretation of the story of life.

From out of the middle air where time knew no measure came thoughts of speculation; without doubt, but with certainty surely he the stranger to this world broke his own mortal bars and came to know not only his own spirit but the spirit of the world.

The instability of human life is necessary to our condition. If it were not for want, desire, and need, the only thing left for us would be the fulfillment of our aesthetic creativity, which of course would make it our highest goal and achievement. Without work for leisure life would simply be a compilation of our moments of tiresome labor. The fortunate thing of leisure is the chance and time for remembrance of thoughts and insight into our dreams. Life moves us on and we have no choice but to keep pace.

It is the cherishing that we do that endears life to us. We have no essential cause but to survive to meet our own curiosity. The question is: What will tomorrow bring? So we endure and wait.

It is the enduring, persevering, and cherishing that we do that gives life its flavor and hue. The question to the philosopher is that how can we imagine and conceive, even perceive, we are going forward when we are just going in circles around and in between circles of greater and lesser proportion.

We notice that the earth revolves around itself and the sun, and even the sun and moon revolve. The greater concept is that the entire galaxy and universe revolve around the great spirit that centers itself in the midst of everything even as it engulfs and surrounds everything that there is. This one notion must have its own positiveness and assertiveness in the elements of nature. We just seem to always return to where we started from; but where that can be who knows?

To think that there is any difference between him that gives reason and him that does not, there is little inconceivable solution nor advantage. Those who tolerate ignorance are like stone and they know not better, but those who search for knowledge gain wisdom and do have an advantage over others just because their enquiry brings them closer to insight, enlightenment, and true revelation concerning their explorations and discoveries.

That we can imagine opens the doors of illusion and deception. That we can think, and reason, opens the doors of mystery to truth and certainty. Our logic knows better as our reason becomes clearer. Our judgment gets keen with wit and the skills of learning.

Impossibility does not lessen the probability of conjecture; it only increases the temptation of contemplation. We live in an age in which there is much talk of independence; yet we are dependent at every corner of our life for some reason or another. A social being can scarcely rise to complete independence, and let us not forget, of course, divine providence.

A Fairy Tale or an Acute Observation

I once heard a story about a boy walking on the beach by the sea. It was early in the morning. An old man walked up to the young one and said, "Why are you picking up those starfish and tossing them back into the sea? What does it matter; there are so many of them." The young one replied, "It matters to each one that they have another chance to live, finding their way under the surf back to the depths where they came from."

It happens like that to some of us; that we are given another upon another chance to begin our lives anew, surmounting the events of constant change. Sometimes a similar coincidence happens to me while driving my car along the back country roads. I come upon an image of something familiar to me, a common turtle in the road. By my nature I just have to stop and move the creature to safety out of harm's way. So people ask me why? And I reply it matters to that one creature who knows no better than to stop in the middle of the road not knowing that a vehicle has the power to send them off into the spirit world where creatures, like humans, go when their mortal end inadvertently arrives at some unknown time and place.

It is the way of wisdom to show kindness and compassion without any prospect of interest or reward. We have these traits within us because we are human, having a spirit true to our Creator. I crossed a stranger's eye and had a true need to respect his condition and address it in the best possible way all the while being true to my own convictions and experience. I told this stranger, "I know what you are going through because I've been there and know the pain."

It is an act of courage to pass knowledge to one another knowing very well the other's perspective may not be the same as my own. No judgment can void the knowledge and experience we gain on our own.

Someone who may never know upon having the opportunity to learn something new might just make a difference in their own life. So by nature we come to pass knowledge to one another for the benefit of humanity as a whole.

So I ask myself: can I make a difference? If I, or we, were not here for some reason than why are we here at all? Though the difference we can make to some significant other may be realized, we can even make a difference to ourselves. There must be some true purpose for everything and every creature. The unexpected discovery, the serendipity of the matter is most amusing and exciting.

The total environmental situation has the most endearing effect on our emotional stability. There must be found the natural balance nature holds within its power. It may very well just be a matter of natural compensation.

Alexis de Tocqueville (1805-1859) once said, "The printed word, achieving cultural saturation, had homogenized the world; and that literacy had significantly improved civilization."

This one notion becomes the basis of an acute observation that demands our recognition and contemplation.

An Evolution of Thought

Danger does not frighten him nor does labor tire; but exhausted becomes his body while his mind labors in thought, tirelessly reaching out in curiosity from the power of persuasion knowledge has on his mind.

Filled with impetuous courage he eagerly faces the masses in the street on their way to work, to the job, early in the morning; he joins the crowd making survival their only cause. We have so much to lose and so little to gain; keeping what we have becomes our duty, not only to ourselves, but to our family, to secure the sanctuary we call home. Home, a place to leave and a place to return to at the end of the work day, a place to spend some time at the end of the work week. The seemingly endless cycle continues. Like the day bends to the evening, while years linger on nature's images often fade away or get tossed with the wind. We collect our wood that holds fire within, reading it, curing with time, for its right and proper use. Likewise we cure our thoughts, preparing them for their release upon the written page.

I am just an ordinary man except that philosophy is my calling. I had no choice but to hear its summoning. Faced with all there is to learn I store knowledge like treasure. Who could answer just a piece of my questions would be a sage of olden times who wrote pages behind dusty covers in old dark used book store shelves. I really can't believe people get rid of books.

Onward to new heights, stopping only to catch my breath and think a bit, I climb life's ladder as age takes me over closing in on the end to reach some new threshold of a beginning. So I have been told many a story and fable and tale, all with the same conclusion: Spirit is the only reality.

All the while we give thoughts to ourselves; from contemplation we are given to thoughts of others. Here we find the common ground of Humanity. We are equals among the great inequality nature has set before us in social rank and tendencies toward learning and knowledge. We find ourselves subservient not only to ourselves but to others as well.

Time has no hold on heaven, so some day to meet with the Maker and have a long talk, perhaps along with some strong black tea and a piece of bread, may well be my destiny.

It's all mine beneath the starry sky; but when morning comes the reality of humanity sets in. Chance comes mysteriously to mend our error, or to make good upon the promise that everything will be all right. Remember the rainbow? And the great flood? The rain will stop and dry land will show itself from the receding water. To err is human. Only machines fail. People just make mistakes of judgment.

The bountiful seasons pour their gifts; except by our labor and memory of it are they stored and hope secured that work is not a vain thing and survival is made by our wit and hands.

It is our desire and passion that the will claims its hold on us, poor humans fated to the extreme limits of our abilities.

No one is exempt, and all is really fair where justice rules. Spring has arrived once again. Jack Frost has retreated to the north. More questions than answers echo in my mind. I hear "Be content," but know no answer to the mystery of life.

We create our own legacy, and history shows how burden is only a trifle that comes with our procuring security and sanctuary. Skill is an acquired character of learning and the accumulation of wisdom.

Misfortune bears down just as benevolence endears our spirit and brings us to the occasion for prayer. But to whom or to what? The Lord and Creator enables Angels to help us along the way whether to our knowing or not; the endearing revelation appeases our mind and soul. So at day's beginning and end, even along the way, we come to peace or anguish of the mess we got ourselves into, or came to us by chance or providence, and scheme a way to better ourselves.

We Pass Knowledge to One Another in aid and comfort to be anticipated but not expected. Mercy comes to us from the sky yet still our petitions rise, and we are all alone, in an empty world, with only a sincere intent to live the best we can.

To wit, reviving useful sense or want of skill relies on the passing of knowledge to one another. A bounty with a humbler name is knowledge that leads to virtue and the wisdom to act with prudence.

Judgment cured of neglect, the philosopher turned just in time to catch sight of a sign that crossed the sky at nightfall. Will miracles never cease? I think not. Our common mistake is to not claim miracles for what they are: acts of kindness from above.

Farewell midnight; the minute hand of the clock passed the hour hand once more. Time sure does seem to slip away from us when we are not giving it the attention it deserves. Another day, coarsely kind, brightens with the dawn. Any single talent well employed knows the task at hand and does it mindful of the reward by sundown.

The water runs downhill toward the sea wearing away at its shores, and we tire from our labor and wear away at our soul with the endless struggle for our sanctuary and survival. Then come more work and eternal rest. For what? Another lesson learned and another bit of knowledge turned to wisdom.

This work is a non-fictional account of life influenced by passions and qualities which are really to be found in conversing with mankind. Though my dialogue is mainly with myself and the reader, the consciousness it provides clears the way for inspiration and metaphysical insight coming from personal revelation and by deliberate contemplation of concurring thoughts, ideas, and notions.

Our curiosity is kept up without wonder at the vast gathering of material open for public inspection, examination, and thought. How can someone be master of their subject when they are taught that nothing is unnecessary? Nothing is still that great something we all have to wonder about. Is it that great nothing that we originate from? Or is it that great nothing that we return to at our mortal end? There must be something going on we just don't know about.

It takes a special turn of mind to grasp formless reality in its essential nature and to distinguish it from the figments of the imagination.

Anyone who sincerely and aggressively searches through history finds philosophers examining and re-examining the same issues we face today except with different points of view. Along through time this constant evaluating is what brings philosophy to its heights of majesty in the field of literature.

Those who labor in thought know the consequences of learning; it is the increase in knowledge from which we derive our individual and social wisdom.

This wild strain of imagination, and creativity, has found its way along the channels of time with readers' curiosity intensified and writers willing to continue the thought. How the mind works is a wonder; but using it is a miracle in that the way it works itself requires only attention and constant review.

Together with that learning which is to be gained from books, experience and insight bring wisdom to the one engaging in acute observations and sincerely detailed contemplations.

Other writings are safer because they are a form of entertainment; but reading from the philosopher's point of view entices our curiosity and diligence to surface reasonable conclusions about the most complex matters. Though we are susceptible to impressions and are constantly and consequently open to the possibility of suggestion, a caution and certain degree of reverence ought to be given to the thoughts of the writers and to our own labor-intensive thinking.

The knowledge we come to may very well be enlightenment, but what develops and evolves from this thinking is our own sense of intelligent wisdom we use in the most practical of life's applications of everyday living. Our own intelligence brings us to the doors of reality as we come to know it, not as it really is, for the simple reason that the unknown is greater than the known and our curiosity aligns itself with fact and fantasy. Illusion can only be conquered with knowledge.

Into the labyrinths of the written word our mind serenely goes about wandering and wondering how to separate the facts from the fiction and find a certain truth.

Somewhere in the mid-level of our consciousness we find ourselves and wonder. We not only wonder about ourselves but of the greater power that keeps our spirit and soul together with the universe. Not only is inside the mind a great place, but outside the mind is a place even more curious. At least inside the mind we can come to conclusions; but outside the mind all is still a great and novel mystery. Even the laws and principles of nature extend themselves into the realm of the spiritual and mystical.

When the adventurer is leveled with the rest of the world and is caught in the universal drama, spectators fix their eyes upon him as if he had the magic key that opens familiar locked doors. Without intervention of the will choice is unrestrained.

The chief advantage of thinking within this sphere of metaphysics is the applications it serves to bring one to new excellencies in common with himself, still under the scrutiny and judgment of significant others in his life. His judgment is questioned, but it really matters only to himself.

Every man should regulate his actions by his own conscience, without regard to the opinions of the world; but we live in a moral and ethical society, and our civilization has some natural base founded upon our getting along with each other by some cultural, moral, and ethical standard. Those subject to live outside this standard are subject to the consequences of their own actions. A large part of human life passes in a state contrary to our own natural desires. Here then the greater good of the whole counts for more than our individual good. Though the whole is made up of its parts, the simple act of conformity generates revolution among the few.

Impatience is to be avoided and patient endurance and submission to forces greater than ourself becomes a necessity for our survival. The chief security we gain from frequent reflection is a settled conviction of the tendency of everything turning to good whether from our own cause or by some higher power, even providence, to live and endure however we can, to the best of our abilities.

What is important to our life is the entertainment of the mind. We strive for peace, leisure, and innocence. Those who achieve contentment are the favorites no matter what condition they find themselves in. Those who have the least have little to renounce. Those with the most have little difficulty finding things to renounce. Those with little have so much to gain. Those with the most have so much to lose. Either way, an open heart and mind lures enlightenment and revelation from the acquisition of knowledge in our constant adventure in learning. It is the whispers of pleasure and the promise of repose that attract our attention the most.

We constantly find ourselves in the middle, perhaps, of a grand experiment, thinking and wondering about it all. Satisfaction not only begins early on but lasts as long as we advance into the world of intelligence. Sometimes we have to throw it all away and find a kind of relaxation in contemplation; but there again we find ourselves in the middle of the knowledge we've gained and that which we pass along to others.

Life is more than a matter of existence; it is how we exist that brings importance to our life. It is not only our observations but our interpretation that affects the way we perceive and, in a round about way, the way we conceive.

What amuses me is how nature affects our thoughts, and the nature of our thoughts themselves. We begin with a curious regard for new information and end up with an inclination to stillness and serene tranquility passed in idle contemplation.

After a thousand thoughts have crossed your mind you find yourself and wonder. The passions which the mind is stirred by naturally hasten towards their own quickening. Any attempt to preserve life in a state of neutrality and indifference is not unreasonable. Our passions are moved proportionately with the condition that faces us in the present here and now. Parallel circumstances bring us to regard the state of our being, keeping reality in the most non-fictitious awareness that we notice we are standing on sure ground or not in this paradoxical world.

Though we draw inspiration from an array of sources, the particular importance here is that we seek inspiration to broaden our own narrow views. To this the universal view of historical genius can be referred to as The Passing of Knowledge to One Another.

The patterns of our thinking depend on the resources we draw our inspiration from. It comes in many forms at all times of a day. At night our thoughts intensify and we are given to dreams and to revelation. Our insight focuses our attention and our perspective narrows in on what occupies the abilities of the mind.

Throughout this work there are a series of thoughts provoked from both internal and external sources of study. By the means of contemplating these thoughts together I've found some that are relevant and seemed worthy of formulating, stimulating further study and explaining their subtleties and surfacing qualities.

The coming to terms with them appears as their theme and consort between the ideas brings to mind their relevance worthy of considering. Learned information and profound thought makes our creative intelligence what it is — something special and a gift to be used wisely.

When inspiration comes it must be seized because a thought not captured is seldom remembered. In this way the enthusiasm of the thinker is ensured and preserved. This is one way of giving an immediate outward aspect to what is going on in the mind reposed to a personal encounter with the greater outward world and as well to the other greater inner world of thought and mind.

We are moved from solemnity to wit through simple and complex sentences with the aim to provoke further thought and reflection. It is the personal context that notions and ideas have which give them their worth. To communicate is natural; to accept what is communicated is an acquired art and requires one to labor in thought and weigh the elements those thoughts bring to mind. We've all been prompted by the same motives, all deceived by the same fallacies, all animated by hope, obstructed by dangers, entangled by desires, and seduced by pleasure. It is no wonder we are lured by our own thoughts.

Our excellence and dignity is conceived in the esteem of our uncorrupted reason and judgmental intellect. Our candor and genius will be made visible by our expression and inquiries after natural, moral, and ethical knowledge. To this effect we seize upon and learn wisdom from each other.

There are many invisible circumstances, those of the mind, which when revealed increase our knowledge and virtue. Those who are content with secondary knowledge from listening and conversing with others in coffee-houses and bar-rooms are indeed passing knowledge to one another; but the deeper knowledge we learn comes from study and contemplation of the facts known to us and the great mysteries life holds in the rites of passage through time.

It is the assertion of one's self into a bolder conviction to learning opinions, ideas, and notions of others that brings us to the embedded notion of our own genius. The media consisting of books, magazines, newspapers, the internet, radio, and television offer particular opinions of fact and theory; but through the ages we have come to know subtle and detailed words meant for conceiving in our mental intelligence. We are equally indebted to significant others for their assistance in increasing our own knowledge and wisdom.

The greater part of students are not born with abilities to construct systems of problem solving, but with proper guidance can develop their reasoning and patterns of logic that enable them to become intelligent in the field of philosophy and metaphysical thinking of abstract concepts only the mind can determine.

Providence has allotted us greater strength than one can realize without excelling in the contemplation of our own thinking or in the greater thinking of others throughout history. It has been the collective labor of a thousand intellects that has brought us to where we are today, and to examine what has already been conferred to us will be a quantum leap in our own intelligence. The necessity of following the traces of our ancestors is indisputably evident in our quest for new knowledge and wisdom.

It might be conceived that of those who profess to forsake the narrow path of truth can still find, on the broad path, the same universal truths, though we deviate towards a different point.

From the wide plains of the open territory that lies ahead of us, the horizon beckons from a distance. Once we reach the point we saw from a distance it is not the same. Our far perspective has changed from a closer observation of the subtleties in front of us, and the horizon infinitely changes with each step towards it.

The boundless possibilities surely open a thousand recesses in unexplained territory and a million fountains of knowledge we can consume for the increase in our own wisdom. It is our employment and utility of our mind, and the endeavoring to form new maxims and hints of theory, content with secondary knowledge, but partial to primary knowledge, to think ourselves entitled to the reverence of a new arrangement of ancient systems of thought.

The hour of earth is visible from the sky. With the dawn the sun's light illuminates and with the night comes the light of the stars and moon; but what is important here is the light that enlightens the mind with inspiration and revelation.

The sage precepts of the first instructors of the world are transferred from age to age, becoming more clear and precise along the way. This is the very theme of which I write. We Pass Knowledge to One Another.

With little variation echoed from one to another the newness of idea and notion becomes apparent in the execution of rhetoric and its elocution in language and conversation.

Every page of every philosopher is crowded with examples and margins full of added explanations in the understanding of the basic principles that make up The Basis of Elemental Thoughts. This expounding and increase in explanation only adds to our understanding of the simplicity concealed in the complexity and paradox of life.

Every man should, indeed, carefully compare his own understanding and adjust his designs with a better estimate of his own abilities therefore becoming more useful to humanity in the contemplation of natural and spiritual knowledge and in the expression of his own wisdom. The wide regions of probability are open to us if only one would be given to the thought of them.

There is a middle path which is every man's duty to find and likewise acknowledge that this middle path is a narrow way, winding through the broad expanse of our universal intelligence — the field of dreams that holds the mind accountable for what and how it thinks.

Nature's bright gleam is a higher revelation where amid all the joy and pain, the birth and destruction, a glorious consummation blends. Brooks thread the many valleys just as our thoughts meander through the labyrinth of reality; and fantasy collects upon the banks of our untamed vision and realization that there is more to life than it seems.

The greening of the world comes in the season of the spring; but we all bloom at different times of the year, in the intervals of our own rites of passage through time. The days go by rustling our thoughts, exchanging fact for theory and revelation for insight. When human beings have such a sense to be inclined to give thought some relative importance in those moments, the minutes turn to hours and the hours to days, increasing our wit to newfound wisdom. Our own indolence is changed to laboring in thought.

There are no signs to follow on the path life leads us on; we must make our way cautiously and patiently through the obstacles that present themselves to us to circumvent and surpass their unique danger of deception and illusion as we search the way for certainty of the truth we all seek and quest for.

It is necessary to distinguish our own intentions and interest from that of others, but also to be able and willing to give thought to differing opinions on the same theme. We must be able to recognize our own strength and weakness in our field of thoughts.

We ought to be aware of our own powers and accomplish a thousand designs without restraint from attempting them. The vigor of the human mind quickly appears when there is no longer any place for doubt or hesitation. Passion consumes us in the Adventure in Learning and in the accumulation of experience creating in us a newfound sense of wisdom.

After a considerable amount of thought the philosopher concludes that the obstacles with which our way was obstructed were only phantoms which we believed real because of our lack of significant wisdom. It was not our ignorance, but our lacking of knowledge in problem solving that comes from experience and study to overcome them.

Whatever pleasure that is awakened in the endeavor to review our distress has been surmounted by the conviction of our own ability of reason and the logical progression of our elemental thoughts.

So we come to this one simple thought: if something is believed impossible the attempt to generate the opening of the slightest possibility would not even be attempted, though those more daring and experienced may attempt through patient endeavor and enduring passion to see past the illusion of impossibility into the probability of things yet still undiscovered, and our powers of intelligence aggregate to knowledge and the happiness thereof, will at last be revealed by the newfound insight into the probability and possibility of the idea and notion we quest to be revealed.

When past unseen reasons veil the illusion of probability that comes to us again and the view seems milder, simpler, and fairer, the conclusions complement the questions that shine in their profusion. From the depths of our thoughts new life returns; from the roots of our thoughts the mind aspires and is itself brought closer to the perfection it seeks for. Never did the Creator constrict the power of Nature nor hold back the thunder from the lightning. So from our sense of enlightenment we come to the light of the mind with an open mind and outstretched arms welcoming knowledge and reason. Is there a measure on Earth? There is none that can contain providence.

Our attempt to disentangle complications causes our wonder a sense of amazement. It is our problem-solving skills and rate of learning that lead the mind to reasonable and logical conclusions.

Wonder is a pause of reason that gives way to our intelligent imagination. It is by these qualities that we engage in problem solving and critical analysis of what we think we know and what we actually know. We discover the interrelations everything has with everything else. We are connected in one way or another with every one and every thing on the natural plane and on the spiritual plane of nature.

Those accustomed to the labor of inquiry, and those who give time to laboring in thought, come to unique realizations and become keenly aware of their own insight from the enlightenment of their own revelations. We become invigorated with self-confidence in the certainty of what we are sure of and in what we believe, with the vigor of conviction, of our own thoughts, and in what we learn from the significant others by our study.

Our own confidence comes with the certainty of our convictions. In the attempt to make a presentation to the average human I do try to use simple words, but for this one notion I will use the word "entelechy," or finding the condition of a thing whose essence is fully realized in all actuality. Also, the enormous task to ennoble thought requires an "ensilage," or storing and fermenting, in this case of knowledge, to form a more perfect union with the wisdom we come to know as our own.

What happens to us is that we find the most amusing and paradoxical results in our contemplations and reflections upon the matters that most concern us in our studies and in our Adventure in Learning experience provides to us.

With the quiescence of astonishment we conceive what has been obscure and too extensive to comprehend; but the rational contemplation we put ourselves to brings the most unusual results. To divide and conquer is a principle easily applicable to those who labor in thought and logical reasoning.

The chief art of learning comes with little steps at a time involving the widest excursions of the mind made by short but frequent flights of our creative intelligence.

In trying to solve the terrifying problems that face us in the world today, we naturally turn to the things we do best. We play from strength, we stave off our hunger for knowledge with study, but as we all know very well time goes on. All we have to show for our progress is the state of things as they are today; and that's not saying much for the human condition as we stand in the present moment.

The proper ambition of philosophers is to enlarge the boundaries of knowledge by conquering new regions of the intellectual mind not only through involvement with thought and the process of thinking but also through common discourse and individual exploration and discovery of the wisdom of the ages.

When nothing more is required than to pursue a path already beaten down, one cannot imagine oneself unequal to the attempt; but upon traveling down a fresh and unfamiliar path the discoveries along the way are unmistakably serene and sequential, leading one to consistent and conspicuous theories of actual truth presented in nature's own reality. In this way we make the most fortunate discoveries by accident or by random chance alone.

To pass knowledge to one another is a necessity and may be considered a principle of nature. Even nature lets us know when storms come and when the seasons are about to change. Man may indeed preserve his existence in solitude, but can truly enjoy the benefits of society by the mutual communication of ideas. By the good use of our senses we learn and increase the ability of the mind.

As one gains time for leisure and the pursuit of intellectual pleasures an overwhelming sense of freedom arises clear enough to articulate as an article of faith that knowledge is power and that power entices our freedom of thought to think what we will without license because our creativity has no bounds but the wisdom and knowledge we store, like treasure, in our intelligent mind.

Understanding the Intelligence of a Philosopher

It has been observed that there are steps to our aptitude for learning: Reading, Comprehension, and Expression. One who devotes their time to these comes to a certain understanding of life and its possibilities.

Reading makes one full; conversation makes one useful; and writing brings out one's exactness. What makes civilization great is the knowledge left behind from generations past and present explorers into the mystery of life itself, including the life we have in the mind. Our physical life is one thing to consider, but our spiritual and mental life is another entirely.

As we unite the sentiments of our understanding with expression we duly serve humanity as ourselves. To read, write, and converse in due proportion is, therefore, the business of the philosopher.

It is reasonable to have perfection as an ideal — that we may always advance towards it, though we very well know it cannot be reached until our spirit leaves our body for another world once past our mortal end. Improvement is perpetual, like creation, and invariably so slow it cannot be realized until one moment comes that brings revelation and insight.

It is those people who inquire into the workings of their own mind who discover in their heart the pleasure and satisfaction of knowing who we really are and what we really know.

At this point in the work here presented, I can see it taking shape and form, clearing the way for a new understanding of our human intelligence along with the development of a certain reasoning we have towards our thoughts and leisurely contemplation. The quickness and agility of the mind shows itself in its utility and abilities. The communication of practical opinion, theory, and idea serves its purpose.

My labor has likewise been much increased because not only is knowledge powerful, it is meaningful as well to our own comprehension and expression of the world we live in, as it is of the inner world of the spirit and mind. In the height of thoughts upon thoughts the metaphysical part of life evolves its true reality.

In understanding the philosopher we have to give due recognition to the printed book. All the wisdom, knowledge, and understanding of the ages is written for all to discover, explore, and inspect for their own satisfaction. As a matter of public record the printed book serves its purpose to humanity.

The wisdom of God has been endowed in the human world. Being aware of it is revelation and brings us inspiration. Striving to work out the problems of the world is a great challenge, but the greater challenge is to work out our own problems and idiosyncrasies.

It is not an exaggeration to say that the future of modern society and the stability of each of our inner lives depend in large part on the maintenance of an equilibrium between the strength of the techniques of communication and the capacity of the individual's own reactions to his or her own thoughts and the common thinking of our society and civilization in a universal whole conception.

Life is more than a grand experiment to see just how far we can progress as a whole unit; it is a personal adventure in learning and the discovery and exploration of our selves and others. So in turn We Pass Knowledge to One Another for the greater improvement of all of us residing here on this little planet we call terra firma, or Earth. One of my questions is: Who named us Earth?

Some may put the statement like this: When a person of greater or lesser significance becomes a legend their work is obscured, and the creator becomes more important than their work.

Keats puts it like this: "The poetry of earth is never dead; when all the birds are faint with the hot sun, and hide in the cooling trees, a voice will run from hedge to hedge about the fresh meadow."

Scholarship today has become fully aware of the ways of treating subjects and the subject itself. With man his knowledge and the process of obtaining that knowledge he calls his own wisdom is of equal magnitude. Our ability to comprehend the galactic magnitude of the universe equals our ability to understand subatomic particles all with our creative intelligent mind.

Neither concepts nor what we can conceive is beyond the imagination but transcends its utility. We are capable of dealing with all kinds of situations, with the one exception of death, because we know not what comes after our mortal end. So the philosopher comes to deduce concepts and theories of that part of nature which conceals itself from us.

Once when I was traveling out in western America an old Indian man told me that the earth would out-last the human race and a new race of humans would start anew, in a different direction than where we had brought ourselves to be. No tale could spark the imagination better than this one.

Though mythology has good grounds to stand upon it was the best human kind could come up with to explain the abstract concepts that occupied the human mind at the time. Then along came the philosophers to do away with the myths and bring to enlightenment the bold facts and theories that ground our present foundations for faith and belief.

Then along came the one called Jesus, and his teachings changed the world forever, even past the present and contemporary. An amazing man he was to expand the culture of humanity; but let us not forget the many prophets that came after him with the same revelations, and the poets, theologians, and philosophers who carried us away in deep concentration of our contemplations.

Neither concepts nor what can be conceived is beyond our imagination but transcends its utility. In this section of the work the mind looks to its spirit for consolation because of its own inherent intelligence. Our spiritual mind is somehow different than our physical mental mind. Though individual implies singularity it does not mean aloneness; but individuality only finds its content and universality in the sociality of universal consciousness.

Spiritual existence and social life thus go together. We can find in our own mind the self-consciousness that makes us individuals and gives us our validity and is united in the collective universal conscience.

The term spirit seems better to render the meaning of universal mind, though each of us has an individual spirit that is somehow connected to that universal concept. Used here spirit designates mind, but spirit is mind taken to a much higher level.

This character, still abstract, constitutes the nature of absolute fact and truth and is the beginning of a reality we have no means of completely understanding.

Spirit in its entirety is more the process from its immediacy to the attainment of a knowledge of what it implicitly or immediately is, essentially to behold itself as part of nature only known in the mind which attributes to it its own consciousness not only of itself, but on the grander scale of the human race, intelligent creatures, and God.

The essence of spirit is not entirely esoteric, but has common qualities throughout physical nature and the reality of spiritual nature, which is the other side, but not the opposite, of nature itself.

Spirit permeates all aspects of its actual existence. Knowledge of its inner depths is true revelation. It is certain of itself and becomes self-evident in our intelligence.

Its universal direction is constantly towards the center of the most high. It deals with reality solely by the characteristics in its own consciousness. It knows itself only in truth, yet it is merely a conception of the mind by the principles that establish it that contain all reality within that truth.

It is something we carry with us in our mortal days and something we evolve into once past our mortal end. No other explanation can do it justice by its own nature and is only a conception we realize that is part of the mind's utility.

Gradually we realize that by studying and questioning the greater and lesser sages of antiquity and contemporary philosophy we are studying ourselves from opinion to experience. The self we discover consists in endless variations set in time in a series of thoughts; we realize as we discover our self we discover everyone.

To study one is to study all; not that all are identical but all are inter-related and have common characteristics. If we connect to the consciousness we move beyond our active mind and discover nature's great depths we hold within us — we find our true self and similarities we have with others.

The ancient and contemporary are both filled with fantastic thoughts. Great minds over the ages have filled volumes of books with the most thoughtful information. Though some are theories and speculation, sure and certain facts have been revealed.

One just has to pursue the path of learning and get involved with the messages on those printed pages. Once brought to our attention we become lured with the need for knowing more and finding greater explanations of the ideas that are secured in the annals of history.

It is the focus of our attention that leads us from the physical to the metaphysical. The surreal is more than fantasy. It is reality of another sort, though abstract; the mind with its utility and ability can conceive and comprehend with all its reason and logic available to it.

The real function of the philosopher is to remove you from what separates you from the actual truth and not just the illusion of that truth. The brevity of thought does not engage the mind more than necessary, but causes an entanglement and mends thoughts together.

It's not what we read, hear, see, or think that is important, though it may be in some way; but what we miss along the way is the important matter and that is what we search for. Though it may be right before our eyes it remains concealed because our attention has other matters it gives way to. Maybe, perhaps, the missing part has all the answers to the questions we ask.

Consciousness is not a luxury for a designated few — it is a necessity for humanity so we can realize our real oneness with the great spirit which makes paradoxically things for better or worse and allows them so we can realize its real power, though subdued. With the spirit of autonomy we endure and survive.

The Claims of Philosophy in its Own Domain

It is our awareness of the flux and enigmatic essence of change that takes place in the world and within our own mind that makes the difference in our receptivity and recognition of the nature of change within nature itself.

In our finding out just who we are and what makes others so similar we realize the truth of human nature and seek counsel not from theology but from philosophy itself — the heart and breath of wisdom.

Philosophy is a complement to theology. They both lead one on in knowledge to true wisdom. The consolation of rational philosophy leads one to question the answers we find, and however obscure the answers may be bring to light the enlightenment of sound judgment and the fine art of distinguishing the truth from its hidden nature concealed in reality, which makes the quest for certainty all the more interesting and self fulfilling as we adventure in learning.

The real attraction of classical philosophy is in its openness to rational examination and discussion of all things and creatures that reveal their true identity. We go beyond physics into metaphysics speculating on the essence of being, knowledge, and truth. We try to find a sureness with certainty beyond doubt. It is the ideal we quest for. The beyond reason and the beyond experience is the nature of our passing knowledge to one another. It is the adventure in learning that has a right to exist in its own domain — in the mind.

The unimaginable that we imagine and the unthinkable that we think about is the human way we explain away the unexplainable. With the utility of our intelligence we can think and reason rightly; as our duty calls we learn to control our will and live within the reality of our situation and condition of our present reality.

To acquire the acquaintance of the skill of reasoning, capture the desire to know, and treasure the answers of your questions; philosophy becomes thoughtful of the most sublime in our reasonable and rational contemplations and reflections. We cannot think without the abilities of our thoughts and though we find stillness, sometimes in those quiet moments the stillness is most refreshing.

By the power of thought we understand the language of the mind. It is not the surface of things that have the complexities we are in the habit of thinking of; the surface is simple. The deeper one thinks about things, the likelier that complexities will make their appearance.

A shallow pond reveals its depths, but the deeper waters conceal unknown mysteries that lure our thought. One must turn a proposition on all sides and think it through and through to reveal what has plainly been concealed by its own nature.

Though caution and slow ascent will guard you against frequent mistakes of thought, the courage to re-consider eliminates doubt and brings us closer to sureness and certainty that we all seek for.

Though the ideal may be to consistently find certainty, we are closer to doubt in our thoughts, so when we do find truth and understanding its certainty can be for sure. Here the improvement of the mind appeals nearer to its own satisfaction and learning finds its end in wisdom from the means of study and contemplation of our own thoughts.

Reason brings upon us our own doubt, but one thing is for sure: our sense of improvement is part of the ongoing process of eternal creation and has no end, only an infinite horizon that we approach which constantly becomes another with each forward step we advance in mind and spirit. Along this path we take spirit more for sure and less with doubt of its existence.

If we too suddenly give up our ascent our idleness brings us closer to no conclusions and increasing doubt; so we must climb to the new plateaus of thought ahead of us while remembering the valley where we started that ascent.

As we continue in the ascent of knowledge and wisdom the clarity of answers we seek become realized with true and certain sureness and certainty as our awareness of the facts we see through their false illusion of the real, pure truth. To this effect we realize and come to actual conclusions of a true conviction of our beliefs.

So it seems it is better not to judge than to judge falsely.

Think with yourself how easily by one turn of thought you can find useful notions and ideas. Think with yourself just how real your spirit comes alive when you contemplate the power of your will and reflect on the power of your imagination. Learn to guard your understanding with diligence and discretion of reason.

Remember that the truth is nearly on the surface and has to be searched for in the depths of life itself. Explore your own conscience for the truth that is suitable to your own convictions. Discover your own consciousness of what you are aware of and all the principles it holds to within its own nature. Reality has many facets that include the realm of mind and spirituality, as well as the reality we are conscious of in our perceptions outside the mind that exist on their own without the slightest thought of them.

Consciousness that does not set out from its own inner life does not start from thought but combines the thought of the Great Spirit with its own from its immediate presence existing within itself along with its recognition of its own reality.

The moment of immediate existence is present in the content of the notion, and present in such a way that it realizes its immediate reality within a greater reality that is above nature but still part of nature in the surreal reality of the mind and the thought of the spiritual side of nature only the mind can fathom that comes into our consciousness of its actual presence.

The moment of immediate existence is reality in the present content of the notion of reality as we know it. We realize our present reality within a greater reality which includes all of society, civilization, and the sublime spiritual reality of the other side of nature. We see spirituality as the earth and moon with two sides and still each are one.

It is neither set up as something thought or imaginatively represented nor of something produced but is part of our real and immediate experience of our existence. The Divine becomes part of our own being once realized and accepted in our intelligent being.

So this is the life and understanding of a philosopher: to subject one's self to rational thought, reason, and to doubt, and to question. Like Socrates once said, "Question everything, even the answers you come to, and pursue a better understanding."

Though we see an end in sight from our wisdom, any end is like the horizon and recedes as we near it promoting further investigation. I wanted to talk with the masters of my field of study, but since they were all out of reach I had to settle for reading their works and bringing my own understanding to a satisfactory conclusion.

Without illumination, like reading in the dark, we can see nothing, but with the enlightenment of the mind sure and certain revelations come to us. Most fundamental principles are clearly stated, and it is up to our rational understanding that we interpret them, not only creating in our mind a basis of elemental thoughts but adding to our adventure in learning as we accumulate the passing of knowledge to one another and establish our own certain wisdom.

Our relationship to the world is not one-sided but is a mutual and reciprocal relationship drawing and giving back knowledge to those dedicated to laboring in thought.

All along our life journey we are exhilarated by following as many highways and byways luring our attention, and though sidetracks often come our way, with our wisdom we overcome them and stay to the main path of our exploration. Though we pass through many varying degrees of skepticism, our quest for truth is a certain end and optimistic results can be expected. The life and times of a philosopher bring to mind many curious observations. With our history of in depth thought we come to terms with what we hold near to the surface of our mind and clean the registry of the depths of our inner mind, making way for new and bold revelations and conclusions.

Time is the most important element in our life. Though its relativity is apparent, only in our present existence does it extend into the realm we pass into once we reach our mortal end.

From our thoughts we find the most fascinating and inevitable variety of contemplations and reflections. Upon the still waters of a pool we can see our reflection underneath the sky, but only the surface of our being is revealed and the sky is what it is, yet above it the universe exists; just the same below our surface another reality exists.

The Absolute Being exists as a concrete actual self-conscious entity that we recognize as part of our own and still exists on its own as the sovereign of providence. Its great spirit descends from its pure simplicity, through our conscience, and into our intelligence. In doing so, having attained for the first time its highest nature, its supreme reach for being comes to us as a saving grace with all its mercy to relieve us of our stress and pain and to increase our joy in its miraculous form that only our mind can recognize.

By doing so and connecting with humanity it has found its own self-fulfillment. In pure thought the spirit has become not only an act of cognition but has realized its own potential in human consciousness.

The actual consummation of this notion brings the Divine Spirit into unity with the human spirit —probably part of its own plan that humans can know it and it can know humans in a reciprocal and mutual relationship.

Many of the problems of philosophy are of such broad relevance to human concerns, and so complex in their ramifications, that they are, in one form or another, perennially present. In the course of time each so called problem, or concept, has to be re-thought in the light of newfound knowledge in order to confront the rapidly expanding reach of the applications that knowledge brings to our attention.

What we seek for is a comprehensive view of what underlies the surface reality we live in, all the while considering the deepest parts of the workings of the inner mind and the furthest reaches of the limits we find in our ever-expanding universe.

We are faced with an Age where it is necessary to return hidden knowledge to the people for their own good, out of necessity against stress and anguish of not knowing the whole truths of matters that concern us the most. Somehow along the course of history it has been decided for us there are things we ought not know; and this peaks our curiosity, for surely we can realize there are missing parts of a lot of stories we have been told.

In esoteric traditions from around the world this concealed knowledge has partially become revealed, and for this reason we come to The Passing of Knowledge to One Another.

That inner stillness in the face of conflict must be recognized and its awareness maintained for us to keep our composure in the face of decision making, all the while reflecting on the consequences of our actions and thoughts that led to those choices.

To explain the phenomena of the activity of the mind and the physical world, including the spiritual realm of our intellectual activity, has been a primary objective of this work, along with achieving some explanatory insight into the activity of thought and the process of our habits of thinking.

Along with knowledge man has long and persistently been concerned with achieving some understanding of enormously diverse, often perplexing and sometimes threatening occurrences in the world around him and within his own mind, as shown by the manifold myths and metaphors he has devised in an effort to account for the very existence of the world and himself.

Not only is there more to reality than is apparent to our senses, but the hidden spirit of nature can be recognized by the sense of the mind to which it is comprehended and relatively understood. This concealed dimension of creation exists in a continuous dynamic interrelationship and the overflowing of one reality into another. The influences in our life are many. The more primary the relationship they have with our being the more powerful the influences become; so to gain knowledge and wisdom influences our perspective of our world.

We come to knowledge by various means. Insight, intuition and experience play important roles in our learning. In its generative and regressive forms, our concept formation utilizes our mind's capacity of intelligence and creative license of invention and conception.

As our understanding grows and progresses, with knowledge gained our foundation and imagination take on similar proportions.

This is the process of passing knowledge to one another and increasing our own intelligence and genius.

It is the conception that is important here. For expression to occur the thought must be there first for the idea or notion to be drawn out of the resources of the mind. You have to have the idea in your mind first, and that ultimately comes from either wisdom or imagination, which lures the thought to the surface of our intellect from the deeper reaches of our own intelligence.

The greatest respect an author can have is due to those whom knowledge has been gained, the insight caused inspiration, and what he or she considers right and useful for whatever stage of intellectual development has been reached by him or herself due to their study and imagination that stems from the passing of knowledge to one another.

The question here is whether it is better to be mysterious rather than obvious as to where the conception of their material comes from, be it from their creativity or study of significant others' material. Of course we all gain some sort of insight from our learning and the accumulated wisdom we gain from our life experience and from the reading of what has already been written in literature and history.

If I can be more like nature I am unpredictable and daring, though most of my probabilities fall in line with the regularity and inconsistency nature brings to our earth and inner mind, thinking of both worlds existing as one. Following nature I am flexible rather than precise, and my plans are alterable rather than fixed. Thoughts of others are only speculation, but I know myself very well. Positive optimism is a necessity to get through what we do; all things usually work out for the best possible situation and condition.

The Freestyle Philosopher

John Kennedy once said, "We choose to go to the moon not because it is easy but because it is hard." And it is the same for all humans that we do the things that are hard because we live for the challenges.

It is the lure of achievement that drives us the way it does. Freestyle or artistic expression in the way we communicate thoughts is one foundation principle of philosophy. The philosopher must use his or her abilities with creative license to portray a thought that brings its significance to an objective observation for consideration and opinion to open a dialogue for suggestion and debate.

Composing and the art of writing seem a suitable means for the passing of knowledge to one another. As we work our ways through life's clutter and chaos our relentless pleasure finds repose in the portents of gladness. We must, for ourselves, create happiness or be satisfied with the bounds of timeless endurance to condition and passion.

We are storytellers, observers, and interpreters. It all becomes a matter of context and perspective, and takes a bit of imagination. The genesis of a thought comes with the idea planted, like a seed, in the core of our mind.

What we're looking for here is the big picture in a little story. Time is everything. Preparation is essential. In a few moments the philosopher must see the big picture in a brief and concise overview. Not only are we exploring beautiful places of the world, we are exploring the beautiful places stored in the composite of our mind.

We are looking for grandeur. Exploring beautiful places requires all the faculties of the mind including our creative and intelligent imagination. The mind is not a vessel to be filled but a fire to be kindled from a single spark of our intelligent creativity.

Our challenges of today forge the destiny of tomorrow. Humankind and their quest for knowledge cannot be denied. For the good of our civilization we learn and pass knowledge to each other that new discoveries and insight will come from previous generations of the students of wisdom to which we all are one. Learning is one thing but applying that knowledge is another.

As time goes on more endlessly the years expand our existence and the thunder of circumstances mark out time between the calling of new days upon no end. Meanwhile, deep inside something awakens and what seems to be the summit we reach, at each stage in our life, is only an illusion to the drama life brings us to notice and give our attention to.

In reality we are, it seems, at the heights of our infinite lowness. Torrents of thoughts echo in our mind in the tireless workshop of our intelligence here at home on our little planet we call Earth. Our terra firma gives us sure ground, but still we have to create for ourselves a solid foundation for what we think and a logic for what we dream and believe.

It is the drama of life that we get involved in that changes us. We change in subtle ways when confronted with situations and random conditions. Our lifestyle changes and all the meanings we thought we had secured need re-definition. Lifestyle changes cause us to re-think how we live and as well to re-define our wants and needs.

For some of us, perhaps most of us, there are more days in the month than money to supply our needs. So we change and find ourselves caught in the constant certainty of change, one of nature's first principles.

We are forced to re-define the everlasting sympathy we have for ourselves and negotiate our values and convictions with our economic stability, just trying to stay within our means.

The drama we play out with the significant others in our life changes as occurrences force their way upon our living soul.

My clock started again. Now I have time, but it is in another time zone than the one I live in. At least its constant tick-tock can be heard, and once the spring winds down I can re-set it to my current time. Living with a clock gives us a closer reference to reality, but sometimes the surrealism of the misplaced hour hand and minute hand brings us to a new reality only our creative imagination can sort and make sense of. Oh, the constant drama of life and all that comes along with it.

In reality we are somewhere beyond the light of our sun enlightened with an infinite amount of creativity that begs to surface in the forethought of our mental activity, in our intelligence, to ponder on and wonder with amusement for our own entertainment.

I've been here just thinking and the thought came to me about what it is that we know about the spiritual plane of our mental activity. It is another reality but connected to ours in the most passionate way. For us to understand the spiritual plane of reality within nature's own bounds, we must first pass to a higher plane of thinking in our mental development, accumulating wisdom where we intuitively apprehend and conceptually comprehend the very significance of the thought itself.

Once this state is achieved we form a synthetic connection between the process of imagination and a real conceptual actualization. It is not beyond our own thinking, because in some way or another all of us have this kind of realization that something is going on here that we do not understand but realize has an affect on us. The concept itself is a matter of faith and believing in matured thought and intuitive speculation gained over the millennia.

The horizon holds the promise of distance urging man to go out and explore, but what is inside has greater depth and grandeur than can be found in the physical world.

One must travel to where the wonders are; their origin held within our mind allures us to challenge the veil of clouds and break through to where our spirit thrives and lives in peace, without confusion but in the reality of truth in the justice of our thoughts.

Our heart beats with high emotion and passion while our breath carries only the inner sound of a silent voice pondering on life's mistakes and gains. The drama continues invariably. The mighty voice of our conscience rings out in our consciousness, and we hear it strongly, weighing against all odds, finding in it what matters most: the preserving and endearing of our soul, the cherishing of our spirit and right to life and living. A great destiny ponders over the footprints in the sand as the ocean's waves wash them away. But I was there once and remember the sea was before me and will remain after me; no matter how many times I walk upon the beach my footprints are always washed away because I walk so close to the water's edge where the land meets with the sea. And if I walk some distance from the water's edge the wind takes my footprints with it, yet I still remember being there.

No one teaches the plants to grow, but people need guidance along the journey through life. Just the same we need enlightenment to survive. Our creative spirit fills this necessity. When opportunity crosses our path we have to make decisions and choices. There our guiding wisdom fulfills the need within our intelligence.

Knowledge, like a stranger, comes to us with a quickening word, a voice that makes us humans amazed at its incredible wonders; it accomplishes in the mind its task of awakening us to unknown things.

Like a sword, the blade of knowledge cuts through our ignorance and ennobles our mind to know that spirit and soul are likened to the universe that challenges us to enter and explore what further knowledge we can discover to add to our own wisdom and genius.

As philosophy is lured by the phenomenology of the mind, our simple thoughts compound themselves into abstract and concrete thinking. Just the pure thought of being and spirit takes on a whole new set of values considering the process of thinking and the actions that thought promotes. Reality becomes sublime and the surreality of thinking becomes our own actual reality just for the simple reason that what and how we think makes our nature what it really is; and the simplicity of human nature takes on the abstract distinction of the Divine within our own intelligent mind.

If we further consider the kind of procedure that pictorial thinking adopts as it goes along, we find in the first place the expression that the Divine Being takes on human form, within our human nature, to think and discover its true reality. Our spiritual nature becomes knowing of itself from our simple human nature.

Wisdom, so strange and miraculous, as if like a dream in hand to him who uses a force beyond compare, takes us by surprise and enters our mind revealing hidden secrets that to our amusement make known the things of Earth and Heaven.

What we learn of is legend and myth, and tales of old. We learn of science and from the poets. We learn from those who write and paint of life. Yet no one actually knows what is happening to us. We are truly part of the ongoing part of creation, and at any one moment we are what we are, human; and we think what we do as intellectual divine creatures.

Our lives are contained in the continual flux of time enchanted with fact and fantasy, imagining reality to be something other than what it really is. The truth is revealed by those who labor in thought.

Moved by many transformations, the age we live in, and the age to come, hold knowledge yet to be found, except in the idle thoughts of a few who reach for the stars.

Between day and night one must toil in labor until their bones tell them their age, and then their mind reflects and ponders on the worth of life and the struggle for subsistence. All is changed with the challenge to increase our own wisdom and to distinguish the divine from the human. As we reach out into the unknown and discover that human is part divine we recognize the thought from its own necessity and realize providence has its place in human affairs.

When one aspires to be like them, the wise and fortunate, then blissfully humble, he rests but then puts his mind to work, studying others as he studies himself in search for the truth behind the mystery that life holds us close to.

So the one who labored in thought grew strong endowed with a steadfast purpose, gained knowledge, and passed it along to others. All education and experience make the blind see and make those who walk to run after the treasure of knowledge beyond compare.

All things we receive in good measure cannot be compared to the knowledge of things divine, challenging life for better answers.

– IV –

Part Four

Creative Thinking: A Supplement to Knowledge

In creative thinking, as a supplement to knowledge, grasping the imaginative idea which belongs to the abstract and pictorial thought group brings the subjective thought to an objective point of view. The new reality of comprehending and apprehending a concept actually changes the way we think because of the impact of this new reality of thought.

It has its importance not only in geometry but in philosophy and theology when thought is given to spiritual matters and matters that concern the working of the inner mind.

Time is very peculiar. When we're having fun it passes so fast, and when we're not it seems to move so slow. It's all relative. It's all so very real, too. And in the end when we judge for ourselves that it's really all the same. It doesn't really matter. Tomorrow is still another day.

What happens to us is that the world and along with it our inner unrest, stresses our mind, and we seek for relief in the solitude of our own mind and replace our worry with the anticipation of hope and faith in what we believe.

Still nothing is greater in either time than wit and wisdom. No one can ever take away these two, though we may lose everything else. It was once true that one could learn only so much and discover that things had limits; but technology changed that and the world of exploration, discovery, and learning has become in all words infinite. Research and development have usurped these limits with new revelations and insight from enlightenment, showing us just how powerful the mind really is when the will to learn is enforced with ambition.

Far off but awe-inspiring invention broke through the illusion of limits and magnified our previous thoughts with the microscope and telescope. From creative thinking our analysis became incomplete so we searched for better answers to our questions. We ought not to be surprised by the ingenuity of the human race. With our creative intelligence we can overcome most any obstacle that gets in our way.

The accumulation of knowledge raises our consciousness to new heights. This movement of consciousness is the totality of its moments. This totality of its determinate character makes wisdom inherently a spiritual reality because it belongs to the inner mind. It becomes part of the mind that treasures its possessions with desire and memory and leads us closer to our destiny with its proper use.

The universality becomes part of our individuality, and the will to know magnifies itself as a dominant force in our life journey. What we call pure knowledge is the absolute connection we make knowing and activating the senses of the mind and the relationship the mind has with its own wisdom.

The consciousness of our wisdom has a connection in our awareness and experience of the learning we come by in the moments of thought and contemplation of what we know and what we seek to learn to know.

In pure insight and enlightenment we can know with certainty that our infinite judgment of the spirit and soul has absolute reality in the mind, because we know of their existence with the senses of the mind as we know of our own conscience by the awareness of it through our consciousness of its energy and power. But the knowledge of these things, without material substance, is not yet finished; they must be known in regard to their immediateness of the moment, essentially as part of our inner reality our thoughts occupy us with.

This mode of experience knows its knowledge as the absolute essential element of our will and the critical essence of our judgment. These are the moments of pure thought, when spirit has reconciliation with its own consciousness proper. By themselves they are single and isolated, but in their unity they are bound together with the absolute knowledge they provide for the mind certain of their own existence. From this certain and absolute knowledge we come to know our own being and the essence of who we really are.

Reality here has no other significance than its own immediate existence bound in unity of the one individuality and the one of the universal, and still all these thoughts compose the inner mind.

Time has a reality all of its own. It is so great a wonder we cannot grasp it entirely. It surpasses all reality and goes beyond its own notion into the infinite of eternity, part of nature's own hidden essence. In the notion, knowing itself as a notion, the moments make their appearance prior to the whole fulfillment of time itself. Grasping an understanding of time is not far from our apprehension. Time is comprehended by our intuition of the here and now, past and future. Though our understanding may be incomplete we realize something is there greater than ourselves. Time appears as spirit's destiny and necessity of a greater life than we are able to know.

Through observation it finds its existence in thought and comprehends its existence in the present, yet remembers its own history and pretends to imagine its own future. Time becomes the essence of reality where we find our true self pondering our own existence in a place prior to eternity that we know only as a notion and concept.

We did not go wrong, nor were we far off course; our thinking circles itself with amusement for its own entertainment. The path to enlightenment comes from the heart and mind in total unity. In this way the unity becomes the essence and substance of our absolute knowledge we call our own wisdom and genius.

It is not of human fault that the mind interprets the heart; it is nature that unveils the truth and covers over the truth with illusion. The mind has an absolute need for re-definition of what we seem to realize we know. Our understanding precedes our comprehension.

Preordained it was, from nature's own rules, not to be restrained from the increase in knowledge. We celebrate when the silver-gray appears and enlightenment comes with a storm of thunder, and lightning sparks the soul into reflection and contemplation.

True enlightenment is when we recognize our own intelligent soul. Just as we recognize our own mind's intelligence, and our creative spirit, the unity we form in our thoughts brings reality to a stand and we devise answers to our own questions where-by our mind then seeks for a better understanding.

The dimensions of time go far beyond our comprehension. Providence has made nature that way so we question reality for our own entertainment and curiosity. Dominion has always been a great mystery; it goes beyond our own imagination. It stretches over the entire universe, beyond what we already know, so we explore and discover realities beyond our own.

That all might have knowledge is our common element, and when silence returns to our burdened mind in our repose we reflect and find more questions to be answered. The mystery remains and we still try to make sense of it all in the common language of the silence of the mind in contemplative thought.

One more progressive thought and another chapter in this work will be complete. The mind is only as rich as the treasures we store in it. Its actual content is made up of all our experience and of the furthest reaches of our imagination. We are not only aware of what we know but realize the limits of our own wisdom. We intuitively know the space and time we exist in. We live in the immediate process of development and creation. We create history even as we become part of it; our immediate and far past becomes our memories and even our learning extends our past as it does our future.

We become all we are from our learning and memory. Our Spirit is externalized and emptied into time. Time is the one thing that contains us and surrounds us even as the Author of Nature does. We become history itself even as we become part of our own future. All our knowledge permeates and assimilates its parts made whole in the foundation of our mind.

Aristotle pointed out that movement can neither come into being, nor can it cease to be, nor can time come into being, or cease to be. We, like time, are always moving into the infinite. Where we come from may not be known even as to where we are going, as spirit and soul; but for sure even as time has no beginning or end, so it is the same for us. In the realm of mind as it is in the realm of Spirit, we are part of eternity and only recognize the present as reality.

Reflections and Meditations

My thoughts were extended as far as I could let them — like sitting beside a campfire, feeling the warmth, and watching the embers soar to the sky like our thoughts roam free and wild, still within some sort of self-control. And then the idea came to me to stir the campfire, like my mind, and a thousand embers took off free at last from their bonds of the fire, and my mind, and soared to the heavens and beyond, carrying my imagination with them.

It's the certain way of thinking we do that brings the metaphysical into our reality. Heaven's messengers are more real than most of us believe possible; but again, it's all in the matter of our thinking. As every age passes into another and generations are born and die, we come into a new way of thinking with our values at hand along with the morals and ethics we consider in our individual minds.

A wiser person could elucidate much more than me, yet I try as a common man with only my sense of genius to relate the thoughts that come to me with the importance of their impression engraved upon my own mind. So in my own words this work comes to life as close to the explanation of the knowledge I have with as much expression as my own mind can conceive. It is the one who labors in thought that can bring philosophy to life, of life, to the common man such as me.

A different clarity shines on the enlightened one passing revealed knowledge on to humanity. Things that have already been said are again said, and re-phrased, in a newly formed way, bringing to those who had overlooked them this new found sense of enlightenment. That's how it is generation after generation finding new meaning from the old.

Sparingly through the times of our life the spirit reaches out in due measure, but few hear the calling; but for those who do the quiet voice echoes in the mind and longs for a new expression. Once probed deeply, life, in a philosophical way, can be grasped in a way that brings out the divine in our human nature. It seems people just don't understand without first fearing and then encountering the consequences; but providence will have its way. And we notice a change in ourselves first and then we notice the change in the world.

Where the spirit is active we too will stir and debate amongst ourselves. Even within ourselves we lose ourselves to wonder; but the sureness we once had returns. Wonder is only the passing of moments in time while the mind is at work with itself. As we resolve our differences within our own mind, and with others through conversation, we find similarities of thought out-weighing the differences. Here we find the necessity to pause and consider our accomplishments.

The release and then the coming together is a natural part of the dialogue we have with others even as we have dialogue with ourselves. Our mortal nature brings us to combat with the part of us that is divine, and while being true to ourselves we direct our will towards those things that supply us our needs and procurement of pleasure.

What course may be the best can well be known by the treasure of wisdom our intelligence holds. From morning onwards there is discourse with others that encounters resistance and submission. All differences once resolved we still store in our mind what will not be revealed; and temporary peace rings calm and rest, and a reconfiguring of all our notions that appeal to our convictions. What we think we know, we cannot be sure, except our belief and faith which is unshaken from its foundation.

Holy Powers joined in unseen thunderstorms conceal themselves, yet in every way can be seen working in our daily path through the rites of passage that move us along a lifelong journey of discovery and an Adventure in Learning.

Oh youth will never return to me, but with time and experience I accept growing older and realize there will be others to carry on my work and studies generation after generation. Literature will always be part of life and culture in all of humanity. This is for sure, a certainty beyond compare. The evening for one is a morning for another and afternoon comes to all because the sun and moon share the Earth equally and in common as we revolve around in a universe full of galaxies. Perhaps even one similar to ours exists somewhere and life goes on just the same with thought and memory in our mind.

From within we hear the call of divinity in our nature as humans. Some choose not to hear while others' receptivity is open to a higher calling. Winds lightly breathing already announce some unusual presence in our intelligence from the other side of nature where spiritual reality is known by the mind to have a sure and certain reality observed by our thinking and our senses.

The travails, designed from above and then carried out here, lead us to wonder and dream and conjure all sorts of ideas, but the truth still remains concealed, waiting for our discovery to be revealed why we have to work so hard just to live. Our enduring cherishing of the spirit of our will brings concealed wisdom to the surface of our thoughts, and revelation inspires us to live at a greater height than once thought possible.

Enlightenment is at every corner we turn in life; while even on a straight course enlightenment brings us closer to the real truth than we once knew. We know that knowledge is infinite and that the variety of experience can be infinitely measured by each of us within our own means.

We know that opportunity has a relative measure of chance and concealed within it the determinants of our fate rest only to be awakened. Consequence and fate are entangled somehow through the use or misuse of our intelligence; but where our creativity roams free our ends are determined by the means we use to survive.

Man is born with rationality and a certain capacity for knowledge, and since no one is born genius, we have to acquire our knowledge through experience and study. As we all know, wisdom comes with age and our aptitude for learning. As does the process follow rules and patterns, so does our ability to apply what we've learned to our everyday life. Who could have thought we would have grown the way we have, and come as far as we have? Not only intellectually have we grown but spiritually as well. The universal consciousness is in every way part of our daily lives.

In all regards we ought not have regret about our study but continue with regimentation, paying attention to detail and considering in all respects the value of the knowledge we find. So our capacity for learning should not have been given to us in vain, and our divine intelligence should provide us with the means of instructing ourselves in a manner of living in which we are led to understanding through long periods of contemplation and reflection.

We ought to consider the idea that the human ego is the prime mover of the will, where all action, intent, and motivation stem from. We ought to consider the quiet satisfaction that comes from the thoughts and actions we pursue in our entanglement with life itself. In this respect, my attitude toward my writing is best expressed by the thought that I write not only for the time at hand, but for all time. Though I am only one there are many with the same concerns.

I would not lose a second of time to be without a pen and paper to capture the thoughts that cross my mind. The fundamental concerns of human values and universal problems will always need to be addressed, expounded upon and sincerely given deliberate thought to. We must conquer the unknown and find, to our own satisfaction, answers to the mystery of life.

For those who consider the benefits of relevance to one's own time as of crucial importance, I will add, in regard to our age, there has never been a time when we have so desperately needed a projection of things as they ought to be and not of just how they are.

What contributes to our well-being is vital to our simple existence. Living need not be a struggle; but no one ever said it would be an easy road to travel, and the journey will be long and full of trials and tribulations to test our character and skills we learn along the way. I only knew as I wrote my books that they ought to have a right to live; and they do as art in literature full of tales, speculation and glory for the human race. We do not just live for living's sake; we live to learn and experience all that life has to offer and in return offer back to life what it deserves.

I wanted to write something real, of true value to the vision man has of attempting to explore and discover the parts of life we retain solely in our mind and the reactions we have to those simple, elemental thoughts. We, like the spirit we carry, need fuel, a primal motivator, or it too will run dry.

There are those who are so satisfied with the way things are they have no regard for how they could be; but in each of us there is this bit of revolutionary spirit that forces us to look for change and act upon the vision we have for ourselves. We have to come to terms with ourselves before we can come to terms with the world. So we look within and then look out into the grand unknown universe that surrounds us.

We ought not to be satisfied with anything less than the vision we have for ourselves in order to change the world and make our mark for generations to come. What I'm looking for is a fresh perspective to compensate for the inadequacies of our present understanding of the personal life of our individual minds.

In twenty-five years we all have noticed how we have changed. In another twenty-five years I will be gone, but these writings will remain, and perhaps someone will find them and add wonder to their own vision of life.

From white light comes the colors of the rainbow; and from one simple man enlightenment may come to the world that will add to readers' own judgment of themselves and the world.

Neither politics nor ethics nor philosophy is an end in itself, neither in life or literature. Only man is an end in himself. From the wheel to the skyscraper everything we are and everything we have comes from a single attribute of man: the functioning of a reasoning mind.

It doesn't really matter anyhow; only a few in every generation will grasp and achieve the full reality of man's proper stature, and the rest will fall short of our real potential. But what is important here is that we continue in our quest for knowledge.

Each of us has within our abilities a thinking mind able to call to reference concrete matters, and as well in our critical, analytical, and rational mind the ability to discern meanings and implications of physical and abstract concepts.

Life seems at times so bizarre and irrational it would be foolish to try to attempt at any understanding, yet we do. We try to make a sympathetic interpretation that creates a sense of normality for our own existence.

We are more at home with ourselves in thought than outside ourselves preoccupied with worldly concerns. It's a miracle how the mind works with what goes on inside it and what draws our attention. Nature is the most common concern. People and things take up a lot of our time, and notions and ideas fill the rest of our thinking.

One of the most obvious concerns of the mind is the work it does thinking about the thoughts we have. Preoccupied with emotion we have to detach ourselves and think clearly and objectively about the how and way we think — not only the what we think about or the why, but the actual process of our own patterns of thought.

In this age of technology we are faced with so many facts we have to discern the truth from the illusion of the truth, all the while considering how we come to knowledge and what we do with it.

We are impelled towards the future with doubt and uncertainty; but the past constantly reminds us to live without regret, because history goes on and is constantly written by the lives we live, thoughts we think, and actions we take from the reactions that our mind concerns itself with in the thinking we do as life goes on.

When contemplating an object in nature, whether in great things or small, I can ask the question, is it the object which is here declaring itself, or is it me? Each and every person really looks on the world in its accumulated finished form suited to one's own measure, but to seize the world without imagination is leaving the one aspect of creation alone without doubting the possible existence of a better or worse condition.

Since this book had its origination almost ten years ago many things have changed, even the thoughts I've had concerning the subject. The way I've been thinking has undergone various improvements. The harvest of knowledge has taken its toll in my creative insight, and through the freedom of expression I've noticed a change in how I think concerning myself and my conception of the world.

What has perplexed the world ever since the beginning of recorded history is how we conceive what is before us and the way we conceive it. The new horizons of knowledge have given greater depth to the mind considering the greatness of the universe and the mind that thinks of it. It may not be too early to decide upon a view of the mind that suits us, but the relative conception most agreed upon is that it is a phenomenal machine that processes information and causes us to react to the discoveries it makes based on the knowledge it has its foundation built upon.

Let me say it wasn't the easiest task to collect information for the building of this work, a compilation of views and thoughts concerning thinking and our thoughts; but as we near the end my conclusions have brought me satisfactorily to near what I've set out to accomplish. The accumulation of my thoughts thus far have been a successful accomplishment in writing, and as for the final chapters of this work I will attempt to bring the collection of my findings to a successful conclusion.

Whoever you are, you're a soul from the ethereal heavens sent to this earth to make your mark and learn your lessons and prove your power and worth. This is what we humans do — empowered to conquer contention and strife and create a bit of heaven on Earth.

You walk and stumble and are expected to get up and move on. There is no standing still or time will pass you by. Endowed with all the miracles of life, your heart and mind configure a reasonable explanation and you live with choice and consequence. Without regard for nature you are expected to overcome obstacles and endure living to the best of your abilities.

What a good thing it is that hope lives in the hearts of humanity. What a good thing it is to find ourselves singing when the music starts. To shape and rule our own lives is a miracle itself, although we live in the spirit of autonomy, providence takes charge of the world around us even as it does of our individual lives.

Those who recognize the value of the spiritual significance in our lives know the power our spirit has over our own will. But in each of our individual lives we know the power of the mind over our will. It is wonderful that those who recognize this miracle know the scale of its dominion.

Our feelings and emotions only heighten our senses beyond the mind's ability to rationally discern and judge the condition that our lives are consumed in. We are reminded by Plato to "do what thou has to do, and know thy self." Whoever should do what he has to would see that the first thing he must do is learn what he is and how his actions and reactions would have some sort of consequence in his own life. What is properly his that he can call his own is namely his own spirit and soul. Scholarship must not tolerate either myth or legend. The scholarly man limits himself to the nearest knowledge that brings wisdom to his mind. You don't have to travel all around the world to realize the sky is blue everywhere.

Everything that liberates the mind leads to our creativity. Like anything else in the mind we have to sort through the good and the bad; the useful and what is no use to us at all. Perhaps this is just one of the natural processes of the human intellect.

Give me the serenity to accept the things I cannot change and the courage to change the things that I can. As for the events and circumstances beyond our control there is no use in getting upset; they are indifferent to our wrath. Perhaps it is just part of nature's mysterious ways. The unruly mind can be tamed. When experience fails, reason and creativity move into action. After our intelligence fills itself with fantasy and dreams sooner than we anticipate we bring ourselves back to the reality of life.

Reason has so many forms that we do not know which to resort to, and experience has no fewer, yet when we deliberate upon a significant matter we resort to our own understanding and judge accordingly to our conscience and better judgment.

Our mind examines what others have related to us and then invents on its own some likeness of what it has found amusing and has a significant relatedness.

The mind works in the most curious ways. How many roads, Bob Dylan asks, does a man have to take before he is free, before he becomes a real man? The answer is blowing in the wind. We don't expect that these questions are easily answered. Our immediate concerns have wide-ranging implications and philosophical meanings.

We recognize we are continuously engaged in a process of growth and discovery. Any one point in time is as good as another. We are encouraged to make our choices wisely and thoughtfully, and to attempt a reasonable understanding of the implications of consequences.

Education is one of the best teachers because it teaches us how to think; but experience teaches us the proper way of reasoning problems. We work hard at life all the time making it worthwhile for us not to be worried, frenzied, and anxious expending our energies on trivialities but rather on the important things that make life precious to us and endearing, finding some assertions that have validity to our existence. You don't have to be a graduate student to realize life is what we make of it and the choices we make have sure and certain consequences. Philosophy opens up our mind to all kinds of possibilities.

My clock started again. Time is on the march. It leaves behind only memories as it carries us along, for the ride, into our future.

It is no wonder that alchemy gets us through our days and nights; it is a better way to search our own soul for the answers to our questions and search through the library shelves for better answers to the questions that raise themselves to the surface of our thoughts. Who knows what tomorrow will bring but just another day.

Out of one subject we make a thousand and sink into the infinitude of molecules and atoms that make up the essence and consistency of our thoughts. Never did two think alike or have an identical opinion of one idea or of many; but alike comes philosophy in its various forms. Though haunted by self-doubt and insecurity we learn our way out of the labyrinth of paradoxical life. Though we all search for a religious meaning to life, God wants relationships not organized religion.

The circus is in town; but little do we realize we are all part of it. What would a circus be without an audience? We all are part of the drama of life. We all are the actors and the audience at the same time.

The peculiar oddity about life is that though we seem to be the same, change is the most constant of all concepts. We are all trained to wear our shoes, but barefoot is most exciting even when we step upon a thorn; then comes the challenge to extract it and we still go barefoot in the park or upon the beach. Think now — wearing shoes upon the beach would take the feeling and emotion out of the adventure and experience we go to the beach shore for.

And what makes the dark side of the moon so special? The answer is that it is mysterious and causes us to wonder how such an existence can be possible. Just the same is the dark side of our soul, something no one knows but us, and the mind wonders how to let light enter upon it.

I was lying on the grass looking up at the sky, watching the clouds, and fell asleep. When I awoke it was night and I found myself watching the night sky. When I fell asleep again I found myself in another world; perhaps I lost myself to my own mind, overpowered by the feelings and emotions that strike at humans in the course of their rites of passage. It's a curious thing our mind is and always will be, so we write and think of philosophy to cure our curiosity and try to make some kind of sense of all we go through.

It can be said that we find it just as necessary to discover knowledge as we do to interpret what we find in a rational and logical culmination of the highest degree the ability of our mind can achieve.

Part of our curiosity as humans is our desire to learn and know. The degree of willingness varies, and the ability to conceptualize our learning varies as well with our aptitude and disposition to learning as a means to wisdom and genius.

What we all are seeking for is an ideology that claims more than mystical rhetoric. There is no end to our learning; even as we cross over to the other side of nature there is so much more to learn. A mind cannot stop itself, like our heartbeat; like our breath we can control it, but we have to take another and add to our own wisdom to endure our survival and to satisfy our will to know.

Our wisdom is not as clever as we suppose; machines fail but people make mistakes, and a machine is only as good as the people who built it and program it. It seems we are so preoccupied with acquiring new skills that will help us assimilate with the new world we are soon to forget that the self needs more than skills and wisdom; it needs stability in its emotional state to cope with an overachieving society.

One idea that has its own importance is that we have to find a state of comfort with our own place in life that comes with our achievement or by random chance of opportunity. We have to learn to be satisfied with what we have even when the power of suggestion lures us on to acquire more. We ought to be wise enough to be able to live within our means and denounce want, differentiating it from need as the basis for our own survival.

We have been endowed with some degree of intelligence to become aware of those things we do not know and extend ourselves to reach out to discover and understand what we find. What we inquire into helps us understand not only ourselves but the world as well, and still we find there is so much to learn we have no conception of. The paradox happens that those who do not know have to inquire, though they need only more rigid clarification; those who know little more than nothing inquire for more enlightenment. The study is the same but the discoveries are more pronounced.

We can no longer claim ignorance to knowledge. The information is everywhere to be found. For the first time in history the flow of information travels at the speed of light over optical fibers of the internet across the world waiting to be explored and discovered.

In today's world of modern technology it is generally accepted that the flow of information has reached all levels of humanity. There have always been conflicts between the generations, but the difference is that today the student is no longer the exception, but the rule. If the purpose of the social apparatus is to create a human existence on the basis of a humanized nature then it defeats its purpose. In today's world we just grow up too fast. The world pushes upon us responsibility to work and live productively.

I owe my tendency to moderation to consult my conscience to the tempering of my opinions and beliefs only due to the wisdom I have achieved from contemplation and study. The world is open to me and I have taken advantage of the opportunity to explore and discover all that I can find to increase my own genius and understanding.

When we meet with the occasion and opportunity of fortune or misfortune there are lessons to be learned to add to our experience. Here we find the courage, strength, and a fresh resolve to our convictions, and explore the unknown that reveals itself through chance and opportunity that come our way by life and providence.

The deeper implications knowledge brings is the ability for problem solving and developing our creative abilities we have been endowed with from the beginning of time. We have a demand for autonomy, but providence always takes its toll in our accountability.

The best investment we can make as a civilization is to encourage the continuation of learning. The best investment we can make is in people, from the smallest child to the most elderly in our society.

We must learn to endure what we cannot avoid but use discretion and sound judgment in what we can, and are, given thought to. Our life is composed of discords as well as different tones. One has to learn how to blend them together to form a more perfect union, creating wisdom from our accumulated knowledge.

We live for the means to live; but it ought to read we live for a reason and for philosophy to explore the reasons presented to our creative intelligence. If you have been able to examine and manage your own life you have achieved the greatest task of all. We live not only for ourselves but for others.

Day after day, from sunrise to sunset, our life earns its own worth. The value we put on it comes from our heart and conscience where God enters and guides us how to live on our own without regret.

Gray skies will come, but we get over it. Pure sunshine illuminates the world; but how many think upon the thought that it is the sun that makes all this possible? And when the gray skies do come the sun shines above the clouds.

My wit is well suited to serve such a mighty cause as my own well-being, and never runs out of specious arguments about anything. This is the life of a philosopher. You are not dying because you are ill, you are dying because you are alive; it's nature's way.

We are demanded for a means to live, not for a reason, but we quest for reason to explain the work and toil it takes to live. We create our own fears, they just do not appear. Education will solve that problem. The greatest task in life is learning how to solve our problems straight on. They have the stealth to approach us, and though the burden is great our intelligence pulls us thru and beyond.

Any outcome from a matter of choice creates our destiny. We have the power to answer the riddles life presents us. Our fate summons us. Our knowledge saves us from the consequences and regrets of choice. We learn to deal with reality and take it a step beyond, answering its questions in our mind all the while continuing our quest for knowledge and a better truth to ground our new wisdom.

We have to step out of the crowd and make a stand for what we believe with conviction and determination with the energy and power of the truth we find from learning and experience. Life may be harsh at times but again no one said it would be easy.

To communicate is one of the most human things a person can do. Communication is a very fragile phenomenon. It depends on trust, clarity, perception, and a very nebulous area called common ground. This common ground is what bonds those who think alike together. At the same time it separates us and brings us into alienation. If you keep your head while those around you are losing theirs, perhaps it is their conception of the perspective and not your own that separates you from them.

There is of course a great deal of familiarity with strife in the Family of Man. One of the strengths of society is a healthy sense of realism in its concern for complex human problems. When I started my inquiry into the philosophy of man my interest consumed me. What I found was the most revolutionary ideas are held by most people but held in reserve for fear of what others may think.

Making our way, by the journey through life, we come across many different kinds of people and things. The reality of impressions clings to our mind like the morning fog hovers over the lowlands. We travel along the margins, along the edge, and if not for the fear of falling we would hesitate less and run the course in place of the slow walk with our attention occupied by everything around us and what is inside our mind that consumes our thoughts.

We occupy ourselves with personal protest against change for constructive purposes; but social protest is crucial to any enlightened society. It is the youth that have the responsibility for building our future. So education and freedom of thought must be our highest concern, and the truth of things must be known without illusion for us to make the proper considerations about change.

We are forced to deal with reality as it is and make our choices according to the facts compiled in our knowledge and wisdom. We wonder what the world is coming to. The answer is what we make it. The motivation towards greatness consists not so much in striving upward and forward as in knowing how to find one's place and remain secure on the edge where reality comes in full sight of our horizon.

One striking feature of our situation today is that we are creating new problems as we go along with time at our side. The same analogy has been with us for ages upon generations. Our capacity to create new problems as rapidly as we solve the old has implications for the kind of society we shall have to design. Of course change takes time; but as we get older the young get older too, and a new generation is faced with not only a new set of problems but continues solving the old problems, but with new skills and knowledge.

Social change takes time. We live in a self-renewing society, ready to improvise solutions to problems it won't recognize until tomorrow. It is hardly surprising that we have come to think of happiness as the absence of problems. We are problem-solvers by nature and the real world imposes itself upon us to a state of frenzy.

One must be able to contemplate both pleasure and pain equally. Time is the ultimate precursor of change itself. We must go deeply into the nature of things to find out what nature's necessity has the need for, to discover and explore the true nature of things and ideas.

Our quest is for more accurate knowledge and methods of judgment to solve the problems of the past and to consider future possibilities. Surely an explanation does exist that we all can agree upon.

Learning as a Skill and Art Form

Truly learning is a most useful accomplishment and a great necessity if we are to survive in this technological society; if we are to become wise in our judgment and if we are to discern our choices we need to know the truth with certainty and learn what we can about present and past knowledge. Learning becomes a skill while the will to know leads us to our own genius.

As our learning progresses we support our beliefs and convictions with reason and logic determined by the how and way we process our thinking. Our intelligence is a powerful tool to be used wisely and only adds to our creativity and imagination.

Only faith can embrace the high mystery of nature. We cannot deny that nature has a physical and spiritual side. There are just too many miracles that cannot be explained by natural phenomena. Our intelligence is just too powerful a tool to deny us the license for our creativity.

Defining relevance has a relationship to traditional and liberal contemporary values. What was important then has no importance now. Times change and so do we and the things around us. Nothing is permanent now; no job or expectation of tenure; not even tomorrow. The crucial issue is the dynamic re-defining of what we think is important. Most of us only live day to day, pay check to pay check.

We want a chance to think for ourselves. So many decisions are made for us. We want independence, but are dependent at every corner and cross road. We look forward to our freedom to make mistakes and learn from them. What we get is a choice between the lesser of two evils. We want a chance to earn a good living and keep our integrity.

Learning is best when it is self-propelled. We need not be forced to learn, but for own welfare it is best to keep our mind active. It is the action of independent study that drives us to newfound wisdom and genius. The real question here is how stress can be humanized.

The world has a powerful effect on our character and disposition. Learning is essential to our growth and development.

We have been transplanted between the old world and the new. Many changes have taken place over a short period of time. We must come to terms with living in a new world order. The socio-economic order has changed not only our lifestyles but our way of thinking about our present and future plans we predict for our near future.

It's the music of life that makes life what it is. No matter what kind you listen to it's the music that strikes your heart. It's not the lyrics, but they make a difference. They all tell a specific story. Combined, the music and lyrics make the grandeur of the big picture what it is. It's the music that goes to our mind, and there we find the peace that we do. It's the music that relaxes us, tames the beast inside.

It is our own intelligence that reasons. We keep the music in our mind. The lyrics remain, and still we create our own. Music has always been a form of communication. It's been part of our culture and civilization even from the beginning.

It is our spirit that recognizes the music and knows our faith, beliefs, and hopes. In the midst of learning we come in contact with different variables that bend and twist our own notions and ideas. But in learning we increase our inner strength and wisdom to make the choices that we have to in order to survive in this rat race of a world. Our quest for knowledge brings out the doubts we have into the open where we can find the certain truth we are looking for.

With the ability to speak and write effectively we can express ourselves and be understood as well as understand. It all comes from within our mind, separate from nature but still part of it. We ought to understand the magnitude of the range the mind is capable of.

We ought to understand the paralyzing power of thought and speech with our creativity from one to another and back again to ourselves. Words are but signs of ideas; and there is more to words than they represent; it is the words that make us think of their representations. The issue of correctness is not important here; it is what the words bring to mind.

We ought to be concerned with the shades of meaning words have. We ought to concern ourselves with preserving the dignity and effectiveness of the words we use as a flexible means of communication. Whoever dares to presume that they know anything and does not even know what knowledge is deceives themselves.

Whatever power we have over our inclinations comes directly from our will; and it has to be conditioned with knowledge to make the right choices at the right time. Man without any apprenticeship in acquiring knowledge does not increase his skills or wisdom but stands idle with a limited resource at his own disposal from the treasures he holds in his mind.

It's a new dawn. Nothing can stand in our way. It's late summer now. The harvesters have already started picking the bottom leaves of the tobacco, and the autumn colors have started to show themselves.

Although literature can do many things, the very best thing it can do is to give the reader an aesthetic experience. Literature moves us to a higher level of thinking. Literature is the story of man's climb to the stars. It reveals the endless journey of mankind.

In so many small circles of friends we have intimate discussions that relieve our minds of the clutter the world brings on or that we bring on ourselves. Remember it's all in your mind. Endowed with all the miracles of heart, mind, and soul all men, women, and children are self-unique in one deep universal consciousness. I would rather stumble a thousand times reaching for a goal than not try at all.

In the world of today the role of literature is becoming more vital than ever. Appreciation comes in part to the words that create thoughts; but even more so it is the opening up of the mind to new ideas of reality and fantasy.

We know what we know really only for ourselves. If I talk to someone else about what I believe I know, he forthwith imagines he knows a lot more, or knows it differently, so I have to turn back into myself with my own knowledge and let each other believe what they want.

Nature tears us from the womb of a woman. As we grow up nature tears us from the world and we become alienated within our own self. We have got to get ourselves back into the world by deliberate compromise and thoughtful reflection. Even if we lose everything and everyone we still have our self, spirit and soul. The mind knows itself better than anyone could imagine. By chance or opportunity we cannot be torn away from our own being.

You turn to speak but you are all alone. You turn, and turn again and promise yourself to make your mark and become a legend in your own time. All your friends are gone but your shadow stands close by not leaving your side. You look to heaven for answers but there are none. And more time goes by without notice because you have no clock or watch and are all alone with the world and at one with yourself.

We learn not to be torn away from ourselves; because even when we have nothing but time, we still have our own self and our spirit. We come to terms with aloneness and find real peace within ourselves because we are all we've got. This is wisdom — not of the world, but spiritual wisdom. Even if the world ceased to be we still would be ourselves in our being.

Man is not so much different that other creatures except that his intelligence allows him to express his creativity and return it to the one he prays to. The creatures have everything they need to survive; but man with his accumulation of knowledge found desire and passion to ask of nature more than it can provide, so we create for ourselves what nature does not. For this reason the mind demands knowledge and wisdom to create from our creativity.

After all, what aspects of our human competence cannot be found in the activities of animals? The only difference is that we can creatively think and reason on a higher level, and we have the power of faith and belief in our own spirit and soul as well as in a higher power that makes our intelligence more powerful than any other creature.

Humanity — man and woman and children alone have the ability to think and realize when they learn something. It happens in the time between the moments of time, perhaps in the realization of a moment we call a second, or even less than that, a half second.

It's the time when we say to ourselves "Ah, I get it" — an intuitive realization that is either deliberate or by chance but comes suddenly. The one who thinks has these moments according to nature's ways. We think things, imaginings, that are not real. And above all matters of concern besides for the ability to think we can remember too, but only humans have a responsibility to their conscience.

The only word I can think of that explains the phenomenon of life is epiphany: a sudden manifestation of the essence or meaning of something; a comprehension or perception of reality by the means of a sudden or deliberate intuitive realization.

In a moment's time we come to conclusions and make judgments, sometimes not even aware of the consequences to come. Reason as if some monumental idea sparked something in our mind and we realize that passion and emotion have overcome us. It happens like that sometimes — life without thinking. Machines fail but humans just make mistakes. The moments between moments seem to last forever.

Life keeps coming at you. You've got to be quick and agile in your mind giving thought its due ultimate consideration. You got to keep focused because life will distract you. Life is the ultimate distraction.

The music keeps playing and the drama gets more exciting every moment of life you can really think about. The decisions and judgments keep coming, like life, and the choices seem variable and infinite. But there is only one choice: to make the right decision.

Every fascinating second of realization exhilarates the mind. To give evidence it's only self-realization. The reality of the external world is beyond definition, but we still try anyhow.

Not only by study and reflection, but by our own observations and thoughts, do we come to terms with the world.

Study and Reflection as a Way of Life

Philosophy is now seen as a practical academic discipline. The caricature of these thoughtful words brings us far around the corner from the ivory towers that detach us from the problems of real life. There is no real instruction book that goes along with philosophy; we kind of make the rules up as we go. There are not only rules but laws and principles that govern thought and thinking.

It was the primary concern of mine to pick out precisely those questions that needed to be addressed and answered. Sometimes we get carried away with a thought by sheer delight of hearing our own brains turning over, but more often we find a new clarity and understanding like an act of epiphany.

The paradigm of life creates the great enigma which consumes the philosopher's attention and fills his or her mind with a tapestry of random, spontaneous, and deliberate thinking potential.

Isn't it curious how a bunch of neurosensors can cause us so much excitement, inspiration, awe, and memories? That is our mind, and it is not a simple thing. So we study and reflect as a way of life.

Time goes on but it doesn't pass us by; it brings us along with it. Hear me now; my own thoughts know my voice. As I listen to myself the words just seem to flow in sequential patterns. I know what I know and know what I do not. If I was not certain reality was not a dream I would be more likely to be drawn to skepticism; but reality has a certain truth about it we just cannot deny.

We should employ our own powers of thought to improve what is most useful for every man, woman, or child in their circumstance of life, even concerning the acquisition of new knowledge that we add to the registry of our experiences life holds for us, including spiritual enlightenment.

We have a necessity for understanding, and due to this necessity our use of words must express what we intend. We must understand the connotations of them and their implications for us to conceive and perceive what their true meaning relates to our intelligence.

There are windows I have not looked thru and doors I have not opened. Man does not live by bread alone; perhaps alchemy is the only solution when life brings us an epiphany of sudden realization.

We should not be too hasty to know things above our present powers or inquire into the depths of knowledge without a secure foundation of enlightened understanding, nor should we be frightened from exerting our strength through our hidden capabilities.

The truth is not concealed in an impenetrable darkness. There is a stream of light that shines thru all things and our awareness just has to realize it, perhaps by an epiphany in our mind.

The mind produces images as fast as thought. People who want more than they need are making a fundamental mistake, one that reduces their chances of being satisfied and causes careless anxiety. We need to know the limits of what we think we need; above that our passion and desire move our will in directions that often lead to regret.

Our life comes with no strings attached. We act entirely on our own. The sober calculations which search out the reasons for every choice and avoidance and drives out the opinions we come to conclusions to are the source of the greatest turmoil for humanity's responsibility to its own conscience, spirit, and soul.

Into the impenetrable darkness of the unknown we penetrate to search out concepts, theories, and principles to add to our own experience and knowledge. As our learning grows, like a pyramid, our base must be secure enough to support the highest tier. We ought to take our learning slowly and build a stable platform for the new knowledge to build upon itself; thereby our wisdom grows with our learning of new knowledge and we gain insight from the combinations of our thoughts.

One can entertain the mind with a variety of thoughts, but too much diversity at one time will fatigue the mind and we will be led astray from our actual learning process. One should take their learning slow and in short steps to achieve real wisdom.

One ought to exercise care, skill, and diligence about their study in a just proportion. This action will achieve great results when interpreting new found knowledge and turning it into wisdom.

The alluring employment of the mind serves as a diversion of thought to enrich our understanding, and pleasure is turned into profit from gained knowledge, thereby increasing the treasury of memories of experience and wisdom.

It takes determination to make a dream come true; you fight until you win or see that it was an unrealistic goal. Essential to our will to know is that same determination to seek and find knowledge that gives true worth and value to our wisdom. Star-guided towards that enlightenment the urgency demands attention and creativity. Something else motivates our ambition: the eternal pursuit of a greater wisdom.

We all must agree that knowledge is power and that same power can accentuate our abilities and capabilities of thinking, even so far as exploring our own thoughts stored in our mind and the capacity of our own creative imagination leading us along to novel and bold discoveries in our exploration of ourselves, life, and the universe our world is contained within.

Man must live within the bounds of nature. Anything above that is just plain surreal. His condition is a very modest one. As for his essential being he has no true privilege above other creatures. What he thinks, dreams, and remembers is just part of life and part of nature within itself.

Nature is constant in her course; there's no denying this. The executive principle of nature is change, and change is constant and plays a dominant role in her essential character. We can always rely on change as a means to any future we can possibly foresee. Anyone who could adequately understand her present state could draw reliable conclusions about the present, future, and past.

We take pride in our fair, discursive reason and logical judgment as well as in our capacity to honestly give thought to the passions and emotions which nature brings out in our essential being.

The wisest, like some philosophers, admit that there is more to learn than we already know, even so much it is inconceivable the amount of knowledge than we can confess to. The unknown is greater than the known, just like the unseen is greater than the seen. Nature is greater than one could possibly even believe.

What we conceive is greater than what we can perceive, and the mind is more powerful than one could even realize except from an epiphany that comes from study and contemplation. What we imagine is greater than all likely possibilities.

The philosophical skeptic doesn't claim that we know nothing, because we do and it shows itself in our intelligence. Our mind confirms that thought, but to do so would be self-defeating. Of course we know something because of our abilities to ponder and think. The skeptic's position is to challenge our right to make claims to knowledge.

The real challenge is, do we actually know anything that has absolute truth and credibility? Of course there are principles that cannot be denied, but our mind plays tricks on us; only our logic and reasoning remains the same. The forces of nature produce the same or at least similar effects in different ways.

It is not language itself that is correct, effective, and graceful; it is the spirit embodied within language; so it is a matter of choice which words we use to express ourselves to achieve desirable qualities of style and form.

Our conception of knowledge is complex and many layered, woven into a tapestry of many designs. But even as we consider the various parts we ought not to forget the grandeur of the whole picture.

Learning is cumulative and associative. The building blocks of knowledge come from the quarry of literature and technological media. We build on experience from birth and continually learn as we grow. As we broaden our experience the demand for quality knowledge increases. It's not the quantity, but the quality, and we need to find ways to express our wisdom and genius.

Another day has gone and a new day has come. I guess I'll just make the best of it and capture a few thoughts, recollect some memories, and perhaps even dream a bit.

There is no occupation sweet as scholarship as the means of making known to us the infinity of matter and the immense grandeur of nature, including matters of spiritual reality and the actions of our own mind, considering its contents and what can be learned.

Wisdom brought from the skill of study, contemplation, and reflection brings our lives out from storm and darkness and fixes them in the tranquility and light, as in daylight without a cloud in the sky, whereby we come to our repose and peace of mind, content with what we know in truth and certainty.

So long as man thinks he has the means and powers, he can transform himself from being lost into being found in the enlightenment, acknowledging the Creator of his conscience with an original state of consciousness. Man does not know the why or how some things got their beginning or their end; but he does know that the here and now occupies most of his attention and distracts him from his own creativity.

As the drama of life continues we all are actors and audience at the same time, both sides of reality watching each other and considering the present, past, and future of what is and was and will be. We create our own destiny.

Learning instructs us to withdraw our thoughts from our mind and form ways of expression for them. Memory produces what it wills but in contemplation we can learn to direct our will towards the comfort repose provides and security of our essential self. What we need is a store of intelligence we can recall to protect our own survival. The simplicity of our intelligence ensures our ability and capability of invention and creativity.

The power of philosophy sends us protection not merely from ignorance and insensibility but for the amusement and entertainment of the mind's potential to logically reason and understand the information it processes in a sensible and rational way.

In presenting closing arguments relevant for discussion it's not the matter of information that comes to my attention but the lack of words to express myself. But that is specifically where our creativity comes to play, like a small child on a playground who must decide which toy to play with. That is a learned quality that comes with our growing intelligence.

Though our progress is tedious and slow, what we gain is a remedy to continual doubt. Consumed with the quest for satisfaction, we think through our speculation and our senses are relieved from the anxiety and stress by probable answers to our most paradoxical questions about life and nature.

When mature old age comes to us we certainly think differently than when we were younger. Life comes at you pretty fast; if you don't stop and give it some thought you might miss the best part.

If chance draws near some opportunity or circumstance becomes part of our life. When we recognize its importance we become wiser in our own genius. Just as life is made better by simplicity, we must draw it out from the complications that present themselves to the drama we all participate in.

There is no room for indolence in our lives. We must excel at life to succeed. But to where one asks? The answer is, as high as one can achieve on their own power. Providence may help, but we have to help ourselves first. The first step is the most difficult. Next comes the second, which requires ambition and effort on our part.

The truth of language is that it can be expressed in more than one way. One must not forfeit their own interpretation and originality but be open to and acknowledge others' viewpoints.

There are others just as temperate, valiant, and inspired as I am. Others are more eloquent; but if I think that I am different it is only because I think I am. Perhaps the other is the different one, but I am not the one who concerns myself about differences; we are all the same.

Who will be the spokesman for society? It is the philosopher with his or her variations of notions and ideas that draw our attention to the reality of reality.

In the history of human culture there is no example of a conscious adjustment of the various factors of personal and social life except in the peripheral efforts of philosophers who deal with conditions and their effects on society. The philosopher is the only one that is engaged in writing a description of the present condition which in turn affects the outcome of history, because the philosopher is the only one aware of the nature of the present.

The philosopher is the one who grasps the implications of the actions and new knowledge in his or her own time before the numbness grows to their remote level of attention and awareness of the social and cultural variations of society.

Initially we set to work with laudable common sense, but even this has its limits. Just too many variables come to play in the drama of life. It is possible to say that the truth lies between two variable points of view, but the problem itself lies between the two, beyond our range of vision, the eternally active life contemplated in repose.

Stumbling blocks of every kind come to the traveler. The philosopher, however, points to the significant places they come along life's long and tedious road. It is the work of the philosopher to learn how to develop the unknown from the known and see what is to come from the unseen.

Look at us now; what we've become has made us numb to ourselves. As concerned as we are about the world, we have to look out for ourselves first. Anyway, collectively we are all one anyhow. Every day another miracle, everyday another challenge — but we will meet these challenges. Still we turn to metaphor for consolation. We turn to the dictionary for words to express ourselves and to explain life away, because it just can't really be explained enough to give us the satisfaction we all are looking for.

And we all live on with the sun rising and setting eternally; so it seems, but there is no assurance it will continue indefinitely. No promises except that the Holy Spirit will never leave us alone.

With no sight of what can be at our mortal end, even this notion carries myth and fable along with our belief, faith, and hope. Who knows for sure what speculation may lead to; the unknown remains the same. We are assured of doubt, and certainty has to be proved by reasonable conclusions a common person can understand; and it has to be believable to a degree of sureness in one's own mind.

And we live on with the sun circling in the sky followed by the moon and along with the other planets we circle the sun and follow in the path we've traveled for millennia, noticed only by the surrounding stars and the one who created them.

With no clear sight of our end we live with a sigh and take another breath because our heart beats of its own accord. We live estranged and indifferent to life because of the impact of reality, but we are sympathetic to ourselves for our own solace if that is any consolation.

We hope things will get better, but it's a long hard road, so if things get worse we can only live with faith and hope outside our fears. Our tears steadily pour from the corners of our eyes but dry with the passage of time, and our memories and thoughts just don't disappear.

Our words "grasp" or "apprehension" points to the process of getting at one thing through another. We live another day trying to avoid regret, living in a state of suspended animation, alienated to ourselves and the rest of the world as if someone actually cared. But time remains eternal, so we live and learn as day turns to night, and it's always today but different somehow.

We have reached the point of suspended judgment, always looking for an anesthetic for the mind numbing our attention to the situation and conditions we regularly face while trying to figure some approach to our own sensibility.

We are a generation with accumulated thoughts from previous ages. We are a generation affected by a whole lot of changes and still are in search of our future. Before we can change the world we have to change ourselves. It is not the easiest of tasks, but it is still possible. These economic times are in flux and carry us along through these stressful and anxious times. There is no other certainty than change. Things can get worse but we hope for the better.

Perhaps it's all just part of our human nature and the progress we've brought upon ourselves. We know for sure, with certainty, it's not all in our mind. The burden of reality affects us all equally.

It is interesting to note that success in keeping up a respectable front in the customary kind can only be achieved by a frantic scramble on the back-side of the facade we put up to protect us from the world. Our social lives have so much to do with our personal lives it is sometimes hard to separate them. Once we start working with machines we become part of the machine. Humans were not meant to keep the pace that they do, but our employers expect us to perform our tasks with efficiency and proficiency keeping the machine at bay.

Many a page has been written, but few read anymore. The spoken word has taken over in privilege, but in literature are found the ideas that give us things to speak about. Consider just how much the brain can think to speak without a proper foundation in reading. Remember there is more to reading than just the words; it's the words that not only give us knowledge and things to think, but ideas and concepts to talk about and converse with our associates.

Language does for intelligence what the wheel did for our feet. It moves us along with ease to distant places in story and tale. It brings us news of invention and contemporary events. It also brings us into fantasy and into a deeper sense of reality.

Language as the power of human extension brings us closer to a world beyond compare, and the written word brings us to our own human creativity.

There is no escape from the movement of the clock's hands; they keep mechanical pace with time and regulate our activities. Time must be one of nature's messengers that reminds us of the infinite regularity of nature's own essence. Time passes but we still remain the same. We say we've changed but really our nature has not — only the facient changes that bring about the reconstruction of the facade we show to the world.

We say we've changed but all that has happened to us is that we got older and hopefully wiser from experience and knowledge bringing us to a new sense of wisdom in our mind.

Though only time will tell we are beset with a widespread feeling of fear and increased insecurity, alienated to ourselves, captured by time with no end in sight on the horizon.

With every sunrise often there is but light and sometimes the sun is hidden by the clouds. So it is with our mind: we see the light but no sun. It's a curious thing. Knowledge acts on us the same; we know and perhaps do not understand, but pay little attention to the knowledge we've gained. It's just part of our human nature.

It's a natural condition that government rules, but the national consensus is that this current economic condition is the fault of the government showing favoritism to the upper class and leaving us, the common folk, to ourselves. The government has abandoned us, being left behind to fend for ourselves while they secure the status of the wealthy, and all we can do is hope for better times while life brings us along for a ride through reality.

We must silence our minds enough to hear the whisper of the voice. I just cannot imagine life without philosophy; it adds so much to the factor of a mind that reasons and gives thought to not only itself but to the world as well. The universe is greater than we could even imagine. As we pass through the rites of passage there are lessons to be learned, and if we don't learn them they come right back at us with greater strength, as if nature knows that the power of acceptance has restrictions and limits in our realizations.

I like a fresh sheet of white paper because it makes me think of the words that are going to appear. I find myself lost in thought seeking for the right words to express myself that surface from deep within without being distracted by the world that I belong to and am surrounded by. Of course we all live in our own little world but one must always remember we belong to a greater world that is greater even than we can imagine.

We are mysterious travelers in a mysterious world, but when we find ourselves we have to decide between two realities and consider them: the real world and the world of the mind. Simultaneously together we exist side by side. As a result of the clock we began to regulate our time, passing the day and night and the seasons. We challenged nature and won. When the printing press was invented the use of language and the word evolved. Literacy became an invaluable tool and the modern age was born. Today we need the skills to use the internet and cell phones; even the mp3 player like any other machine requires skill so a new technology brings with it new knowledge and wisdom.

Electricity came along and gave leave of day and night. Now the night is full of light and the clock is meaningless except to remind us when daylight will come. These notions bring invention to the creative mind and with just a thought we change the world just a little bit.

These memories, reflections, and contemplations are relevant to contemporary thinking. It's something we all come by when dealing with the world accumulated in our mind that reasons to the best of its ability the facts of the day. We contemplate at day's end, trying to make some sense of it all where there is none; but we come close in our thinking about the matters that draw their importance to our attention. Being sick with mediocrity we try to excel, but there is no recognition in the ambition to do better when we can. So we find our repose in knowing we did the best we could and that is enough.

We've reached a point of great decision. What will benefit us may involve a temporary set-back, but we will meet the challenges. If the decisions we make are consistent with our dreams, what will benefit the generation to come is a wonderful sight is on the horizon. We have to find the means for relieving our insecurities in the here and now is of vital importance; but to just relieve the burden of survival would be sufficient.

Like a wind up pocket watch or an old pendulum clock they need winding. When time stops for them it does not stop for us. Our relationship with time is part of the drama of life. I do not just speak for myself, I speak for humanity in a voice that is as close to my own as it is with the spoken and written word.

Our logic and reasoning have the need for a new basis, an elemental foundation for how and why we make decisions and come to judgments.

We live in a constant state of want and giving up meeting the challenge of the day to get along without regret. We live with complete disregard for antiseptics and survive in an infected social phenomenon where the complexity of life overshadows its own simplicity.

To prevent further undue wreckage in society the philosopher moves from the ivory tower to the contract tower to escort society through these changing times that overwhelm our own psychic consciousness. It is the philosopher's duty to improve and transform the image we have of society and that we have of ourselves. Change comes upon us so quickly we have to allow ourselves time to comprehend and understand its complexities as an extension of our own being.

From our learning and experience we grow wise, but it is our wit that solves problems and expands our dreams. It is not surprising that our earth-based natural means cannot conceive knowledge which is divinely based. I think if we confess honestly to ourselves we can realize we do not only learn from our strengths but from our weakness as well. Our judgment draws its strength from experience by both its own weakness and power of reason. Life becomes a miraculous thing as we live and learn as we grow and mature.

Can we delay the inevitable? Perhaps just for a while; but providence will have its way. We must help ourselves first for Heaven to help us. We have to think clearly, without distraction.

Well as usual the drama of life continues. Every day is today; tomorrow will come but we will call it today once more. Generations will pass and it's all the same but different somehow — today is always and yesterday is still only a memory that fades until it is forgotten. Once again lost in thought my mind wonders and wanders.

Whoever sets out to find something eventually reaches the point where they can say that they have not found it, or, that they are still looking but need direction so to not be led astray with false notions.

Philosophy is divided into these three categories. Philosophy is just the training of the mind to be logical and reasonable in this enigmatic and paradoxical world.

We ought to remember that truth is certain, but the appearance of truth may be deceiving because we just do not understand clearly the principles of our considerations.

Within us we have the means, by our intellectual abilities, to seek out the truth from falsehood. We must distinguish the merely probable from what actually is. We must find certainty reasoning out the appearance of truth from the actual truth. What is deceiving is the knowing of partial truths that we speculate upon but are not sure of. Philosophy distinguishes reality from illusion, the appearance of truth, which is a dilution in the fantasy of the mind. So we study and apply our learning, develop a philosophy, and endure life with amusement for our own entertainment.

A soul safe from prejudice of one opinion or another has made a wondrous advance towards peace of mind. When the intellect is stripped of all human learning it is left above all only with divine inspiration. If I remember correctly there is a verse in Ecclesiastes that goes something like this: "Accept all things in good part, just as they seem . . . the rest is beyond thy knowledge."

Exercising the Mind

It is one of our innate abilities to use the mind; for better or worse, our thinking and creative abilities have many practical purposes. It is the pleasure of exercising the mind that is important to the conclusions we come to and the judgments we make. In our learning we refine what we think we know is the truth and seek for a better explanation of what really is and dream of what could be.

Our mind takes us anywhere we want to go. It is a powerful tool to be used wisely and nurtured. It is a machine that needs servicing regularly, constant upgrades, and the freedom to actualize its own potential.

How can we explain the diversity of the human mind? Perhaps it is the social nature of our status. We have to consider our needs first before we can even think of the desires and wants that persist in our thoughts. Even though our sun is the most distant thing in the daylight sky we can look beyond it or even in the other direction and see further; our imagination leads our thoughts in many ways.

Knowledge is power; it enables us to expand our thinking in many ways. It increases the ideas we hold and brings revelation to our creativity. Knowledge is part of our very essence and character.

One illuminating thing about the mind is that it is self-revealing. Our thoughts wander all over the course of human events and even lead us into the sublime world of fantasy. Though through technology we have seen further and deeper into nature our curiosity has not ceased but has heightened with amazement at its splendor.

What makes philosophy so interesting is that it is a grand adventure in thought. A spark in the void comes so naturally; and the revealing of what was once concealed brings light to our minds.

The voice inside me is whispering, "find answers." So I look to philosophy, and like a voice from the past I hear what I am looking for. The thought is paramount in that it creates all things within our own development and evolution. One has to realize they can dream of infinite possibilities and the answer matters as we look at possibilities and potentials — the revenue of the mind.

The brain fires new sequences when the addition of knowledge accumulates and we are open to the other, that which we know little of. We are questioning beings and answers are what we seek in our quest for a fuller life. There is more to the here and now than we can realize. We have to stop the routine way we think and redefine a new pattern of thought that includes new realities.

Every civilization is a reflection of its knowledge. The fragmented view each of us has reflects its incompleteness so we quest for a more accurate and complete world view. We exploit what we think we know and act upon this wisdom even with its incompleteness.

We cannot change reality but we can change the way we perceive things. We must increase our understanding to achieve the fullness we are looking for in life.

The day is the beginning of great thought. What we keep in mind or discard depends on the attitude and perspective we take of life. We have to dream of infinite possibilities. The answer is to look at potentials and probability of their existence. The revenue of the mind is knowledge; and knowledge becomes a treasure the more we know and understand. The day is something new of creation and along with creation is the furthering of our thoughts.

Thoughts create our reality within the greater physical and spiritual realms. Our observations affect directly our attention. Even as we project our thoughts to the world it replies back, and there we make decisions and judgments of what we will accept or deny.

Even as life slips through our fingers like an hour glass filled with sand the residue lingers in our mind and we have to resolve what it actually is. Reality goes further and deeper than we can even imagine. The ultimate decision we have to make is what part of reality do we want to believe, the surface or the deeper part that requires a deeper exercise of the minds own power.

What ever way we observe the world comes back to us. We do

not have to accept the way things are; we can change the world with just a simple thought.

How things are in the world is a matter of complete indifference for what is higher. Our God reveals himself in many ways, shapes, and colors, and in all kinds of things and Creatures. Some say it's all in our head, but the wise know different. It is not how things are in the world that is mystical, but that it exists and we are part of it determining for ourselves what to believe or not.

The answer cannot be put into words, neither the question: but all the same we format our own interpretation. Doubt can only exist where a question exists, a question only where an answer exists, and both circulate in our active imaginative mind. What we cannot speak about we must pass over in silence, but in the silence our inner voice can be heard whispering to us in quiet tones of philosophy.

The process of philosophical thought typically moves from first, inadequate but ardent apprehension of some novel idea, figuratively expressed, to more and more precise comprehension, until language catches up to logical insight. Revelation from study brings this quality to new heights; but it may be wiser to let go of unfinished thoughts and half-spoken answers, and the mystery of life remains the same: unanswered but hypothetically speculated upon.

Since man was so desirous of making himself an equal to God, it would have been better to bring the properties of God down to Earth and turn them into human attributes rather than send our human attributes up to heaven. I looked to the sky for answers and all I found was blue sky with a passing cloud. When nightfall came all I found were specks of light we call stars, in recognizable patterns but too far to make out their qualities. I realized life is the same, too far from us to recognize the simple qualities we have as human creatures. The dream persists; the answer remains secluded in the quiet silence of our inner mind.

Man cannot be other than he is; he cannot have thoughts beyond his reach, but in both cases we still try to seek out the unknown, expect reasonable explanations, and bring the furthest answers closer to our own understanding.

Critical thinking is an absolute to the philosopher and to the theologian. Yes, it's the certain way of thinking that makes revelation into knowledge and wisdom. Thinking rationally, questioning assumptions and embracing complex abstract thoughts lures the mind to its potential.

We live and learn and then we negotiate our learning with the knowledge passed along to us from the ages. Then we discriminate that wisdom into the believable and probable with the likelihood of false assumptions and impossible, keeping in mind our sensibility and the variations of possibilities.

Though the value of an open mind is self-becoming to the one who labors in thought, it is a necessity for one who studies and reflects on knowledge to consider the objective as subjective while observing the reactions we have to our own thoughts. All things have a surface nature and a hidden nature we have to reveal from their concealment. Nature is just enigmatic poetry; when we read into it we exercise our ingenuity and all the abilities of the mind.

Learning passes the way with suppositions, and knowledge with theory. Reason and logic are found in the way of wisdom and critical thinking to those who labor in thought. Grandeur is found in both the physical and mental realities our mind gives thought to.

Every age in the history of philosophy has its own preoccupation, not for obvious practical reasons but for deeper reasons of intellectual growth. It is the mode, or technique, of handling problems and their subject matter that assigns them to a specific age.

The genius of a great philosophy is characterized more by the formulation of its problems than by its solutions to them. It is by the angle of perspective that we come to the conclusions that we do. In our questions lie our principles of analysis, and our answers may express whatever those principles are able to yield to.

There are a thousand or more fantastical patches in our learning network and their contrivance, their clearness, amuses us with its ingenuity, with the cleverness of the mind. Clearly a well planned out thought must have some reason behind it from our own ingenuity.

The experience of any moment has its horizon. At any given moment that horizon may change. The infinite moments between recognizable moments too have their own horizons. Each can be experienced and shared by others, though any two people looking at the same thing may see something different.

There may always be more than one explanation for any event; and the view of one can be added to the experience of all. That new horizon of which we speak is our ever-evolving part of creation and is always appearing as something new. This newness is the amusing part of life.

Different minds will take the same event in different ways, depending on our interaction with that event. As time will tell the philosophical horizon widens in all directions at once as horizons do whether looking forward or back or in any direction. The event horizon is something different than the visual horizon; it is the threshold of some action or reaction to a stimulus or from a cause to an effect that affects us in its own particular way.

Even if we go back from where we are in the here and now there may be something new brought to our attention from missing it along the way, as often happens when we re-trace our steps through history. The limits of thought are not so much set from outside the mind, but by the fullness or poverty of experiences that meet the mind in our curious world.

In the end all we are left with is the metaphysical; insolvable problems whose statement harbors a given paradox and follows a real labyrinth of an enigma full of variables and possibilities leading to a variety of conclusions and possible answers.

All the principles of knowledge bring us back to the creativity of the mind in conception and in the notions of different perspectives depending on the perspective the mind chooses to view them by.

When we apply ourselves to thinking of things in a spiritual way we must first start with the inner self and traverse great distances in the mind to see the other side of reality we believe exists.

It is such that our thinking never leaves ground unless we think of either spiritual matters or abstract metaphysical philosophy; so I indulge myself to let my mind soar because in the air it is most comfortable. Neither fantasy nor illusion have a place in pure thinking; so we use our rationality and logic to keep a level plane of our thinking on this higher level.

All the unknown things remain hidden in the majesty of nature. Providence made it that way to keep our curiosity in suspense. So it seems that after we find some answer we lose the attraction it once had to our curiosity; but we move on as usual to some other matter. And still we are caught up in speculation and opinion.

Our observations and discussions revolve around in circles with each holding to their own point of view; but there is better sense in making the choice for a unified conclusion with mutual agreement among the audience discussing matters of more or less importance to society.

From our individual abilities we root ourselves in the earth of our mind; and unless nurtured by knowledge and experience we are bound to make mistakes in thinking and bear the consequences of our thoughts that lead to actions resulting in a variety of reactions that affect social and cultural unrest. It is the differing of opinion that affects the effects; and life goes on with cause and effect just like supply and demand; and the price we pay is always inflated above its real value.

Where all the first principles of the Ancients and Renaissance thinkers are found I cannot see any objection why we ought not to accept them, because ethics and morality have one standard: that of conscience and consciousness of the grounds we base our thinking by.

Base yourself on admitted postulates and you can build up any case you like; from the rules which order the original principles, the remainder of your constitution will follow on easily without self-contradiction. If we can only live without regret we would continue in increasing our knowledge base and foundation.

The Renaissance crystallized a new outlook on life and

challenged the human mind to make sense out of its bewildering world. This new era of thought had a mighty and revolutionary generative idea: the dichotomy of all reality into inner experience and outer world.

We take for granted the immediacy of an internal experience from an external world. We've determined the difference between what comes in the mind and what comes to the mind. Both realities exist simultaneously, forming a congruent and coherent consciousness we can accept and come to terms with.

The mind is always fertile, though sometimes dormant, but it is ever creating and discarding ideas from considering their importance. The rise of technology is the best possible proof that the basic concepts of physical science are essentially sound, but strangely enough the so-called mental sciences have gained very little from the great adventure of the human race.

Our mind is built upon the foundation of our "Basis of Elemental Thoughts," and as we expose ourselves to "The Adventure in Learning" we do, indeed, "Pass Knowledge to One Another." As well, we learn from one another, accumulate knowledge and find our own wisdom worthy of thought and consideration.

Human beings are curious creatures. Each of us uses our mind differently. Some just think and react, others think and act; some just examine what is just below their feet or their surroundings; but others scrutinize great tracts of the heavens and search within themselves for substance and essence. Our intelligence is but a thought which our spirit revealed to us.

No one has yet discovered how purely mental impressions produce ecstasies and stimulus that are astonishingly amusing which capture our attention and nourish the wealth of thoughts we treasure in our limited mind; though expansion of the mind comes along with the increased wealth of knowledge and experience we accumulate in the span of our lives. Our lifelong journey truly is an Adventure in Learning as we build upon the Basis of our Elemental Thoughts. If we reason knowing that human reason knows anything at all, it must be its own essence and its own domicile. It is domiciled within the spirit and soul in the center of our mind; being either a part of it or one of its activities.

When we have to assay anything reason is our touchstone. But it is, most surely, a touchstone full of falsehood, misconceptions, errors, and defects, and must be constantly improved and upgraded. How better to test that then by reason itself logically imparted to our creative intelligence. If we cannot trust reason when talking about itself, it can hardly be a proper judge of anything outside itself, so the world remains the same but our mind constantly changes.

The time has come to adjust our considerations of ourselves and the world. We've become so complex the necessary adjustments are crucial to our behavior in action and reaction to the stimulus of thoughts and events that come to our life. We ought to come face to face with ourselves and the world and look at what we wanted and what we've become. No one person can change the world; but we can change the way we see ourselves in the world and make a difference to ourselves which in turn may, perhaps, change the world.

The nature of our spirit and soul is really not known, whether it is innate or slipped into creatures at the moment of conception or at birth. This is part of the mystery of life; and what happens to it when our bodies cease to exist is the other part of this great mystery; but one fine day or night the answer will be revealed to us and the truth will be made known whether our study or lack of will have a purpose.

The constitution of these thoughts determines part of our character and the outlook we have on life. This brings me to the conclusion, and only one, that I know myself and just how incomprehensible God is, yet I confirm my own beliefs with my faith and wisdom from the Knowledge Passed Along to One Another. Though the verification of my beliefs may be tentative, it is the hope I have that carries me along. I alone can think of the good ole days and dream of my future.

There's more to mind over matter than one thinks. Our senses tell us one thing and our mind another, yet the mind is different than the world it belongs to. The mind interprets what is inside it and as well interprets the world outside itself. It still wonders as a constant activity. Even as we interact with both our interpretations are constantly changing. We even interpret the thoughts we have.

Life is a window of experience with no pane. Life is an open door with no hinges. Life is an experience we grow and learn from. Perhaps that is the reason for living; to experience the interaction we have with our experiences we have on Earth. We experience the inner and outer world simultaneously as one complete experience. Our interaction with ourselves and the world makes us realize just who and what we are.

The frontiers of our research are lost in the dazzling light of the fountainheads of history in the making. We push our investigations to extremes, and still they, like dreams, have to be realized.

Those who penetrate most deeply, and thoroughly, into the highest matters are engulfed by their own curiosity and recognize their own ignorance to the knowledge that is available for learning.

Our simple-mindedness is only glorified by our intellect and from our creative imagination. Even if the truth were to drop right into our hands we have no way of seizing it; reason does not have enough power to establish any rights over the principles. Every single idea which results from our own reflections may be suited as subject for doubt and uncertainty, but in the real world we know for sure what our condition actually is at any given moment.

The question arises: Who is so powerful and endowed that we can trust them to act on their own, allowing them liberty of judgment to sail upon the seas of knowledge and responsibly assert notions and ideas beyond accepted opinion? Those at the top of the social and political ladder, or pyramid, make their own rules because we let money rule us, and those without it are like the serfs back in the 1300's; except for the change in technology our social structure has remained all but the same.

The human intellect guided by sense and reason, in a logical way, can go only so far towards understanding natural causes and considering issues of the world and mind; but when it reaches the original first cause it proves blunt and has to stop, either because of its own weakness or else because of the difficulty of the subject.

Some 15 billion years ago, if one could imagine that far, the process of creation might have had its start. In that spirit we evolved from the first atom to what we are now, just simple-minded humans with a great imagination.

So the question is, who cares? The answer is that nobody really cares and we all are just living to survive because we have no choice. If we could evoke change we would just call to the sky for help and mercy; but first we would have to believe something would hear us. So we are brought to a situation where we have to have emotions like faith, hope, and a positive belief that could be verified beyond our own suspicions.

Have you ever been in a very good mood? The experience is the letting go of our doubt and truly believing help is on the way. Today, as it always is, is as good as you want it. How bad do you want it? The mighty quest is on; our curiosity leads us to seek causes, just let go of conditions, and just live and be happy, because though we live in a world we did not create, we do create our own world in our own mind and live with the music we hear and think of in the moments of our creativity. Time waits for no one, so we have to keep pace or fall back into our own co-existing time plane, like in a frame of mind, or having an attitude towards something, perhaps about life itself.

This is a moderate opinion which holds that the intellect is adequate enough to bring us to the knowledge of things and thoughts, but there are definitely limits to its power, beyond which it is unreasonable to believe in an unlimited expansion of the mind itself.

It is difficult to fix boundaries for the mind, yet they exist. Even though centuries have passed we really are all the same.

Where one man's intellect cannot penetrate to avoid that some things are more likely than others, he concedes to his own judgment the power to incline towards one probability than another. The propensity may be there, but the conclusions are inconclusive and clearly unsubstantiated because of speculation and personal opinion.

Let us leave aside that infinite confusion of opinions and just stay with the facts which we can see among the philosophers themselves that enable world-wide debate about knowledge. The sky is above our head, and the ground below our feet is our Earth. Some things are sure and certain; all else may be just make believe.

Apart from the infinite diversity of people's thoughts we can easily see that the foundations of our present powers of judgment are insecure, causing us uncertainty about how we feel within ourselves; but first we must find some agreement with the thoughts we have of the world and ourselves. We need to find a way past our present condition, in time, within the state of current affairs.

Maybe we went wrong somewhere? Perhaps there was a human error somewhere along the time line we live by and are subject to. Sometimes we move on and sometimes we just stop in restful dormancy. Maybe, perhaps, we just need to realize a new way of thought?

When in the course of accepting and receiving, with understanding, knowledge from one another, most thoughts come with their own ground. We understand what we are thinking; yet can we receive anything without changing it? If our human grasp were firm and capable of seizing hold of the truth by our own means, then truth could be passed on from one mind to another, one person at a time, using the basic principles that we know as the grounds of our judgment and decision making, we by far could say we've evolved along with time.

Our conditions remain the same with a consenting opinion from the masses. Among so many concepts we could find at least one that all could believe with universal consent; but the fact is that there is no single way of thinking or proposition that is not subject to debate or reasonable discussion.

When we find something new our reasoning about what we thought changes from our recent discoveries. We no longer think as we did but evolve in our abilities of processing knowledge. It is our new way of thinking that brings about invention and change.

I think the real question is: How can there be so many brilliant minds at work and still we have some conditions that are unbearable though we do endure? The appearance of rationality which each of us constructs for ourselves causes us to reason a thousand contrary reactions to the same subject; but if you are clever and have a certain wisdom to you, you can learn to shape and mold it to adapt to different conditions and circumstances. We must be willing to change before we actually can go through the process.

A thousand chance emotions, feelings, and curiosities are unbolted in me in the storerooms of my mind. Just so many words can express my thoughts; and when that time comes this story will be finished. Oh so close I am, but still so much further there is to go. I can see closure on the horizon, and it is still there even as the horizon changes, like a beacon drawing me nearer to my destination.

Even with my own writing I cannot recover the original thought; yet as close as I come it seems to appear just as I thought it. Within my mind I go over the material, make corrections of my thoughts, and find a new meaning revealed from that same original thought. Just as we sometimes do our best to confine our thoughts we do the same to refine them in expression.

Time changes the nature of all things, as each stage must be succeeded by another in a never ending process of creation. The same thing happens in our mind; as we learn we change and in turn create more changes in our thoughts and way of thinking. That is the power of knowledge in the present immediate, past, and future. Even our own concept of the Creator changes. But the concept of time and eternity cannot be fully explained, though we can explain the time continuum; the contrary contrast of eternity is still sublime.

Greater Thoughts On Knowledge

That which is eternal is Time, for time is a thing of movement where nothing stays still. It appears like a shadow in the eternal flow, never remaining stable or permanent. We keep track of time only because we are creatures that regulate their life by the cycles that time affords us. It is not a thing, but something full of awe inspiring moments that are recorded in the books of history.

Knowledge has its price on us; it endures time and collectively enables us to evolve and mature. Knowledge is the power horse that moves civilization, building upon itself with the increase in wisdom and technology. With leaps and bounds we've become as we are.

It is commonly held that good sense is the gift of which nature has most fairly shared among us. And is that not reasonable? Yes it is because without it we could not survive with the decisions and choices we have to make to survive.

Who recognizes the worth of learning more than the one who labors in thought and pursues intellectual activities. It is learning that is essential to our nature. Our mind was created for that purpose. My sympathies change but not my judgment. The more I can learn, the sharper my reason, and my judgment will be from the foundations of the knowledge I've built my wisdom upon.

It is a remarkable example of the mad curiosity of our nature that we dwell so much upon the future while having to deal with the present conditions we live with. Though we are all almost the same, in varying degrees, furnished with the same conceptual tools; our judgment and diversity of opinion takes us to the extremes of both ends of the spectrum; except at one end is pure light and the other is full of color, and between is a range of the spectrum that we can only envision without technology. And still our world has to be interpreted by the inner mind with one prejudice or another.

Above all we gain mastery of ourselves. We cannot evade philosophy by immoderately pleading our human frailty. Philosophy is merely constrained to have recourse to her unanswerable counter plea; living in necessity is our common answer, but it brings out our best intellectual activity.

What concerns us the most is the impressions that ideas give us. Ideas are undoubtedly made out of spontaneous or deliberate thought, that which interests the mind; and we interpret ideas in many ways according to our level of competence, skills, and range of knowledge. Only a part of our behavior is practical and belongs to our common sense. The remainder serves simply to express ideas that the mind calls forth from our creative intelligence.

The great contribution to the philosophy of mind has been the realization that human behavior is not only a strategy but also a language. The language by which we communicate ideas leads us in our learning, developing our reasoning and judgment while guiding our behavior. The language of the mind is the same that we use to communicate with the world even as we communicate with ourselves in the silent moments of contemplation and reflection.

When we employ our learning we ought to be better at judging in our choices and decision making than before we learned anything at all. One must enjoy learning and savor the power it gives us in our ability to reason on logical grounds. Enlightenment comes with understanding and integrity. Knowledge is a power that elevates the spirit to new heights; as our wisdom grows we evolve and quest for a better understanding than we once had. The better our understanding the more apt we are to take a new perspective on life.

As we live we have situations and conditions come upon us. We have to learn our way around, explore, make discoveries, and live, enduring with our capabilities; but if we learn along the way our wisdom becomes our own genius.

For those who want to learn you first have to apply yourself to the experience of living the life of never-ceasing learning. Knowledge becomes a primal motive in our succession of the rites of passage ever improving and evolving as we go. We claim learning of ourselves and of the world because we have a certain wisdom endowed to us in our creative mind. Oh if people would only understand their learning just a little bit better what a world we could have.

Learning is a great and useful instrument of the mind's abilities. It is not the knowledge itself that is important here, but the life experience we endure and learn from. Let the diversity of judgments and opinions set before us be diligent and reasonable with all the logic available to our own reasoning powers.

Look around, choose your own ground, but keep your principles sure and certain. Perhaps it's just all a matter of attitude. The profit we possess after study is to become better than before and wiser in our own fashion and style. The greatness of the spirit and soul come from the greatness of the mind; enlightenment comes from study and contemplation.

One thing we ought to get from learning is the bringing of new frontiers into perspective. Having a clear-cut view of the past helps us in looking side to side and forward and up, imagining new horizons. Though our perspective of our horizons takes many forms, we border the edge of a massive reality.

We ought to judge the infinite power of nature with more reverence and profound awe at its splendid power. We ought to be realistic about our abilities, capabilities, weaknesses, and strength. One of the qualities of philosophers is that they recognize they know little and have just so much to learn. One ought to excel at what they do with deliberate intention. One ought to recognize the wealth of resources that are available and the use of technology.

Learning as such is creation, a never-ending process of exploration and discovery, all the while learning applications and processes of thought and reasonable thinking. We learn to question the probable and possible and come to terms with reality as it is.

We must distinguish the unusual from common opinion and make our understanding relevant to our logic and reason. What is important here is the culture of improving the mind, and its abilities, all the while considering the capabilities that are within our range of optimizing our foundations of reason and logic. We must find the fine line that distinguishes the possibility of our believing.

We ought not disregard what we do not understand, because there is more to the meaning of something than appears on the surface. As soon as you have established the frontiers of truth and recognize what error is and then discover that you must, of necessity, believe some things even stranger than you once rejected, you find that nature is more complex than the simplicity you make of it and come to terms with what you once rejected as possible, even probable.

Sometimes an impression on the mind is in need of qualification and distinction in the direction it leads us to wonder upon. We ought to concern ourselves with the imagination a thought provokes that is beside the actual truth of a matter.

We ought to concern ourselves with the investigation of nature and the essence of all things, even our own natural being, through our primitive curiosity that leads our imagination to conclusions even of unknown things our knowledge has not yet tasted nor understands.

So it turns out that nothing is so firmly believed as what we know the least about, and that no person is more sure of themselves than those who tell stories about what the appearance of truth really is because it is unknown and its explanation is only our creative imagination at work underlying our interpretation of a thing or event.

Though opportunity and fortune come with different measures, from the equal balance of necessity we must experience both sides of nature's essence in order to justify the events we go through in our life experience. We must take the good with the bad with reasonable distinction and indifference and make the best of our experiences, learning all the while in our journey with our knowledge and wisdom.

Sometimes it seems fortune is playing with us, leaving chance and choice to decide what it seems is important at any given moment. Fate may be of our own making, but chance and opportunity have more to do with nature; and if one could believe in Providence we would be more likely to take life less seriously than it apparently seems to be. The complexity of life ends up mysteriously in complete simplicity.

Though we have similar human attributes we only differ in opinion based on our wisdom and knowledge. I more readily acknowledge our similarities than differences but contemplate my own attributes in order to improve my own quality, so I devote any extra time to study from my available resources to quicken my judgment according to the truths I've found in my own accumulated knowledge.

As a part of human nature we ought to come to an understanding of our conflicting emotions of the variables of opinion and pursue the debate that surrounds the appearance of truth from the real truth.

The mind uses a metaphorical veil, or cloak, to cover over our passions and emotions. It is crucial that we find peace of mind to keep our focus and attention to our present duties in the conditions that surround our lives. Behind the veil are tears of joy and pain that enflame the heart, which our reason distinguishes from the causes and events in our lives. The response is a natural effect of our interpretation of these circumstances and events.

Everything changes, and things get old, and we just get older.

Still some ideas are forever young, and the older we get these same ideas keep their freshness. Consider that a person thinks of an idea, say a point on a page of paper. Then the person thinks of another point to connect the points to create a perfect line. It is true that those points put down on the paper were preconceived, showing that some unknown ideas materialize in thought before they materialize in the real world. Perhaps it is one of the functions of the mind to preconceive ideas before we realize their true meaning.

We cannot consider history in its own right before we consider the present to give history some relationship. In the same way we cannot consider the Creator without first considering the Great Spirit whose own thought brought into the world not only itself but the Creator as well. Just as a thought and idea have similarities they also have differences, being that one leads to the other and something always comes before nothing to give that nothing some definition and place it in the relation of thoughts and ideas.

This is part of the nature of the universe. Even the light of the sun comes in waves of new light upon previous light without interruption; but our mind contemplates matters in different ways. It separates thoughts and reasons them with many angles, with a variety of perspectives to take in the whole picture and the grandeur of it all. With this in mind the horizon becomes only a shadow of what lies behind it, where we bring our heart and soul to contemplate in a metaphysical way superior to the reality that presents itself to the actual reality we live within.

Let us leave aside those long comparisons between the solitary life and the active one; each of us has the liberty to their own nature. Everyone knows you can get lost in a crowd of people, and though we live united on the planet we live out our lives in the solitude of our own mind. It rained today and though the world around me went on as usual I spent the time alone in my study thinking of all of them.

The spirit and soul turned inward upon the self and contemplated in thought history the present and the future. The rain beat down against my window and though I thought of my condition, believing at the moment a solution was possible, I could hardly see one, nor could I conceive one, but surely one would be revealed from its concealment.

I fought off depression and surrounded myself with music, and a variety of conclusions came to me; but it would have to be me who would have to decide what future I would make for myself, with the choices available to me. We live such public lives when we return to the sanctuary of our home we are left to wonder if our judgment is fair enough to make the right choices of the opportunities we have.

Every man must decide the road on which he will travel. There is just so much time we can spend idle in one place before moving on. Time passes so quickly and we do not want to be left behind.

Sometimes a stranger would pass by and would have time to talk and you would listen to their tales and fortunately you would add their opinion to yours; but the final decision would be yours alone.

So with a little patience I should be able to find my way out of this labyrinth I have been drawn into, being amazed to see myself ensnared and as it were imprisoned by the latency of my own thoughts.

If the road one chooses to take has never been taken, one should be perceptive and curious to what lies ahead, for no counsel can be given except by one's own resources of the mind.

From the mind's resources we can determine our treasure and with the worth we give to our own knowledge gain wisdom from what we have learned. When we consider the gift of a moment in time, a door seems to open to another reality, always present in our memory yet rarely witnessed; because time passes so quickly, each moment is recorded and subjected to our wonder and amazement, increasing our bewilderment of it and increasing our own curiosity into its own depths of reality.

In this time we find ourselves beyond the confines of the ordinary and realize for a brief moment the extraordinary that nature has to offer for acceptance or rejection by our own logical reason.

When we find ourselves beyond the confines of the ordinary we enter into a brief moment of the extraordinary that nature has to offer when we achieve the awareness of it. So grand is this adventure into enlightenment it seems like a quantum leap forward into the unknown. We are captured by the amusement and amazement of what our mind beholds in the realization of our gained insight.

We know we have experienced something out of the ordinary that is almost beyond definition. It is the moment of realization that captures our attention in its novelty and grandeur. We know we have experienced something unusual, but all the same it became part of our own reality in a sublime way.

None of us is so clever to allow our sight and insight to be dazzled without realizing it, so that by keeping in mind the continual changes in human affairs our judgments on them may be more firm and enlightened from the experience we gain throughout our life experience. Our power of judgment is a tool to be used wisely on all subjects and can be applied anywhere with reason and discretion.

Human intelligence is a curious thing; if one door is closed to it, it finds, or even breaks, another entrance to the world of the known and unknown to discover and explore its innate qualities.

If one symbolism is inadequate it calls on its treasure of resources for another explanation. The limits of language can be surpassed by our creative intelligence and accumulated knowledge we call our own wisdom. When we think of the impossible we are at the same time forced to think of its probability and possibility.

When we speak of language as a means for communication, and thought where we use language to interpret even our own thoughts, we are forced to think of expression and the means for constructing meaning from a simple idea; even in its complexity a sort of simplicity must be found. So we are left with breaking through the limits of expression into a world of symbols and an understandable language we can relate to.

Nature speaks to us through our senses and ends in the realm of mind where we interpret, with all of our experience in the world as its subject and object of our contemplation according to our capacities and abilities of our mind's own resources, which lead us to learning — the combination of understanding and expression of what we think we know and of what we actually know.

The utility of the mind is our natural asset and is all that we can depend on for our survival. The seasons have changed again. The autumn has come with the morning frost. This is my fourth year in the creation of this work and we've come a long way with our thoughts. The conclusion of this work is near, but while I even continue in its conclusion new ideas continuously come to me for another work.

Necessity: it is a requirement of life. We can depend on its principles in exchange for the ability to decipher and interpret the knowledge we gain from experience and from study and contemplation.

We can never learn enough because all there is in life is continual learning and advancement of humankind. We learn to apply our knowledge in the achievement of new wisdom. We surrender to our imagination all that we still don't understand.

It seems to me that we are being constantly involved with ourselves, with the veering opinions, and in a state of unresolved conflict due to the changing conditions of our present environment.

We question ourselves for answers where none can be found, yet we search ourselves and make up answers to resolve our questioning with the desire, ambition, and motivation to bring to conclusion and resolve our doubt of the future while dealing with the situations that present themselves in our enduring for survival.

This questioning we do makes us think on a higher level than we would ordinarily do if our environment were to be stable and sure. What a wonderful thing it is that we can separate ourselves from the "I" in "me" and come to terms with the "me" in society.

When people fail to understand everything they hear, read, or give thought to it is only the words that fail to give up their meaning and not our understanding of them that rears itself to our reasoning and logic. It is the words we use to interpret things that cause us confusion, so our increase in knowledge is a necessity. We Pass Knowledge to One Another so we should not ask that our definitions be general but precise, and that our decision making be certain and well grounded with concise meanings and accurate in the highest degree available to our judgment.

We ask that our judgment should comply with our knowledge and wisdom to make the right choices from the treasure of our thoughts. As we journey through life we convince ourselves that we know where we are going, but we know not. We are unsure of anything except for our present condition that is constantly changing; nothing is for sure, and doubt surrounds us unceasingly. Though we can be sure of where we came from our destiny remains unsure, and we deny the present without regret because our deeds and thoughts have been pure and our intentions sincere. We seem to distance ourselves from ourselves because of our own uncertainty. Our end is assured and is at our doorstep; while we endure surviving our only recourse is to find good reason for continuing on this journey we call life.

The transformation of experience into its concepts is the motive we use for learning and finding a means for expression of the thoughts that present themselves to our mind. If not for learning than what else is there for living? We live to learn and experience life in its fullest measure. What we do understand is only an appearance of an understanding that comes from our knowledge. There are reasons for things that are beyond our comprehension, but we imagine ourselves understanding only for the sake of convenience. Only occasionally are we given a glimpse of the true meaning we seek, but most often we are unaware and confide in ourselves some theory for the events that are part of our living experience.

Although we may have good intentions, sometimes fate does not turn our way and what seems like failure is just a test of character. The greatest achievement of success is overcoming the obstacles that get in the way of our success and fulfillment. To survive we have the necessity for achieving success at our endeavors. Surely we are destined for success acquiring the skills to ensure our survival.

Though we tumble in upon ourselves, and the world seems to crash around us we will rise, like the phoenix, and recover what surely belongs to us: peace, health, and comfort of mind overcoming the shadows of the mind with the brightness of the noon day sun.

The light which we all think of as optical light is different than the light of enlightenment. To solve this mystery we come to an insight of the universal consciousness and of our own in relation to it, raising us to a state of awareness, so dazzling that it becomes overwhelming. We realize that the spark of enlightenment opens to us concealed doors of perception that were never revealed to us except from the enlightenment of the mind from our learning experience that comes to us from the life we live that is open to memories and dreams. Our soul cannot reach so high while remaining in its own place. We must constantly face change and move along with time at our side. We must break away from the bonds that hold our spirit and confront ourselves with the reality of our own spiritual nature.

Reasoning and education cannot easily prove powerful enough to bring us actually to do anything, unless we also train our spirit for the course on which we set her.

So though I study for my own instruction, perhaps someone else might benefit from my treasure. So it is that We Pass Knowledge to One Another. For many years now the target of my thoughts has been for better understanding of myself and the world. In following such a roaming course, I've been consumed with penetrating the depths and inner resources my mind beholds. That which makes us who we are has innumerable characteristics, and who we are is contained in the many thoughts our knowledge is contained. No description is more difficult than the describing of one's self, nor is it easy to describe someone else without knowing some of the details of their inner thoughts.

To prepare yourself for public view you put your thoughts in order, arranging them as you would if you were preparing to measure your own self-worth. The portraying of the words of thought of a shapeless subject, which manifests itself in knowledge and wisdom, we learn from one another identifying the similarities and differences we have, discovering a thousand minds leading to discovery of the essential qualities we bear for ourselves.

It is not one individual quality that makes up the human character but many more than we think of or choose to recognize. If you want to know the world you first come to know yourself. Tradition has a long line in history; but sometimes we have no other choice than to break the mold and create a new form from re-assembling the pieces of what we once thought had a sure and solid foundation. Little did we understand that change is a constant factor in all things except in the notion of an unchangeable balance between Spirit and God.

When I gave this thought considerable reflection, I determined God could no more change than we would allow our own thoughts to accept that God may be more human than we once would allow.

Concluding Thoughts and Reflections

This work is an accumulation of years of study into the thoughts that a common human reflects upon in deliberate concentration. Our observations cover a wide range of concepts and notions that do, indeed, entertain the mind with curiosity and amusement. We are most certainly amazed at not only our perceptions but with our conceptions that reach far beyond the reality presented to us by nature. Just the thought of the other side of nature, the spiritual side, our intelligent imagination leads us on by its own luring.

This thinking that we do is totally unlike any other. Even as we explore the unknown our discoveries make the unknown less and the known more. It has been a melancholy humor, a most inimical endeavor finding truths that are not and sensitive qualities of a truth that has become more certain than ever before.

In the many days of solitary retreat my contemplations, both deep and shallow, contributed to my own generated wisdom. I've incorporated knowledge from the recent and past and developed a new generation of thinking. Surrounded by the world I've drawn into myself, come out of the shell of my existence, and entered into a world and universe greater than myself. The understanding I've come to is relative to contemporary thought along with the concepts that have spanned generations even back as far as antiquity.

So from "The Basis of Elemental Thoughts" through "The Philosophy of the Worker: an Adventure in Learning" to "We Pass Knowledge to One Another," the simple consideration of our thinking draws us deeper into knowledge from gained insight and thoughtful reflection.

It has been just a remarkable journey, this Adventure, we've been on these past years; and now the new conclusions we've come to have surely compounded our faith and belief in nature and all the qualities held to her. Not only is this life of ours more exciting but the evolution of our society and advances in technology have brought us into a new era of human ingenuity making our home, this terra firma we call Earth, into an envelope open and ready for the delivery of a message to some distant place in the future.

When I first put my head into this raving concern for writing thoughts, ideas, and notions my only anticipation and expectation was the study of myself and humanity and our interrelationship.

I offered myself to myself as theme and subject to a closer inspection than one would ordinarily do. The conclusions I've come to have been sincerely revealing and quite curious in the amusement and entertainment of my own mind.

We need not place all of our attention on just action-reaction sequences but on the attention of our condition and situation in the present here and now, by our focusing of attention not only of stimulus and response but by the supply and demand of the resources in the treasures of our own mind.

Truly the Laws of Nature, that is instinct, are stamped on all creatures and things. We have a natural fear of being hurt or wounded so we distance ourselves from each other, ending in the solitary alienation from society in our own little make believe world. But it is more than that; we cannot live without social interaction while we overcome the interaction we have with ourselves.

Because humans believe the dream is real they take it very seriously; but the dream is just our imagination getting the best of us and the drama invariably becomes a comedy.

For our own self-preservation we avoid what seems harmful to us including the emotional value of our own spirit and consider the compassion and justice not only from us but due us. The slight discursive reasoning we do should reform our own sense of will and judgment; but nature would not allow us to be swept away by her power alone; reason and the capacity of our individual mind subjects itself to our will and inclinations, justly according to our own ethical and moral nature we impose upon ourselves.

One thing we do learn from our accumulated knowledge is how to manage our affairs in the course of our daily and routine livelihood. We learn to restrict our own rules and habits and take to what is appropriate and comfortable to our nature.

The world of objective contents, of our thoughts, leads us to their discrimination and reasonable interpretation in the most logical and rational utility of our capabilities in the most subjective way.

What we need is to have sufficient reasoning power to select and embrace things according to their merits where one would allow themselves to be led by their intelligence rather than by the emotions from natural impressions that act upon us alone.

Though our bodies are protected by the armor our mind provides, what comes from within, our emotions, are held to the limits of the armor and turn our lives into the drama of reality. Now we can choose to play out the drama with the poison of our emotions or we can turn it, the drama, into a comedy and laugh at the ridiculousness of the unfolding nature of the reality we create for ourselves.

What we need is to have sufficient reasoning power to select and embrace things according to their merits where one would allow themselves to be led by their intelligence rather than by the natural impression that acts on our emotions.

Knowledge and truth can be lodged within us without judgment; judgment can do so without them, recognizing our own ignorance is one of the surest and most beautiful witness to our judgment that I can find. Of course we can be sure of what we do not know and still what we do know comes under our own scrutiny because of the doubt that remains in our mind, apparent and related to our opinion and value of our judgment capabilities within our reason.

I would very much like to grasp things with a complete understanding, but I cannot bring myself to pay the high cost of doing so. One cannot enjoy learning without the leisure time that proves to be invaluable to the one who labors in thought.

I freely say what I think about things for the purpose of discussion and verification in the enjoyment of debate. Some things may very well exceed my competence, but an opinion of a notion or idea may be worth a thousand words by its explanation, so I've treated my subjects with as much dignity and integrity with as few words as the subject matter would allow, concluding with a sense of certainty.

What we all strive for is some kind of inner fortitude that helps us get along in a world of trying, just to get by. One must learn how to sustain inner conflicts and debates which one has with oneself, which is part of our nature, more than attributing one quality to another as we grow and mature, when life gets wearisome and the struggle is more of a challenge than ever just to maintain a satisfactory disposition in our moral and ethical social and cultural environment.

When we reach what seems to be our limit, and emotions get the better of us causing us physical and mental fatigue, we need to call on our inner fortitude which has the most saving power our spirit can provide.

Our sustenance must be maintained for our own well being. Consider just how many people go through the perils of life to be worthy of a destiny theology teaches and philosophy believes. Our temporary lives are full of improvisation and spontaneity. The permanence is believed only to be illusion; an endless day is not beyond its possibility, and isn't it a peculiar thing that we are always brought back to reality from some extraordinary stimulus.

It is difficult to rid ourselves of hindsight and preconceptions, but our imagination thrives in the mind which thought is given to.

The most powerful influence on us is our own philosophy so the encouragement of the will must come from our own mind and by the influences that surround us.

I think what we need to consider is our continuing relationship with not only the Earth and other humans but the relationship we have with ourselves and the honesty we have in that agreement.

We are our own listener and speaker; we are our own actors and audience in the same moment of thought and action. Our reactions are at the same time well thought and spontaneous, prompt and decisive. Not only are we responsible for ourselves, but we also carry some of the weight of responsibility for our significant others.

A virtual reality, that most of us believe is true, can be completely indistinguishable from inside or at least from real life. Put simply, we can only get an intellectual grasp on reality from within our own conceptual framework, which is determined by a complex scheme or combination of factors including our culture, history and personal philosophy of life. But the fact that we cannot step back from, or outside of, our particular conceptual framework and take an objective view of things does not mean we cannot get to know anything. A perspective has to be a perspective on something, and by sharing and comparing our different views we can hope to bring our various beliefs into relief and to achieve a fuller, rounder, more stereoscopic picture of the world. Consider that the panorama view is greater than just a single image of the world that surrounds us.

It is a long way from nothingness to eternity. Resistance is meaningless where there is nothing to apply the force of the will. Nothingness is a fulfillment of apprehension. Where there is something it is possible to consider the meaningfulness of resisting against it. From the beginning of time the great nothing we call an empty void had to have something to give it meaning; and this great something was the spirit of nature itself, born from its own thought to be the force and power of the will of nature and the natural essence and substance of thought itself.

Curious as it is, the power of the mind comes to us as natural as the power of conscience if one is so inclined to be aware of it. Life is a curious event. We can expect the unusual at any time. Living without regret is difficult. We act and react often without concern for consequences. The moment seems to overwhelm us. The matter of conscience has personal variables. What we can plan for is within our control; but what we cannot plan for we must have contingencies dealing with chance and uncertainties for our future. So here we are in the present here and now with what we are faced with and our self.

It's a long process of the mind finding its own identity. We have to separate our physical needs from our emotional needs. It is these needs that make us aware that we are human and nothing else. Once you overcome the needs of the body the mind becomes enraptured with itself and a sense of wonder is an expression of ecstatic feeling.

We fight a war for freedom from the dream that controls our life. We hunt what is inside us, the emotional fears and pleasures that overcome our intelligence. We look to the sea and to the mountains and all we can find is our own reason and logic which is under the influence of perpetual change.

We interpret everything with the mind. Whoever controls the belief controls the dream. The dream is only kept alive by what we keep in the treasures of the mind. Those treasures only have a value by what we believe is of worth. So by and by we learn to control the beliefs we have, give worth to our treasures, and make for ourselves a life which is our living dream.

It all happened in a moment, without any provocation — a thought came to me about reality. I can't pretend it's not real, but the circumstances cannot be denied. Beyond the fact that there is a reality outside my mind, it is my own interpretation that makes it so.

Sometimes you just have to get off the bus and look around at where you are. You discover your real self and come to terms with what you find. The only thing you can change is your mind. So you wait for the next bus and hope to find your real self in another place and time. Little do you know that you have changed because of the way your thinking has progressed.

This is reality; but every time you move from one place to another the past becomes a dream, the future remains the same, and your present condition is just a dream come true and you believe it. In the present we create our own reality from the thoughts we think, the actions we take, and in the reactions that come from our interpretation of the reality that is within and surrounds us.

Sometimes we just get caught up in our own thoughts and time means nothing because of the dream world we enter from within our own mind. Time passes unnoticed and the reality of the dream is all so true to us that no one else can believe it, and they think something is going on but just don't understand anything but themselves. That's just the way it is; we live our life inside ourselves with the world at our side shadowing our every movement and thought.

It confuses us and is something our personal experience has to come to terms with. The certain way of thinking, living without regret, living without doubt of our beliefs, all the time searching for clues to the answers we seek — life will supply our needs but our wants endure and do not go unnoticed. Surely the discipline of the mind is at the forefront of our wisdom, and the knowledge we come to know and understand is still open to discovery and amendment.

We must constantly battle the inward mind that occupies our time and come to terms with our vices and virtues. Nothing but the will can control us; yet the will has to answer to a higher power not of our own but a conception of the power that controls nature. Though we and nature act autonomously, the greater force of the Holy Spirit seems to know what events will bring about change for the good on its own terms, faithfully acting without regret or misguided intention because it acts with absolute knowledge. There is nothing that can compare to it because within itself is the beginning and end of all things except itself which is eternal.

The senseless is degrading to man's estate; we're told this is the truth and we must look at life the realistic way. You have to look above, beyond, down, under, and around, but life's worth can be found. Our spirit is on parade for the world to see. What we really are shows through, revealing our true self. My heart whispers in quiet retreat until life compels my strength to turn my thoughts to the serene and divine captured by my own mind. And hardly knowing why or how, you'll know yourself inside. Let your mind relax and play while glorious adventures lie waiting all around.

Though we try to reach the summit of knowledge by gradually building up and consolidating the wisdom we attain, we have to examine day by day how the spirit of the age furthers our effort and learn to absorb or dismiss what is harmful to our endeavor.

We must mainly concentrate on the renewed analysis of the content of our knowledge. We must learn to see the difference between the fact of truths and simple theory. Let everyone examine themselves and advance their thinking with serious intention.

One day the thought came to me that I came to think was important: our attitude towards ourselves and the world makes all the difference in the way we participate with the world and interact with our own will, disposition, and nature. Most of us find ourselves talking to ourselves on occasion, thinking things through, examining the different perspectives available for our consideration. It was for me a real coincidence that the truths we've been told are conditional and subject to individual interpretation. My own beliefs had led me to the conclusion that the truths were permanent and consistent with well-founded basis in their elemental form concurrent with contemporary thought.

We live our lives with memories of the golden past, the parts of life that have silver linings; but with all the good we just cannot deny the rough times we go through. Without a doubt or regret it's just unavoidable to remember and not forget, everything juxtaposed with hope for our present days and future glory.

We can predict the seasons but the weather is always unpredictable; and a reliable truth is always subject to verification and opinion. How many people think alike? Perhaps that's what makes us all so individual and the thoughts we have multiply with time.

The sun hangs high in the sky, occasionally crossed by light clouds that shimmer in its brilliance, and I wait for the evening to come just to see the splendor of the sky changing colors as all the thoughts of the day congeal in my mind, and from there I try to sort them distinguishing one from the other.

Given the vivid physical world and the lucid inner world of mind our multi-layered inheritance becomes a fantasy come true. In our formative years we did not know we were being deceived, and in the later years of our development we have to look beyond the deception and find for ourselves some certain truths. Our sampling of life has sincere effects on our outlook and affects what we conceive as real and imaginary. Both chance and opportunity pass our way at the same time; both convenient and inconvenient are the moments we endure through the rites of passage.

There's more to music than just sounds and lyrics. Music is a universal language all of its own that everybody understands in their own way. Just the same there is more to reading than words; it's the thought-provoking ideas that stimulate our brain's power and emotional response, luring us to where we might happen to go.

Our thoughts multiply in the consideration of life at each stage in our development and become exponential as we mature. We procure and discover knowledge along the way as we explore each aspect nature affords where our attention is captured from the individual perspective we take on our own accord. The infinite variables make the difference in our thinking subject to our own thoughts that have mastered us over our reality. The relationship to these phenomena make choice a chance of the will.

You know we can't avoid learning. It's always something that chance and opportunity afford to us. It's just a natural part of living; and perhaps one of the best parts. If we can apply our learning it's even better, and satisfaction comes easily. As we grow and mature the fantasy of life changes into a harsh reality where wishful thinking ignores the hardship and the fairy tale becomes a true-to-life realization, a grand drama being played out in our own front yard; and if only for a moment we can find some kind of relief and repose for our disposition with not a thought rather than any thought at all, we can find actual peace in that brief moment of time and be thankful for that moment of relief.

We learn that living is not easy and the effort we put into life brings great results. We learn mediocrity doesn't get us anywhere and learn to excel at what we do. The accomplishment of being able to excel is an exponential achievement. We learn that moderation is a good thing. We learn what to avoid and become familiar with what attracts us. We learn that economics is an essential part of living. We learn the meaning of worth and value. We learn the meaning of sentimental. We learn the value of our emotions and learn not to regret as we continually improve our decision making and reasoning. We learn the logic of consequences.

We are encouraged through our early years with expectation, and have great anticipation for our later years; but I've learned in all my fifty-plus years that living just doesn't come easy and we learn to control our emotions and discover the potential of our will.

Our life is like a poem, a ballad you may say, and the lyrics play on our mind as we sing to ourselves and to the world. We learn to be our own best friend and listen to ourselves as we think through our own thoughts.

So you say you remember when you were young and now say how much has changed. Incredible isn't it. We've come so far and still wonder where we're headed towards. And what about the little kids?

Bright winter days to remember. Warm summer evenings to remember. All the good in the world makes us momentarily forget that there is bad too. What occupies our time is the movements of the minute hand and the hour hand; the second hand is only a nanosecond in the grand experience of life.

There will be warmth and cold, rain and snow, sunshine and cloudy gray days — all this we have to come to terms with. We stand and watch the world go by and all the while give some thought to ourselves. Where do I belong? Where do I fit in? Only in the present here and now can we find our real self.

So do you think we have to defend the notion of being different? Well it seems so. Our individuality overcomes our similarities, and the human race is still one civilization at each progressive stage in history. Each generation is one, each era in time is one; and all together we are all one but retain our singular individuality. So where do we go from here? Back into ourselves and out again to get involved with the world to which we belong. We learn how to wait, and wait some more; it's just part of life. We know that time goes on even without us.

Do not be anxious for tomorrow because it will arrive soon enough. Be thoughtful of today and take care of what is at hand. Tomorrow has its own set of complications just as today has its own special needs to be addressed. What can be more important than dealing with today because we are not assured tomorrow will even come; and if it does we know not what form it will take.

Life starts for us as a dot, a linear expression, and goes on to another waiting dot; but perhaps there is another side from the first to the last that makes us wonder what we endure through on the fragmentary line we call our own life.

I sit on the bow of my little boat watching the great sea for fair weather, remembering my own port of call and imagining the journey to the awaiting port on the other side of the sea.

Because of the multitude of thoughts in our mind we must learn to distinguish one from another and keep our mind clear from the drama of life we so often get involved in. The intellect with conceptions imprinted in it, of the opposing forces of life, makes it necessary for us to find the stillness we search for despite of the opposing forces of nature that keep us from finding our goal.

Inner stillness seems to be the most sacred of all qualities because it means when we do find it we are free from worldly concerns and spiritual impurities from the forces that keep us from achieving that specific goal. Inner stillness is being content, having no desire for want of anything more than that state of stillness.

As we look into ourselves and out into the world we take notice that there is a bigger problem than we once thought. It is the matter of consciousness, of the expanse of time between the moments of one's thoughts. As a matter of mathematics the notion of an infinite space between one and two has a similar power to the notion of the space between one and a thousand. Though the relationship is the same while the numbers are of a different nature, these relationships can be compared to the time between thoughts.

I took notice of the sky last night and discovered while considering it was the month of December that the sun sets further to the left of where it usually sets in the summer, but the moon still sets in the same location as the summer sun. I realize that we are on the path around the far side of the sun and it brings to my mind how sometimes we are on the far side of our own thoughts and the waves of our thoughts, like the waves of the seas, are continual but not consistent in shape and form. This particular wonder creates a vast amount or room for further thought.

Consider for just a moment, without interrupting the moment into its own infinite particles, that two lines which seem parallel but are not by such a small degree that they will converge at some distance which is close to the limits of infinity. The degree is so small that the largest atom we know would not even fit in the angle of declination. Though these two lines will somewhere in space converge it takes a large amount of imagination to realize.

Perhaps what makes me wonder the most is this: Where has the passion for thought gone? Re-phrased, it could be: Who cares anymore about what thought really is? Thought is actually one of the greatest endowments the Creator has given to humanity.

I sit here at my desk in my study and look around at my world contained within these four walls and have the slightest regard for what is outside the window I sit by. We ought not to forget that the big picture can be broken down into detailed parts and those parts have their own essential being.

We all have struggles at whatever level we achieve in life. We ought not to take some of these struggles personally because of the socio-economic conditions that present themselves to us and take them just as something we have to use our wits to overcome. All other factors we ought not take so personally and adjust our perspective of the situation and conditions that matter to us the most. Perhaps it's not us who are different, but the world that is different.

Today is the day that your mind has made and just maybe the world ought to go along with you for a while instead of you going along with the world, even if just for a moment, so you can collect your thoughts and align your schedule to be accommodating to the multiple facts of reality.

The night moves with the darkness. The morning moves with the dawn. And the day just moves along like every day is today; and it really seems just like it is.

It seems to me that we could say that nothing ever presents itself to us in which there is not some difference, or indifference, and the act of distinguishing and discriminating compounds the thoughts we bear. Just as well if no one was around and you thought you were alone you would not be, because you have to be beside yourself and with the spirit of your own conscience, always. You are always a witness to yourself even if it is in your own mind.

Since philosophy has been able to discover no good way, or method, to tranquility we must rely on theology and incorporate the idea into our own sense of being, and at some time cease questioning ourselves where no answers are to be found. Learning is the key to discovery, and for this sole reason we explore what we are able to on the way to wisdom finding ourselves and the true meaning of life. But continually we ask what's it all about and all we hear from ourselves is "I don't know." And all I can say to myself is "I forgive you."

And then I think to myself: that's all there is, compassion for myself and others and forgiveness when events bring themselves to our attention that were no fault of our own.

Should we find a hidden meaning in life? I think so and it is life itself. Every day our mind ceases to wonder at the hesitation we come to approaching the meaning, and just lives. Humanity is such a big word and I am still alone, still and alone in thought.

The weight you carry is that of responsibility to yourself for your own preservation. You cannot forget yourself; you always remember and take notice of others as you do of yourself because they are just like you though different but the same.

We must find our own inner fortitude secure against the assaults life brings upon us by chance or opportunity. We must be valiant in our association with motivation and ambition to succeed which is more than our own survival. It is the reaching for the aesthetic heights of the pyramid, striving, not being content, to reach the summit; but there is none. As we climb to the summit, it, like the horizon, moves further away from our sight and reach.

Since not everyone has the same determination let us follow after reason with constancy to carry out our responsibilities faithfully and reveal the truth from its concealment in the action of achieving knowledge and passing it on to one another. We ought to remember what we leave behind, as we leave our mark on society, for all it has done for us; our own wisdom may become invaluable as a tool for introspection and discovery of the world we live in.

It's a beautiful day; don't forget it's all projections and interpretations from your mind; we can make it better than it is. You have to make yourself happy before you can make someone else happy. The overcoming of the power of our emotions has to have some restrictions and liberty of the intellect. It's all I can do to keep my own sanity; why should I be concerned about the world? Well, just because I should. They say the start comes from me, and I can't be responsible for the world; but I can make a difference by having compassion and sharing the great mystery with my own interpretation for the betterment of humanity as a great collective.

Sure enough I can go on, but not by myself. I alone am less than if I am joined by the Spirit; so be it, and so it is. My life is not less without myself, but greater with the spirit within my own soul. Perhaps it's just a matter of belief, but we all need comfort as we are subjected to the forces of the world.

Sure there are people out there like us, but no one like you. Who knows better than you; so why call on me? I am just an ordinary philosopher and theologian and only know as much as I have learned. I can only relate to you as much as I've experienced and let me say some of it has been miracles and very powerful revelation as insight comes in mysterious ways; but understanding comes as plain truth.

I've found a way to move on from this place; but the memories contained within me I will never forget. Sure we all look for safe harbor, but the safest one is sometimes sheltered from the storm outside ourselves. The river of life takes you on a long journey; the current is so swift we only get a short look at what we pass, and while looking for a place to shore up we can't help but remember all we passed, all the experiences we missed. But more untold stories will come to mind as our lifelong journey continues. Echoes stir us and the great wonder continues in our mind of what's to come, because we already know what has been.

We're riding on a great mobius turning the outside in and the inside out; we know what side we're on but the changes of life just seem to overcome us with pure strangeness and our imagination seems to carry us to the edge so we can look over and see the other side of ourselves and the other side of reality all in a single moment.

"I've come a long way just to be with you," the spirit said. How about we spend some time together; there's a little left. There will always be tomorrow. City streets need crossing. Skateboard parks need courageous young people to play and do their tricks. Books have a double meaning; the one presented and the one you interpret. We ought to give thanks for everything, but sometimes that is very difficult — sometimes, almost impossible.

So we learn it is impossible to stop our mind; it's even active in our sleep without us having knowledge, unless we remember a dream. Although it's within our power to feed our mind with worldly knowledge or spiritual enlightenment, our concerns are based on the day, and it's always today.

Everyone has a story about how things are supposed to be but that don't change much considering how things really are. We become really self-conscious but we really have to remember to keep up with our hopes and truly believe there's a silver lining to everything. Rainbows don't just appear, they need the rain; and sometimes we need tears to dry our worries and concerns.

Without the gift of discrimination no other virtue can stand firm to the end because it is the mother of all virtues. The sun will not set once before we are called to discriminate between one thing and another; and by this we learn to control our decisions and choices. How I got here to where I am is not important; but to where I go from here is my most concerning thought.

True discrimination comes to us only by learning humility, and it is not only what we do, but what we think that ought to concern our thoughts of worldly and spiritual things. It would take me a long time to give account of the judgments I have made, but our concern for consequences is at the summit of our thoughts. I too am gray with age, but my heart is young and eager for new experiences. Everything it seems is just a test of our abilities and the courage to use what we have learned and dive into the waves of the world without fear, always with hope that times will get better and we will meet the challenges of the day boldly as a warrior goes into battle.

The truth is one certain thing; it never varies and is permanently constant. There is no more reliable witness than each man to himself. As for me, I only exist — my purpose is still to be discovered. Against all odds the challenge increases as do the rewards for finding what it is that I was sent here for. Of course all are of varied opinion; but ourselves we know the best of our true nature.

In these last days of writing this discourse on human nature I've come to master some of my own conclusions in accord with the masters whose care and tutoring I have been under. No challenge is too small for the courageous in mind, the brave in heart, and the creative in intelligent thinking to conquer. Not one of us is secure from doubt so we naturally indulge in study and thought.

Perhaps we cannot leave the security of our own mind, but we must reach out. We'll be there soon, in the safety of the north, a place where the atmosphere rises to the sky along with our prayers and we know someone hears our calling and sees the tears we cry in desperation.

Fifty thousand islands form a chain in your mind so that you can swim to one and then another, but not in a lifetime. The midnight sun shines on the Arctic Circle, at tree-top level; I've experienced both and it's a miracle. But we always have to return home where we find rest and can lay our head to sleep to face another day with renewed strength. The telephone rings but no one answers; I wish I were home. It could have been important; I'll never know because I wasn't there; if only I would have picked up the phone, I wonder.

The destinies of half the world are unknown; another quarter will go forgotten, leaving just one other quarter of which half of them will only be remembered because of their success and the remaining, those who left the world leaving their mark, will soon be forgotten because people just don't think enough to give them the least consideration. It is neither fame nor fortune which those of history follow, but a simple life of study and contemplation brings the favor of a treasury of fortune to our door.

Whether we open our life to knowledge or wisdom of the ages our place in time will soon vanish just like all those who came before; time waits for no one and everyone waits on time for their calling. Every generation passes and as we round the sun again the seasons change and new life forgets from where it came from.

Relax and have a laugh; it won't hurt. And what the heck, it's a funny thing that happened to me; it just gives me more material to write about.

No sooner than a hundred years from now we will be the ancient ones except for those who know to read between the covers of old dusty books; and what becomes of those before us live on in antiquity.

Whoever will be reflective with due measure and proportion will bring to the forefront of thought all the storms that passed through the eras making creation more than just a scientific endeavor of the Master of Nature but a simple progression of equal thoughts with due balance leaving no room for resistance among the creatures. We learn that nothing is for free, and those who once had a name no one can remember. We are so consumed with work that living just doesn't give us enough time to sit back and think as we ought to; maybe I'll just take some time and wait for the mailman to deliver my check. Maybe, perhaps, this economic thing I got caught in was a blessing in disguise. We put in the till our hard-worked-for money that the government takes and now they've got to give it all back. Thank you Mr. President Roosevelt. And who said they don't know what it's like until it happens to them. It's not sympathy we need but some real compassion and a job.

What really makes a difference is the language we use to talk with ourselves; in the quiet unspoken we hear ourselves thinking with images and rhetoric only we can generate and understand. There must be more to being common than outstanding because there are more of us than them. Those who labor in thought are the minority; but they are the ones who know more and act less because they are aware of the consequences of the masses, the majority, having the ability to think for themselves. So they call for leaders and happily follow the leader to their own graves working for a living and living just to work. There must be a better, another, way to endure survival. This study of knowledge is filled with extreme variation; but that is what makes living so amusing and entertaining.

In many ways, shapes, and forms, all things come to pass. We live in a temporary condition with the permanence of change. Creation is a perpetual reality that brings together life and death and rebirth because nothing is wasted away. Things and creatures just fade away, and we build castles in the sky. The odds are just random chance, fate will make its way; the house rules, and the rituals we play are just part of the game. If your number comes up then you get the chance to play, and you don't have any say over the rules.

We have to access our judgment within such a deep labyrinth of difficulties in understanding one upon another of decisions, and choices, and so much disagreement and uncertainty in the school of wisdom. Those who have been able to reach any knowledgeable conclusions about the world and themselves can find a simple coherent commonality in most every other being; we are just human.

Whatever thoughts that come to mind that are the products of intelligent reasoning, in a sincerely logical way, rarely satisfy the stringent requirements of our certainty. So I find the desire to know is just an affliction and an affection destined to man that one should learn all he can and increase his understanding of nature and human nature, find his own God, and deliberate on the conclusions. Then he must pass along this knowledge to one another in discourse and further debate.

The affliction is the pain of study we learn to overcome because of the affluence, quantity, and abundance of resources. The affliction is the partiality or emotion we have towards our studies, and like other pleasures becomes an addiction in our quest for the nearest complete knowledge we can achieve. Our affinity, our natural attraction for exploration and discovery, so it seems, is a natural principle of humanistic behavior; and like in other studies we seek for affirmation and verification of what we think we know as well as the theories we assert with the relativity of truth our reason can afford.

The climb to the summit is the most challenging, but the higher one gets the view that is much grander, exposing the horizon to what was once out of sight. Miracles do happen in our ascent; the clock keeps time with our progress, jet planes leave their marks in the sky with the passing clouds, and our inner fortitude and courage find increase in our persistence, accelerating towards the final goal. Each step of the way gets us one step closer, but we need not forget where we came from because we will return; and we will always remember the difficulties we experience along the way and the first view we take from the summit.

It is from necessity that our curiosity is aroused to seek for the answers to our eluding questions. It is from necessity that they are answered so that we can move on to deeper questions.

What we allude to, make an indirect reference to, is our theories and interpretations that seem in the present to satisfy our needs. Our curiosity heightens when we think we come close; and still the mystery remains to life's persistent questioning. Everything that happens to you will teach you of the magnificence of life. Through the experience of ourselves and others we learn what life is really all about. Do not refuse to learn; for when the intellect grows and matures it finds the wonders of life.

Once you deliberate and advance in your thoughts, you come to new conclusions of old matters. It is important to take counsel in others as you do in yourself. So I sit here at my desk counseling myself, in remembrance of what I've been taught, thinking of where I've been and to where I am led, towards my own destiny, thinking of all I have learned, wondering if it will be enough. But I will head out on the road I've chosen and make my way, remembering God and my own conscience.

There are three measures life gives to us: remembering the past, living in the present here and now, and dreaming of the future. The latter two require much thought because we can change the now and the future, but the past cannot be changed.

We should be quick to learn, after long practice, to keep to the stillness of the heart and mind to recover our sensibilities of thinking clear without distraction and to consider each thought with its own implications. We ought to keep our heart as we do our mind, attentive to our learning, so that reaching out for spiritual wisdom increases the likelihood that our knowledge of the physical world will find truth and certainty.

Everything unanswered keeps us in suspense from the mystery that surrounds it. Reasoning has no other basis than experience while the diversity of events offers us infinite examples of every kind. Even the least knowledge is seldom enough. It is commonly held that good sense is the gift which nature has most fairly shared, yet there is not anyone among us who is not satisfied with our allotment.

We ought to walk the world proudly, but humbly, giving thanks for what comes to us and for what we bring to ourselves from the decisions and choices we make from our judgments and conclusions.

Books can be your best friends; they don't talk back but make you think and give way to discovery and the adventure in learning. We ought not to say "Oh, those were the days," or "Oh, sometime in the future." We should live in the here and now and just deal with it, with all that comes to us or we bring to mind, and accept patient endurance.

You know it's a wonderful world when things are going your way but at some time you run out of cards and are all in and you've got to play with what you hold and just hope random chance goes your way. And still when the odds are against you, you still have to have the courage to go on.

Anyone who would look past this would be looking beyond what his sight could reach. If anything at all is becoming then nothing is more so than life, than the contents of your entire life all rolled up into today and the outcomes of your thoughts, decisions, and judgments. We never neglect ourselves even for a short while, for the moments that life consists of.

If you are adept and have discovered the entrance to the mysteries of life, and standing before God at dawn, you will understand the meaning life has; but be watchful in your mind for new clues from your own exploration in learning. If you have an aptitude for learning your discoveries will show the magnificence of life and all of creation.

What we have to do is to look beneath the words and find the truth that we understand in its simplest terms; because there is more to reading than just words, like there is more to thinking than what is thought. In clear boldness we interpret our thoughts and give meaning to them as we see suitable to our own level of competence.

If we are given to believe in conscience than believing in the spirit is not far behind. If this is true than we can believe in heaven, and heaven's messengers are not far behind this thought. If we believe in the power of our own will than the power that drives the will also drives our spirit to challenge the new knowledge that comes to our understanding not only of physical things but of spiritual things as well.

I like the crust of bread. It's like the perimeter of life and contains life itself. I like the end pieces, mainly the crust from the loaf, because the crust accepts the baking and is just as full with flavor as the bread from the middle. This one thought makes us perceive what we can conceive of the contents of our living. It is not only the thought of life that reveals its magnificence but our perspective and attitude, our disposition, that makes this notion boldly alive and vibrant.

So I sit back in my work chair, where I think and watch the sky and see the clouds brushed by the wind as time itself goes by. At my desk in my study my typewriter keeps pace with the music I listen to, considering each thought that comes to my mind of which I give my attention to. A jet plane passes by my window, the same as the birds of the air and creatures of the land we call our Earth.

So what we believe is what we perceive and what we conceive may not be so. We have to think past the illusion into true reality. Our own conscience confirms our spirit, its essence, and our being even as we are becoming signifies that we are not yet what we will be. So you ask yourself: who am I? You realize that you are nothing but the will of the Creator. Each day I am as good as new even though I am old and getting older. Skill is born of knowledge. From our knowledge is born our true wisdom. From our wisdom we learn to control our reasoning and judgment. Combined, these qualities make our living just a whole lot easier. From these qualities we learn discrimination and bring this complicated world into simplicity.

Nature has vouchsafed us a great talent for keeping ourselves occupied when alone and often summoned us to do so in order to teach us that we do owe a part of ourselves to society. But the best part of ourselves is in the activity of our own mind.

Nothing is without compensation. For both right and wrong, good and bad, the rewards we harvest have justice as their measure. It is the Spirit that mystically confirms its presence within us. Our own conscience confirms the ethics and values we hold to in our convictions. If you engage in spiritual warfare be still in your heart and call upon the powers endowed to you with your present abilities and sense of mind. It is almost impossible to look at the sky or stars without awe or walk the Earth without air and your heart beat continues even as the mystery remains.

Much have I traveled and still there are so many places I've never been except in books where the world comes to life beyond our sight. Social smiles and the chains of freedom link us to the morality of the mind. Our judgment tossed and turned by one decision — the better choice of two bad choices or perhaps one better than another. So much material to write about and both dreams and reality bring us to wonder. Forever passes into nothingness; but something is there and eternity can be explained, but not in human terms, and the universe seems to expand into infinity.

It was fun being on the far side of the sun, but winter is leaving now and spring will be here soon once we pass through February, the hardest month of the year. Every time we circle in our orbit we find more material to write about as our experience with life fills us with its magnificence, awe, and grandeur.

Be still in your heart and mind. The unimaginable may happen. Solitary thinking leads us on. The naked brain can overpower our emotions. The drama unfolds one chapter at a time, one day and evening at a time. Time holds the scales that balance life with certain accuracy. In the stillness of your thoughts you imagine all that is possible and perhaps probable.

The elements fill the space between the Earth and the ethereal heavens. Our stubborn mind will not rest until, in contemplation, we find what it is that we are looking for. Entanglements everywhere cause us alarm; but there is none, just misinterpretation and representation from misguided conceptions. And as always some answers will follow to our persistent questioning; and once more we find that stillness in our heart and settled mind.

We ought to remind ourselves that a controlled mind leads to controlled emotions, which is a good thing. The exigency or state of immediacy that our watchfulness of the intellect requires is most useful when finding the stillness of the mind that serenity needs to find that calm and repose we seek for. This mental philosophy or practical wisdom is useful in achieving spiritual knowledge.

Sometimes it seems we force our imagination into reality, and just as well, at times we force reality into our imagination. In time each variable has its own measure by the degree of thought we put to the subject and object of that which we think.

So what we are trying to do is to take a look at the story behind the headlines, read between the lines and see into our reading the thoughts that the words provoke. Ideas come to us in many forms, notions with many backgrounds; and all we can do is interpret to our own satisfaction.

I tried to catch a glimpse of myself, and what I saw I did not dislike. I was finding the real me hidden inside this shell of body and mind. We all have to grow up, but it's amazing the crazy paths we follow in doing so. We have to find a representation of reality we can live with. Living on the edge of thought, of wrestling with the fundamental problems of being human and finding an appropriate means of expressing them.

The writer must be qualified to impose order on chaos. The writer must be adept at handling experimental works portrayed in the words of thoughts. The writer must display a skill in drawing conclusions from notions and ideas relevant to humanity. The fact is that the writer must have an understanding of where he or she is going and how he or she proposes getting there.

I caught a sense of what literature in the grand sense involved. We live in a world of human behavior, stark, cruel, infamous, and dramatic, worthy of an exposition to think upon. Unless you have a strong sense of blood coursing through your veins, when you write significance won't be in the words, which is the essential nature of literature. We learn that life is full of passion and emotions that in some way have to be dealt with.

We find ourselves pole-vaulting from one level of thought and expression to an entirely new plateau. We find ourselves being led into the broad avenues of learning so much grander in design than the limited country roads we once knew in our life experience.

What kind of people are we, crying in frustration as we labor to untangle their lives and motives?

Remember the sovereign rule: "If it's not written it doesn't exist." A thought not written is often lost forever unless its significance is regularly brought to our attention. It is the writer's task to provide society with a fresh and sometimes necessarily acid portrait of itself. To excel I must live with a burning intensity — to have the courage to pay whatever price is exacted for the pains and labor of my own generous thinking.

I think my readers, as you call them, also have serious concerns and wrestle with ideas nested in their own minds. I brood over them constantly, and it is my dedication to those visions, as it is to my own, that sustain me through my years of study and meditation.

There is a lot more to writing than just creative expression. There must be first a topic of which its concerns can be addressed. Sentences must have grammatical structure and preserve parallelism, a parallel congruent pattern of thought with composition style. It, the writing composition, must have well-constructed paragraphs with sentences full of well-placed words within the sentence.

With words properly used the composition becomes a work of art formatted into a basic unit of human thought that can be easily related to. The writer must maintain coherence, integrity, and respect for each given thought and idea. The writer must be hungry for every bit of knowledge to relate to the reader.

Writing is a cerebral process that evolved not primarily from the brain but from the soul. The goal of writing is communication between the souls of the writer and reader, and mastery of the art consists in the ability to utilize words to ignite flames in the readers own soul.

The street becomes a local university available to anyone who wished to utilize it. This is how dozens of the best minds find their material to write about, from sincere human needs. Why else do you think you were put on this good Earth? In one word it is "intensity" — to explore the intensity of the human endeavor.

I didn't have to graduate college to find a unique story to tell. Once properly organized the lead sentence sets the agenda with the rest of the material reinforcing the concept being addressed. During the years of my study I became caught up in a hurricane of emotion, in both my professional and personal lives. I found myself following not a single point of light but an entire aurora borealis that flashed in all sectors of the sky.

The mission of the artist is to elevate him or her self through study and insight to the highest attainable level and then to communicate with his or her peers, to seek them out, to exchange concepts with them, and to write, paint, or create music so as to illuminate the problems or issues that concern them.

We have an obligation to communicate with not only the brightest minds of our generation but with the most common folk who walk along the main streets of our own communities.

Anyone who can read, or has heard of history and man's long struggle to achieve meaning, knows that the journey started many eras since humans began to think and communicate with the significant ones around them. When you come upon an abstract principle you find yourself with a very long tale. The infinite intelligence that presumes to explain human activity no matter how bizarre grows tedious within its own right. What we do is to find a binding matter to bring together scattered and diverse ideas.

We people find two ways of acquiring wisdom: by patient accumulation and analysis of the evidence available, and by epiphanies that in an instant illuminate continents and centuries. Drawing on experience acquired, I defend my selections that could be accepted not only by myself, but by well-grounded people who can appreciate what I bring to the light of day and enlightenment of night.

We learn to work in silence, with the best brainpower we have. It's not impossible to believe you really can do what you think you can. So we sharpen our pencils, break out a new cartridge for our pens and put on our thinking caps.

What has happened to me is that I see human capacities, human variations if you will, in a new and unique different light than I once did before. I began to read and write as such happened never before since I began to study with the intensity that I have now. So with one more sentence I will have sufficiently completed this composition, which I am rather satisfied with. So it is done.

Afterthoughts: Looking Back

Our life consists partly in madness and partly in wisdom. Whoever writes about the paradigm of life merely and respectfully leaves more than half behind, though not unnoticed. So out of consideration for both I find what is most appropriate to the theme and subject of this discourse and relate what I can, addressing the passage of knowledge to one another in substantial individual thoughts and the notions that ground the ideas and raise them to the new heights they deserve.

I weigh the thoughts with an equal measure and bring the sections of my divided mind into one grand subjective object of consideration.

Then I hear the calling of both sides of the conversation, having within my own intelligence the capacity for constant deliberation without distinction of bias or prejudice towards one particular view or any other, keeping a liberal, but conservative attitude of the relationships those ideas impose on my own thinking.

If you try to reduce life to rational rules you will simply give yourself the task of going rationally insane and discover the madness that is just part of the rationality of nature itself.

Our mind travels in all directions at once, in the same time as thoughts layer themselves and separate themselves near and around each other, creating the grand panorama of a horizon in a three hundred and sixty degree world which also includes the aspect of the realms of vertical and descending nature of the qualities inherent in deep space where everything and nothing collide.

There is nothing in us during this earthly prison either purely corporeal or purely spiritual that is as much injurious to tear a living man apart as his own thoughts that come from the heart of his mind in both forms, unconscious and conscious, that Angels and Demons bring to our soul.

It is a good thing to keep our soul in a state of innocence. It is the duty of the philosopher to inquire and understand himself in order that he may know the world and his own God in a more perfect comprehension. A reasonable mind is a curious thing, often set to a little thought and wonder.

Even if everything that has come down to us by means of knowledge passed through generations by written and spoken word was reported to be theory of known truth, that would be nothing compared to all that we still do not know.

A hundred times more wisdom is never found or lost that comes from study and learning from the sources of knowledge available to us. Though knowledge is a powerful tool when used to create wisdom, our curiosity drives us to find out more and make less the unknown, increasing our own adventure in learning through the exploration and discovery of knowledge and wisdom we can call our own.

There is no idea so frivolous or odd which does not appear to be fittingly produced by any mind dedicated to laboring in thought, which does not occur to be having some potential worth.

Knowledge is a very weighty thing, an integral principle in our reasoning; it brings our common sense to common ground where the ordinary and the extraordinary have equal measure.

It is clear that I have set out on a road not merely traveled but on a road as a way of life. This has been an extraordinary composition to write. It is not without toil or ceasing as long as the world has ink and paper to accumulate my thoughts.

Life is a delicate thing, easy to disturb and hard to fix when it is broken, easy to handle when things are going well and most worrisome when the tangled web gets knotted.

This remarkable composition has brought the tangled web of life into the consciousness of our thinking mind. Life ought to be "woebegone" but it isn't, so I've managed to consolidate my thoughts and carefully consider life in a serious and provocative way. Our own spirit and soul is torn at the root, compromising with life from conflicting forces. But live we must, dealing with it as it is.

It is not an easy thing to abandon our thoughts completely, but some are more or less not worth quite the effort to keep when we live with doubt and the need for verification of the truth.

Now that the show is over we lead ourselves to remember the finer points of enlightenment and see just how to enact a response. Traditionally at this time we could decide the implications of what we can remember or decide to re-read for fear that we might have missed something important.

The enlightenment of the students' understanding has clearly become more than a dialogue in their inner mind with themselves. It has become essential wisdom with recondite knowledge and newfound appreciation.

The sagacity and meticulous wit of this composition, in all three parts, has been a noble endeavor and actually most satisfying. What we do in spite of our conviction to be self-reliant is to indeed "Pass Knowledge to One Another."

Any knowledge we do find in the course of human events, those slight traces are enough for a keen-scented mind to draw out of our universe and safely lead one to discover just what else can be found out and known.

The ascent and advance of society depends on its individuals and their interaction with each other. This is and has been the principle for expressing in composition "We Pass Knowledge to One Another."

All the rest of the mind is left to the imagination; but even it has to be willing to seek and accept newfound wisdom and the knowledge it affords to us. Enlightenment is the golden means to self-proclaimed wisdom. Special thanks to all those individuals who promoted the well-being of this composition and study in human nature. ■

www.ingramcontent.com/pod-product-compliance
Lightning Source LLC
Chambersburg PA
CBHW031130160426
43193CB00008B/96